DESERT SNOW

One Girl's Take On Africa By Bike

Helen Lloyd

Take On Creative

First published in 2013
by Take On Creative

Cover Design by Helen Lloyd
Cover Photography by Helen Lloyd and Lars Bengtsson

ISBN 978-0-9576606-0-1

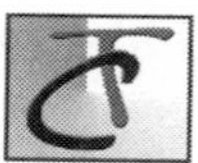

www.takeoncreative.com

Preface

The hardest part with Desert Snow was deciding what to write about. There are many stories to be told from two years on the road, cycling across a continent. It would be much easier to write about only one place or one event, to delve deeply and describe the little details that bring the words to life and take you with me on the journey.

It could be a book about cycle-touring, the philosophy of travel and exploration, or about Africa and its history, cultures, and geography. It could be a light-hearted tale of adventure, or a solemn and serious account of a single country's chequered past. It could even be a work of fiction. Whatever the subject or genre, it should at least be an interesting book.

This is not the book to read if you want to know how to undertake a long cycle tour or become an expert on Africa. There are other books that tell you these things better. Though, my advice is: don't read them. Instead, get on a bicycle and start pedalling if it is a cycle tour you want to do or travel to Africa and learn from what you see and who you speak to, so you may understand more about the rich, colourful continent. Not everything can be learnt from a book.

If, however, you are still reading for the simple pleasure, then I shall tell you now what this book is about. It is the story of my journey through Africa and all I enjoyed and sometimes endured. It is a mishmash of people and places, a melee of misadventure, a medley of emotions and a mixture of images and impressions. It is my Take On Africa.

But this story does not begin in Africa. It begins with beer.

Helen Lloyd
England, May 2013

The Author

Helen Lloyd grew up in Norfolk, England. She studied Engineering and has worked in industry. Travelling has been a part of her life since she was sixteen. In 2009, she quit her job to embark on her first long journey by bicycle, from England to Cape Town. She has since cycled in North and Central America and plans to cycle across Asia. Between journeys, she spends her time in Norfolk and Buckinghamshire.

More Information

There are a number of extra features online including trip statistics and photos not seen before with galleries relating to each chapter of the book. See www.helenstakeon.com/desert-snow/extras

'If an important decision is to be made, they [the Persians] discuss the question when they are drunk, and the following day the master of the house where the discussion was held submits their decision for reconsideration when they are sober. If they still approve it, it is adopted; if not, it is abandoned. Conversely, any decision they make when they are sober, is reconsidered afterwards when they are drunk.'

- *Herodotus, The Histories*

ROUTE MAP

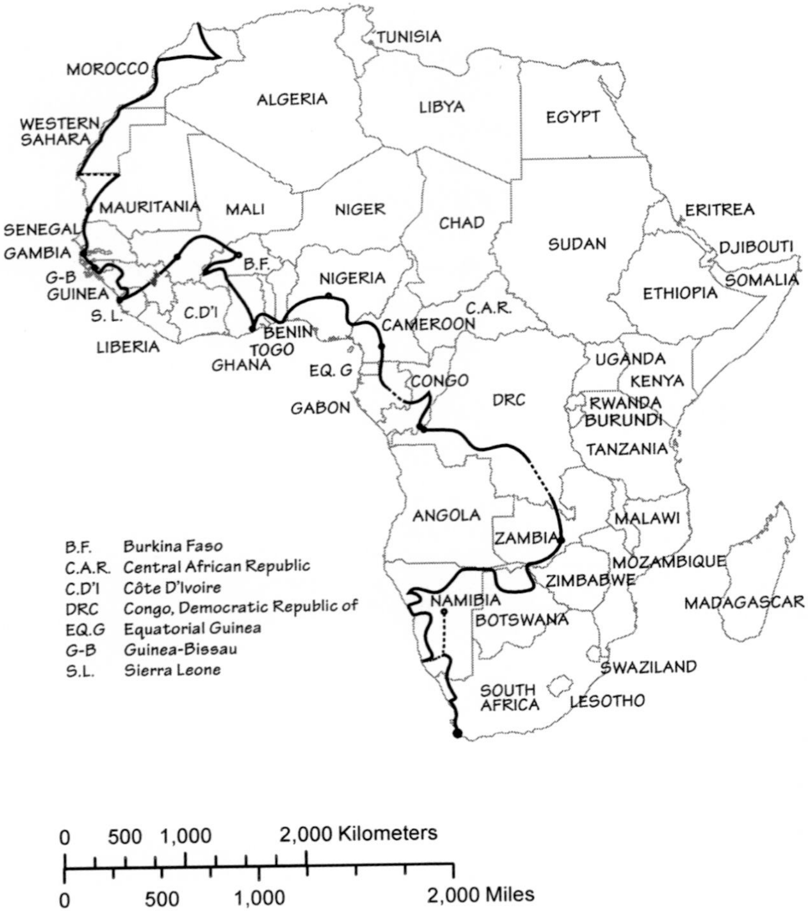

TUNISIA
MOROCCO
ALGERIA
LIBYA
EGYPT
WESTERN SAHARA
MAURITANIA
MALI
NIGER
CHAD
SUDAN
ERITREA
DJIBOUTI
SENEGAL
GAMBIA
G-B
GUINEA
B.F.
NIGERIA
ETHIOPIA
SOMALIA
S. L.
C.D'I
C.A.R.
CAMEROON
BENIN
LIBERIA
TOGO
GHANA
UGANDA
KENYA
EQ. G
CONGO
GABON
DRC
RWANDA
BURUNDI
TANZANIA
ANGOLA
MALAWI
ZAMBIA
MOZAMBIQUE
ZIMBABWE
NAMIBIA
BOTSWANA
MADAGASCAR
SWAZILAND
SOUTH AFRICA
LESOTHO
B.F. Burkina Faso
C.A.R. Central African Republic
C.D'I Côte D'Ivoire
DRC Congo, Democratic Republic of
EQ.G Equatorial Guinea
G-B Guinea-Bissau
S.L. Sierra Leone
0 500 1,000 2,000 Kilometers
0 500 1,000 2,000 Miles

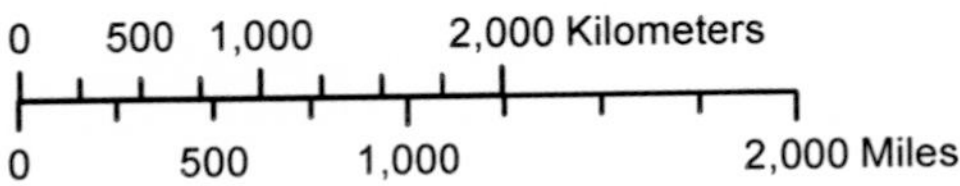

Contents

Part Four

From Beer To There

1

Before the Bike Ride Began

Europe

'Where to this time?'

'Africa. I'm going to cycle to Cape Town,' I slurred between swigs of beer, while taking a break from post-operation, one-legged crutch-wielding dancing at a local best-not-named club. My knee was hurting and the painkiller-alcohol combination was not proving effective.

I guess if I'm really going to do this, then I should tell as many people as possible. There was no turning back now and that was fine by me. I had finally found something I really wanted to do.

'OK, that's cool!' was the enthusiastic and equally dismissive, uncomprehending response that I was to hear many times before the trip was over. 'Ready to dance again?'

That was more or less how the conversation went. After all, it was several years ago and I was quite drunk.

Almost two years passed before I set off for Africa. Preferably, I would have gone sooner, but I wanted to leave in the summer to get the best climate for crossing the Sahara. I ignored the fact that I would hit the rainy season further south. The truth was that the scale of this ride was beyond my comprehension. Although I had mapped a route all the way, I hadn't thought about the practicalities beyond the first few months. Crossing the Sahara Desert seemed like a major challenge when considered from the comfortable sofa at home. The rest I would deal with when I got there.

Two years gave me time to save enough money and for my knee to heal. I checked my passport wouldn't expire and counted the blank pages. I researched which countries I required a visa for. Then I went on with my life. I spent less and saved more; I 'danced' less and did the exercises my physio prescribed.

Desert Snow

I thought about where I would take my next annual holiday. By then my knee was well healed, so I took my mountain bike (only bike) to Cuba. I took my passport, wallet, camera and bikini, and filled the rest of the borrowed panniers with clothes and books. I cycled enough to know that I could cycle more, but not so much that I didn't have time for sightseeing, photography, diving, hiking and horse-riding, and a token afternoon sun-bathing. After three weeks, I returned to the office with a suntan, convinced that this ratio of cycling to not cycling was perfect. Cycling to Cape Town would simply be a series of three-week holidays. Then I went on with my life.

Weeks passed by, merged together, and were forgotten as weeks do when you work nine-to-five, instead, distinguished only by how you spend the weekends. I was eager to begin the trip and have seven days of memories every week.

The New Year dawned and as the summer drew closer, I awoke from the monotony realising that now was the time to get organised. I created a website for the trip where I would write about the journey and upload any photos I took. It would be my Take On Africa and that's what I named it.

'What bike are you going to ride?' someone asked. *Good question – I'm going to need a bike.*

'One that is unlikely to break or need many repairs,' I replied.

I searched online for a bike that met this detailed specification and bought it, along with some waterproof panniers. A company selling outdoor gear agreed to provide some camping equipment in return for a series of articles for their blog. The rest I bought second-hand on eBay. And then I went on with my life.

My last day at work rushed by and my final pay cheque for the foreseeable future arrived and was readily spent – I had a wedding in California to go to. While there, I stayed with friends and went mountain-biking.

Climbing over tree roots was a breeze and downhill was a rush. I cruised over rocks and glided down drops, switchbacks on single-track and another drop. And then I was flying mid-air, detached from the bike, with my head rushing towards the trail. Crash. The bike landed beside me. My head was spinning. Don't move. Can't move. Not the manoeuvre I had meant. There was an intense throbbing in my right thigh and any attempt to move it shot a pain down my leg, taking me to the verge of unconsciousness where my vision was blurred and sounds were muffled.

I eased myself into a less awkward and more elegant sitting position, instead of sprawled with my face in the dirt and arse in the air. Attempts to stand failed, although I felt fine once the nausea went away, as long as I didn't move my leg.

Light was fading on the forested hillside, so my friends called the emergency services. Eventually, the rescue team arrived, put me on a stretcher, and began the slow walk off the rough trail. After transfer to a truck and then an ambulance, I finally arrived at the hospital. I felt as though I had been a real inconvenience and that I should have made more of an effort to walk down myself – I was high on multiple shots of morphine. Now that the pain was manageable, I could move my leg cautiously. An x-ray confirmed there was no break. Take On Africa was back on.

Fortunately, I had the last-minute foresight to get travel insurance or it would have been a costly fall. It served as a reminder that it would be wise to get cover for the Africa trip. I was sceptical that any major emergency in rural Africa would result in a timely evacuation considering it took several hours to get medical care in a nearby American town. Better safe than sorry though.

So began the minefield of specialist travel insurance. Few insurers cover trips of two years and fewer cover cycle-touring unless it is an incidental activity. Starting from a list of thirty, the options soon dwindled to two possibilities; I called one.

'Hi, I'm going travelling and need some insurance. I checked your website but wanted to confirm something.'

'Certainly. What exactly are your concerns?'

'Do you cover worldwide trips of up to two years?'

'Yes.'

'Do you cover cycle-touring as the main activity?'

'Yes.'

'Excellent. In that case, could you provide a quote for a two-year cycle-tour in Africa?'

Silence.

'Hello?'

'My apologies. Yes, of course.' A flurry of questions and answers were batted back and forth, and a quote was given. 'Would you like to arrange the cover now?'

'Not now, thank you. But could you please provide the quote in writing, explicitly stating that it will cover a two-year cycle tour in Africa?'

'Of course. I can email that to you now.'

Later that day I received a new message from the insurance company:

> It is with regret to inform you that we cannot provide cover for a two-year, cycle-tour in Africa. We hope that you are able to find suitable insurance elsewhere.
> Kind Regards.

There had been a complete reversal in the ether of telephone wires and Internet connections. I didn't know it then, but this was a sign of conversations to come: to be adamantly told a fact and then have it refuted or outright denied later was not unusual in Africa. Dignity and respect can be honourable traits and are highly regarded in many cultures, but not when it comes to admitting you don't know or don't understand. It is better to say something, and if you say it confidently with certainty and conviction, then it becomes a fact. It is not outright lying when there is a possibility it could be true. Even a stopped watch tells the correct time twice a day. The last insurer was more amenable.

There was nothing essential left to do. Instead, trivialities began to assume epic proportions. I did, however, go to the doctor and try to get malaria treatment for my medical kit, in case I got malaria and was far from medical help. It would be possible to buy treatment cheaply in Africa, but the chances of it being counterfeit and containing insufficient amounts of the active ingredient would be high.

'Good morning, take a seat,' said the young doctor I had never seen before. 'How are you today?'

'I'm fine, thank you.' But, since doctors don't expect patients to be fine, I clarified the reason for my visit.

'No, you don't need malaria treatment.' He began a well-rehearsed drone of how prevention is the best medicine, and that I should wear long sleeves and trousers in the evenings. 'You should also take a malaria prophylaxis. Besides, there are many other diseases that are worse than malaria.'

I nodded my head in agreement, but judging by the condescending tone, the doctor clearly thought I was retarded.

'Yes, I realise that. I've had all the recommended vaccinations and will be taking a prophylaxis.'

'Would you like me to check which vaccinations you should have? Which country are you going to?' *Did you not hear what I said!*

He reached for a reference book, and I subdued a sigh and stared down. His fingers were long and his skin white and smooth; I wondered if he had ever done a day's hard work besides thumbing books in the library.

I tried again, 'I'll be travelling all over Africa. I have been through this before. All I need now is the malaria treatment.'

'It's not just the diseases,' he added. 'Africa is a dangerous place. There are wars and wild animals and …'. He stumbled into silence, pondering other potential threats. 'The best solution, if I were you, is don't go to Africa.' *Seriously?*

'I am well aware of the risks. I'm still going. Can you prescribe a course of Malarone?'

The doctor flicked through the book and spoke into it, 'You cannot use Malarone as a treatment if you are already taking it as a preventative.'

At this stage I was unsure who was wasting whose time. 'I know. I will be taking Doxycycline as a preventative.'

'Unfortunately, I am not allowed to prescribe Malarone as a treatment, unless you have actually been diagnosed with malaria. There could be serious consequences if I prescribed it and you then misdiagnose the malaria or take the incorrect dose. If you died, I could be liable. I'm sure you can understand my position. If you suspect malaria, you should seek medical advice immediately.' *You could have said that at the start.*

The doctor had now found the relevant page and was doing some maths. 'So unless you have malaria now, I can only prescribe Malarone as a preventative, which requires a different dosage. For example,' he was on a roll now, so I listened closer, 'a treatment would require the same number of tablets as would a preventative for a three-week holiday.'

This conversation was not getting the desired results. I accepted defeat and thanked the doctor for his time.

'No problem, I'm only sorry I couldn't be of more help. Is there anything else I can do for you?'

'Well, there is one more thing. I am going on a three-week holiday to Africa and need a malaria prophylaxis. Can you prescribe me some Malarone?'

The departure date arrived. I loaded up the bike for the first time and realised I had far too much stuff. During a process of removing excess baggage, when the contents of my panniers were strewn across the lawn like washing drying on a riverbank in Africa, a woman from the local paper appeared. She carried a camera around her neck and notepad in her hand. She asked the questions I was to hear a thousand times again and then hesitated briefly before asking to take a photo of me with the loaded bike.

I set upon the task of packing up my mess, feigning a casual air of I've-done-this-a-thousand-times-before-and-of-course-it-all-fits.

'It would be great if we could get an action shot too.'

'What, as in me, cycling?' A mild panic ensued when it dawned that I had not yet ridden a fully loaded bike.

'That's what I had in mind. Perhaps down on the road.'

'Sure.' *How hard can it be?*

Never ride a fully loaded bike for the first time in front of a press photographer with your shoelaces undone. The paper kindly used one of the photos of me stood in the garden.

* * *

Most changes in life, like evolution, are gradual. Discontinuity is solely an illusion of time, created simply by looking away and failing to observe every moment. Just because it is dark when we go to sleep and light when we wake does not mean there is no sunrise, which is the most beautiful part.

It is the same with travel. Flying, by its speed and disconnection with the land, is like sleep. In less hours than a full night's slumber, we awake in a foreign land thousands of miles away, jerked suddenly from the comfort of what we know into a strange new world.

With my first ever flight, I woke to the strange world of Delhi. A timid, sixteen-year-old blonde girl from temperate, rural England was thrust, eyes wide open, into the heat, sweat and stench of a chaotic city that never seemed to sleep. The scene remains vivid in my mind, as the most powerful ones always do.

My feelings were purely sensory though. I saw the crowds jostling, heard the rickshaws tooting, tasted acrid smoke in the back of my throat, and smelt the reeking rubbish piled in the streets. But I was merely an observer; I don't remember 'feeling' anything. It is a gift of youth, the ability to cope with change and adapt to a new environment unaffected. 'Culture shock' is an adult phenomenon.

Walking to the hotel in Old Delhi, down a dirt road lined with wooden shacks with bare-footed men selling umbrellas and mending pots, where everything was unlike anything I had previously experienced, I didn't want to close my eyes for a moment, should I miss something. I barely slept for days.

But Delhi had always been there. Only, on the other side of the world, its incoherent rhythm had never reached my ears and its multifarious soul never touched my heart. Now I wondered about all that existed between England and Delhi and elsewhere besides.

Travel overland, slowly and surely, and you see the changes right in front of you; although imperceptible between each passing mile, the cumulative effect is undeniable, the result more impressive and compelling in its entirety. You begin to understand that the world is a collage of history, languages, people and cultures; of territories, terrain, and climate; with the pieces continually moving and overlapping.

It is no surprise that Africa, brimming with such diversity, overflows its geographical boundaries. It should have been no surprise that I saw pieces of Africa before I set foot on the continent. There are pieces of Africa everywhere; perhaps there is a piece of Africa in us all.

You may be wondering, of all the places in the world, why did I choose Africa? I think maybe that Africa chose me. At the least, it has been a part of me for longer than I care to remember.

Once when I was young, I was lying on my back on my bed looking up at the damp-stained ceiling of my room. It was the place I retreated to when my little world no longer felt safe. I was sad; life seemed just too hard for such a small person. There were things happening around me, the problems of a grown-up world and not one I was a part of. I caught only snippets through doors stood ajar and raised voices muffled through the walls. I wanted to hear it all so that I could understand and at the same time to cover my ears in ignorant naivety.

Parents exhaust themselves doing the best for their children, by protecting them from the world for as long as possible, but what they don't realise is that kids understand more than they let on – their muted expression is simply not having the words to explain what they are thinking.

It seemed like things were bad, but I couldn't help thinking that there must be people in this world worse off than I was. I don't know why, but one of the images that sprang to my mind was of the news coverage of the famine that gripped Ethiopia in the early 1980s. Children with emaciated faces covered in flies sitting silently in the dirt on twig-thin limbs, looking through the camera lens with black empty eyes, is a haunting image for another child.

There were, I realised, plenty of other children whose lives were far harder than mine. They never complained and, instead, suffered simply to survive. I decided there and then to stop feeling sorry for myself. I wiped the tears from my eyes, made one last snotty sniff and told myself to buck up, cheer up and grow up. There was no point in feeling sorry for myself. I could either accept things the way they were, in which case I should not complain, or I could do something about it. Acceptance and silent resignation, or defiance: those would be the choices, except I didn't use those words then because I didn't yet know them.

There was nothing I could do then because the issue was money, or lack of it. So I made a promise to myself: never let money get in the way. I would not argue because of it, and I would not let it stop me doing something I wanted. It was very simple in my childlike innocent mind. It still is.

Later, when my mum told me about the time she had spent teaching in Kenya in the late 1960s, I was fascinated. There was so much more to Africa than pain and suffering. There were children like me who went to school every day, played games after class, and had hopes and dreams just like any child. It made me realise there was more to a place than what we see on the news.

There was wide-open savannah, and wild animals in the flesh and tusk that weren't stuck behind bars in a zoo, but roaming free and fighting strong. There was a place where roads were long and empty. You could spend your days without it costing a penny, and you wouldn't eat much because it was always hotter than it ever got on a clear English summer's day, but when you got hungry you could eat mangoes and tiny sweet bananas from the trees. It struck me as a very simple and good life where you owned little, needed less and owed nothing.

I wondered what else there was to these places I had never been. One day, I thought, I will go to Africa.

Now that day had arrived.

For the first time in my life, I had no plan for my future and the freedom was liberating. Yes, Cape Town and my path were destined to cross, but the route I chose to get there was unconstrained by commitments or promises. The options were infinite. I purposefully made no plans beyond Cape Town. After all, anything could happen between here and there. Instead, I was enraptured with the here and now, revelling in the liberated moment where the present was dissociated from the past and future.

* * *

I wheeled my fully loaded bike off the ferry in St. Malo, France, not knowing where I was going to sleep that night, except that it would be in a tent, and not knowing which way to go, except if I headed south I couldn't go far wrong. I didn't even have a map. Actually, I had three maps covering the whole of Africa, but no map to help me there and then.

But fortune favours the brave, so I boldly struck up conversation with the other stranger wheeling his bike off the ferry. Paul showed me to a campsite, and the following morning he handed me a large road atlas of France and said, 'A gift to get you off to a good start on your ride.'

Those first days were filled with smiles, despite the rain, and filled with croissants and coffee, French bread, cheese and tomatoes, a profusion of fruit, and a steady flow of red wine. It was a welcome discovery that I could justifiably devour everything I desired because of the energy I was expending on this journey south – although I was as often heading east or west, as I meandered along cycle routes or followed a tow path, going with the wind or where my fancy flew.

It was in Rochefort that I had my first glimpse of Africa – at an open air concert where a lady from Chad with a powerful voice and evocative presence sang captivating songs from the stage in the dimming light of day. I watched, mesmerised, as she swirled her bright orange dress that shone under the stage lighting, and I was taken in by her voice as the drum beat louder. Rather than memories, my imagination took me into the depths of a hot and dusty Sahel, and I was excited with expectation and anticipation of what was to come. I almost forgot I was in a maritime town in France.

I smiled all the way to the Pyrenees, even when I got lost despite having a map and when I had to go back to collect things I had left behind. My days were filled with cycling through pretty villages and along quiet roads until I was tired, and then I stopped to rest or sleep wherever I cared. I had time to read and relax, and time to visit cathedrals and castles. Life in the French lane was one long holiday, and I couldn't think of anything else I would rather be doing.

I cycled on into Spain where I met up with a friend. We meandered from hills to coast and back on country roads, and crisscrossed the Camino de Santiago, but my pilgrimage was not a religious one, so we wound through the beautiful mountains of the Picos de Europa, and then headed directly south over the sun-baked Central Plateau where the searing midday heat of August was too much to bear. We cycled early and late, and in the afternoons we sought shade and welcomed the siesta.

If there were one thing I learnt, it was to watch and learn and do as the locals, for they have lived on the land much longer than I, and in that time they have become the master of it. If I was to survive nature's fickle ways, then I would have to do the same. So we slept in the afternoons and then when we came to a town in the evening, we stayed up late and savoured the cool air, and ate tapas and drank beer and had a good time.

Then my friend left, and I cycled on through Andalusia alone where I saw signs of the North Africa I knew – Moorish architecture adorns the cities of Cordoba and Sevilla – like the Giralda, which is now the bell tower of Sevilla cathedral, but was built in the same style as the minaret in Marrakesh, Morocco.

By the time I reached the southern tip of Spain, I had been cycling for two months and was completely settled into my new life on the road. I was happy to find a quiet spot in the wild to camp, and it took little time and no thought to set up my tent. I had sweated up hills and whiled away tedious hours on long stretches of road in quiet contemplation or by drowning my boredom in music, and I had cycled through dull days of rain and the searing heat of Spain. And I loved it all.

Africa would have new things in store, of that I was sure, but when it came to cycling, I was certain I had it all under control. I only needed to continue the same way – take one day at a time, enjoy every moment and make the most of the freedom I had.

I was ready. So I took the ferry across the Strait of Gibraltar and, finally, I was on the African continent. The Africa of my imagination and Morocco of my memories were still far away when I walked off the ferry into the Spanish enclave of Ceuta. Then I reached the Moroccan border checkpoint …

Part One
West Africa

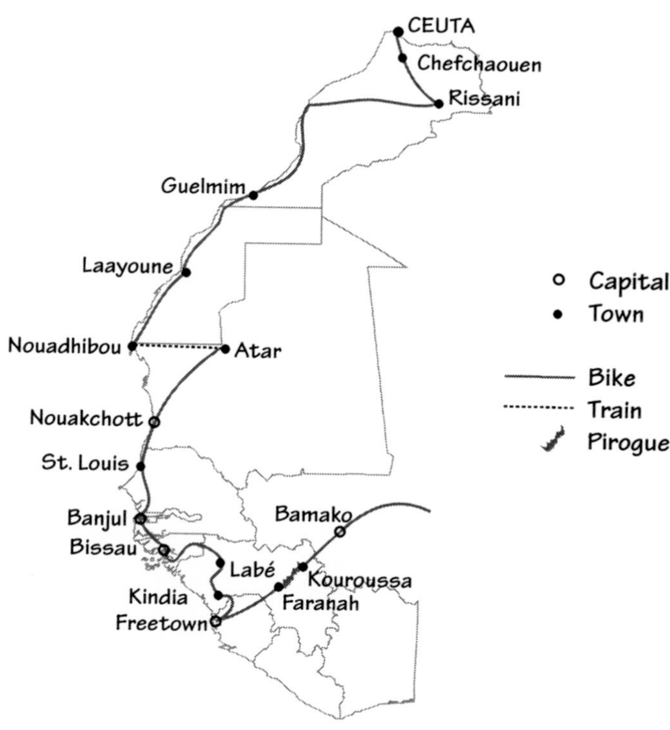

2

Kif and Gnaoua Music

Morocco

Chaos.

Cars crammed, log-jammed in the crush. Horns blasted, and fists waved, with holidaymakers and bootleggers bustling. Dodging bumpers, I weaved through the confusion of cars, black market money changers, and people sitting and standing and sometimes selling goods. *This is more like it.*

But calm returned as I pedalled away from the border, and I settled into a rhythm and enjoyed the passing scenery from the saddle. The sights and sounds were a sensory overload. What a delightful contrast to the Costa del Sol where I had cycled the previous day. This was nothing like the sun-soaked Mediterranean hot spot of high-rises and hotels and sunburned Brits with football shirts or no shirts at all.

Now with the sea on my left and rolling hills to my right, cattle grazed and egrets stood alongside, and a snake slithered away from my path into the darkness of a drain. The camel strolling in the distance was a reminder that I was leaving Europe behind and entering a different world that would be impossible to understand unless I looked upon these new scenes with a local perspective.

The palm-lined seafront turned into a pretty town of whitewashed houses trimmed with sky-blue windows and matching doors and roofs. Passing cars and trucks and buses beeped their horns. Passengers waved, and drivers shouted encouragement. The warm welcome was a welcome reminder of why I wanted to revisit Morocco.

The road south to Chefchaouen was along the edge of the Rif Mountains. Although a detour up into the mountains on small tracks was appealing, I was unsure this was wise. Looking back, I was mostly unsure of myself. My time in Morocco had been short so far, but it was clear that as a female, cycling, and alone, I was conspicuous on all three counts; attention was guaranteed and unavoidable. While being a single female could be an inconvenience and concern, I later learned it could also be an advantage. For now, the Rif, renowned for lawlessness, was not a place I wanted to attract attention.

Morocco is one of the world's biggest producers and exporters of hashish. The Rif region, which is closely controlled by mafia, is rife with the industry. The government turns a blind eye.

The indigenous Riffian Berbers have always done as they liked, especially in defiance of the rule of government. Throughout history, they have repelled external attempts to take over the area. Considering the cannabis plant took hold in Morocco's Mahgreb following Arab invasions, it is surprising that cultivation of the plant in the Rif did not begin for another 800 years.

By the time Morocco gained independence in 1956, although illegal in the rest of the country, cannabis growth and consumption were authorised by King Mohammed V in the five historical *douars*, or villages, of the Ketama and Beni Khaled tribes in the Rif. This was nothing new; Hassan I in the nineteenth century had done the same thing. Regardless of the current law, it is not confined to the five *douars* now.

There were numerous police control points along the road from Ceuta, and some trucks were stopped and searched. While the Rif is generally overlooked in all matters, the current government is taking some measures to tackle the export of the drug. Unfortunately, these controls are more for show. The big players pay off the police or simply employ drivers who will drive high-speed and not stop at the checkpoints. There are always people willing to accept incidental casualties by reckless driving when they will be paid more than they could ever earn in another job.

Chefchaouen, founded in 1471 as a base for launching attacks against the Portuguese, is one of the most beautiful towns in Morocco. Perched on the hillside, it was always up or downhill when walking within the old town walls. The cool blue hues of the medina exuded peace and calm, in contrast to the effect created by hundreds of feet pattering along the cobbled alleyways as the sun went down and everyone rushed to the Great Mosque, urged on by the *muezzin's* call to prayer.

My guidebook included a list of recommended cheap hotels, but I rarely paid much attention to it. Sometimes it is better to arrive in a town with no expectations or plans and wander without aim until you see a hotel that takes your fancy.

That was how I found the Hotel Sahara outside the walls of the old town. I didn't stay for the cell-like concrete room in the corner that was barely big enough. I stayed because the owner was welcoming and friendly and talked to me about his family and the town, and there was not another tourist in sight. I stayed because I didn't have the energy to walk up through the medina. It was cheap, and had a bed and a shower; that was all I needed.

As the sun lowered in the sky and the shadows lengthened so that the sidewalks were shaded, all of us who had been cocooned in cool confines emerged outdoors to enjoy the dying heat of the day. In those last hours, the sun's rays give the best heat there is – gently warming, not only your exposed skin, but also your insides, so that kindness and generosity radiate outwards. It is also the best kind of light for taking photographs, when buildings are bathed in a golden glow. I was going to take photos until it was dark, and then sit outside in the plaza while a multi-lingual waiter served me soup and a hearty *tajine*.

Sauntering through the narrow streets of the medina, disorientated but perfectly content, I found myself in conversation with a young Moroccan. Wary of his intentions, for it was easy to assume he either wanted to sell something or steal from me, I listened carefully and kept my eyes open. Youssef, however, saw me as a foreigner alone in his hometown and was curious if I were enjoying myself.

'I assume you are not Muslim,' he said, 'but if you have not eaten yet, would you like to join me to break fast?' When I hesitated he went on, 'It's nothing fancy, just me and my brother and a few friends eating together in our shop. We break fast there every evening during Ramadan. We'd be honoured if you would join us.'

'OK, sure. That would be lovely.'

It was a far more enjoyable way to spend the evening than alone. The town would still be standing to photograph tomorrow. Besides, not everything can be seen through the lens, even a wide-angled one.

While almost every Moroccan will consider themselves a Muslim, not everyone goes to the mosque or prays five times a day. With few exceptions, however, everyone fasts during the Islamic month of Ramadan. For the less zealous, it is worth it for *Iftar*, the festive gatherings of family and friends to break fast once the sun goes down.

I walked with Youssef to collect fresh water from the public fountain before returning to his small shop. *Iftar,* breakfast for them and dinner for me, was soup, bread, figs, milk, and tea served on the shop floor.

It was a quiet evening flicking between a Spanish football match and a reading of the Koran on the TV, which was set up in the doorway where the signal was best. When Youssef's friends arrived, we climbed the wooden ladder to the upper floor that was piled high with an array of colourful rugs. We piled in too and settled down to enjoy a flavoursome, slow-cooked chicken dish typical of the Sahara. We tore the tender white flesh and sopped up the succulent yellow juices with pieces of bread torn from the loaf. I had not yet mastered eating with only my right hand as is customary and could not eat quickly. Occasionally someone broke off pieces of chicken and passed it to me, noticing that I struggled to separate the meat from the bone with only my thumb and finger as though trying to eat with chopsticks for the first time.

After dinner, Youssef asked whether I had ever smoked kif and I said that I didn't think so. I was not even sure what it was although I had an idea.

'Oh that's OK, you are not the only one,' he said. 'You know our king, Mohammed VI? Well, he visited the Rif Mountains once. He was without his usual entourage of aides and guards, and was driving up through the hills when he came upon a small house with an old man smoking outside. Piled up high beside the little house was kilo upon kilo of the cannabis plant, but the king had no idea what it was.

'He stopped the car, stepped out, marched up to the old man and demanded, "What is this?"

'The old man explained, and the king replied, "Well, in that case, you must let me have a smoke."

'When the old man refused, the king got angry. "Do you know who I am?" he shouted, "I am the king. Now give me a smoke."

'But all the old man said was, "You certainly can't have a smoke – if you believe you are the king now, you will think you are God once you smoke this kif."'

We all laughed at the joke and laughed because we were high and it is good to laugh with friends and not to take life too seriously.

* * *

A hundred kilometres after Chefchaouen, trundling steadily along and absorbed in my thoughts, a Land Rover overtook, pulled over and the driver, leaning out, shouted back to me, 'Helen! Helen!'

I approached apprehensively, not knowing why anyone should know my name here. I was greeted with a wide smile and, 'Helen! It's Radi! Remember me? Youssef's brother.'

Of course I remembered, only I barely recognised this buoyant man in bright yellow t-shirt and bandana as the same one who had sat pensively in a deep blue hooded *djellaba* last night in the store.

'I'm going to visit my family. They are having a feast tonight. Would you like to join us?'

The only reason not to go was that it would mean accepting a lift and foregoing cycling every kilometre. It was the moment to decide what was most important about this journey. It was a quick decision because I only had to remind myself that I was cycling to enable me to see the countries I travelled through and as a way to meet people.

If I turned Radi down for the sake of a few lost kilometres on the bike, I might just as well return home, cycle as many kilometres in the gym and read a book about the country.

So I strapped my bike on the roof, which was harder than continuing pedalling when all I had to do was cycle until tired and then look for a place to camp. Now I didn't know where I was going or what would happen next. While freedom to make spontaneous decisions is liberating, breaking free from routine and the familiar never comes easily. Because something is easy does not mean it is better or more enjoyable and it would not always make me happy. Since regrets usually come from those things you don't do, I generally make a habit of accepting the offers that come my way.

Regardless of the dimming light, Radi knew it is nearing the time to break fast because he was hungry. I could tell because Radi's foot was pinning the accelerator to the floor, but he was only speeding up the Land Rover and not the setting of the sun. It was contentious whether we would make the feast in time or an early grave.

Hunger makes for short tempers and bad driving. I have never seen more fights, speeding and traffic accidents than during Ramadan. It is not just the male Moroccan psyche – I saw women arguing too, and it was the same in Pakistan when I travelled there. Besides, I know how irritable I get when I have not eaten.

We had barely entered Radi's aunt's house before being whisked to the fully laid table because no one would begin until, as the guest, I had taken my first spoonfuls of *harira*, the filling Moroccan soup of lentils, chick peas, onion, garlic, tomatoes and spices that tantalised my taste buds. The soup was followed by onion-filled pizza, *kefta* balls in a spicy sauce, hard-boiled eggs and then a main dish of chicken *tajine*. Desserts were sweet and sticky – sickly pastries, almond paste, chocolate mousse, and cakes too.

Once dinner was over and the plates cleared away, the girls disappeared into an adjoining room and shut the door behind them. Radi and his aunt and uncle remained at the table, and mint tea was poured for all. Hajj, respectfully named because he has made the pilgrimage to Mecca as all Muslims are expected to do once in their lifetime, removed a pipe from his pocket, carefully packed it, and lit it. The aunt, who did not smoke or approve, said nothing; instead, she poured a shot of whisky, which was her guilty pleasure.

'What are the girls doing?' I asked, curious about the reels of laughter coming from behind the closed door.

'Go see for yourself! You're welcome to join them if you like,' Radi said, although he did not dare go near what was clearly the girls' domain.

I cautiously walked over the thick pile carpet, soft under my bare feet since I had removed my shoes when I entered the house in the customary way. As I slowly pushed the door ajar, smoke wafted through the crack, and I curbed the urge to choke.

'Come in, come in,' the girls shouted through the dense smog.

'And close the door quickly,' Izza shouted over the top, and volcanic laughter erupted again. I took a seat on a cushion on the floor and partook in the epitome of passive smoking, staring through the haze at the pile of kif on the table, which explained everything. I listened to the gossip without understanding because I did not know much Arabic. I wished I did.

Later that night, Izza took us out to her local bar where a band was playing traditional Berber music with a group of women dancing. The audience was male-dominated, but so is general life on Morocco's streets. Izza was not perturbed, so long as there was a hookah at the table.

We returned in time for dinner before sun-up, and then we all settled down to sleep. As they had a guest, all the girls slept downstairs. They liked the company. So we each took a space on the cushions that lined the intricate green mosaic walls and covered up with thick heavy blankets, and we slept until the first person stirred when the fasting resumed until sundown and another celebratory meal.

'We have an old Berber saying, "When you come to our house, we are your guests, for this is your home." We would love you to stay for as long as you want, a day or a week or longer, it is up to you. However long you stay, you must stay for the party in a couple of days' time though,' Radi's aunt said. It was a sentiment I heard many times in Morocco. How could I refuse?

Whereas Christmas dinner preparations at home require buying a pre-packaged frozen turkey from the supermarket, here we all hopped in the car and drove up into the hills of the Middle Atlas playing eye-spy for goats. When some were found, we looked for the shepherd to ask whether we could buy one. A manic goat-chase in a muddy field ensued, but the goats we caught were not fat enough yet. Instead, we returned home with leg-tied chickens bought fresh and clucking from the market.

After the feast where there was even more food than usual, everybody moved upstairs. Three musicians were sat on a carefully laid rug at the far wall. The old *maalem* was a friend of Hajj and was here to play traditional *Gnaoua* music.

The word *Gnaoua* probably originates from the Berber word *aguinaw,* meaning 'black man' and was used to refer to the enslaved black people of West Africa who came from the kingdom of Old Ghana in the eleventh to thirteenth centuries. When the slaves were freed, they migrated to North Africa bringing their own customs and beliefs to Morocco. They settled in Marrakech and Essaouira, which were connected to the trans-Saharan slave trade.

The *Gnaoua* music spread to Berber and Arab groups, and today it is being modernised by fusing it with blues, jazz and reggae. Sometimes called the Moroccan Blues, there are many young artists popularising it, although the spiritual meaning is being lost; though the music here was nothing like the trendy tunes I later heard on Essaouira's streets.

The *maalem* sat cross-legged in the centre strumming the *gimbri, a* lute with a long rectangular body covered with stretched camel hide and a palm neck. The sound from the three thick strings of wound camel hair resonated deeply in the enclosed, bare room as the *maalem* plucked complex tunes on the outer strings and his thumb kept the beat on the central string.

The other two musicians, both in their early twenties, kept time with *krakebs*. I sat and listened, and was mesmerised by the rapid repetitious rhythm of triplets emerging from the din of the metal castanets, with the strongest beat alternating between the left and right hands.

When everyone was assembled around the walls of the room, the two young musicians stood and danced hypnotically while keeping the rhythm on their *krakebs*. What sounded like one continuous song was really a series of chants and they lasted about fifteen minutes or possibly longer because in the entrancement time stood still. When one song came to an end, the musicians carefully laid their instruments on the floor, sat back against the wall, and poured tea from the silver pot into a small glass. A heavy silence descended the room as they each took a slow sip before passing it on.

When the glass was empty, the musicians took the *maalem's* lead and raised their instruments and recommenced the rhythm. The *maalem* sang and it sounded like speaking in a low voice with an uneven crackle that some men get when they are old, but it was no less beautiful for that. Instead, it sounded wise and true.

A frail lady wrinkled by weather and age was helped up by her daughter and began dancing. She stood facing the musicians, barely moving at first, but as she absorbed the music, her feet began to shuffle in time, and slowly the movements became clearer and more defined. All the while her feet moved with the rhythm, her eyes were closed and head drooped and arms dangled loosely by her sides. Gradually, the pulse quickened, and the lady started turning and swirling faster and faster, her arms swinging and flailing and her legs moving frantically. Then Radi took a silver plate that was burning incense and wafted the scented smoke below her face. As the tempo slowed, barely perceptible at first, the lady's movements calmed until finally the music stopped, and she came to rest. Then she opened her eyes and walked slowly, like the old lady she was, back to where she had been sat as if nothing had happened at all, and she eased her frail body back onto the cushion.

The music continued deep into the night, and the men stood and danced and twirled, just as I had seen Sufi mystics do in Pakistan, on the edge of entrancement and possibly enlightenment. However, they never let their souls be completely overtaken by the spirit of the music, unlike the smooth-skinned young woman who, at the height of one chant, collapsed to the floor writhing like a trapped animal trying to escape. Her screams cut through the fragrant air, and during her outpouring, Radi took a thin red cloth and let it float down and shroud the lady like a thin veil, protecting her from the world.

Later, some people were covered in a black cloth or yellow cloth for different colours symbolise different functions in nature. While I didn't understand everything I was seeing, I too was mesmerised by the music and realised there is much more to our world than meets the eye, although I doubted I would ever see far beyond the physical because that is all I have ever been taught to see.

3

Middle Atlas and Desert

Morocco

It felt good to be back on the bike, riding the rough tracks through the Middle Atlas Mountains. Two weeks had passed since I took the lift with Radi. It was a pleasant evening ride until the black clouds filled the sky and the rain began. I arrived at the source of the Oum-er-Rbia River cold and bedraggled, but it was nothing a hot shower, hearty *tajine* and sleep at a typical Berber hotel could not fix.

The rectangular room had no window because in the mountains that only makes it colder. It was carpeted from corner-to-corner, so I left my muddy shoes at the door. There was no furniture, so I laid out the large woven mat of green and gold embroidery as a table when the food arrived, and when I was ready to sleep, I simply laid several blankets on the floor as a bed and used a cushion as a pillow and covered myself with another blanket. And that was possibly the comfiest hotel bed I slept on in the whole of Africa.

At the river's source, the water gushed from above and plummeted into a bright mud-orange pool. The recent rains had rinsed the earth and stolen its rich colour before flowing down and giving life back to the valleys. Across the river, the track wound upwards through cedar forest until I came out on an open plateau where sheep grazed and the air was crisp and clear.

I cycled across to some makeshift tents beside the turquoise lake, milky with mineral riches, and asked if I could take water from the lake because I had none left to drink. The shepherd indicated I could if I stopped for a drink with him first. So we sat under the shade of the trees and drank tea, which he poured from an old recycled tin that was balanced above a small fire by three flat rocks.

We walked down to the lake's edge and I was dismayed to see that he scooped water from a little pool sectioned off by rocks that had donkey shit floating in it. To allay my fears, or just ignoring them, he filled a container, filtered it through an old rag into my water bottle and drank some himself. Satisfied that as it was good enough for the shepherd then it was good enough for me, I greedily gulped down the cold refreshing water. I was thirsty enough to take my chances. The mantra, 'if the locals drink it then I will' served me well on the journey, with one exception.

The road to Itzer was much longer than I was led to believe. Local estimates varied from 20 to 30 kilometres to the town on the eastern side of the hills. It did not look far on my map covering the whole of North and West Africa. On my map of Morocco, which was still very large-scale, the road looked a little longer and more winding too. But the devil is in the details, and it was with me on that dirt road. After 25 kilometres, I saw a sign telling me there was another 74 to go. By nightfall, I was still high in the mountains when I had expected to be in town.

Traditionally, Berbers were farmers living around desert oases and here in the mountainous regions of the Middle Atlas. In the valleys, I saw temporary shelters where semi-nomadic farmers, whose flocks were grazing on fertile pastures, lived until they returned to their village homes for the winter. Today, about eighty percent of the Moroccan population are of Berber descent. Now mixed with other races, it is the Berber language that identifies them. It is unclear where they originated, but their ancestors have lived in Morocco since Neolithic times. The term 'Berber' comes from *barbari* meaning 'foreign', although many call themselves *Amazigh* meaning 'free'.

The Berbers were quick to convert to Islam during the Arab invasions. However, they were still discriminated against by the Arab-dominated caliphate, which considered them second-class Muslims and sometimes enslaved them. Eventually, the Berbers revolted in AD 739 and established their own tribal kingdoms. Although few survived their own troubled histories, some towns, like Sijilmasa, that lay on the principal trade routes across the Sahara, flourished.

Several Berber dynasties were strong enough to threaten countries in Europe, and through the eleventh to thirteenth centuries, the

Almoravids and Almohads controlled much of North West Africa and Spain. Their legacy today stands in the great cultural Spanish cities of Cordoba, Sevilla and Granada.

Although the Berbers were repeatedly marginalised and discriminated against – as indigenous tribes often are, for we need only look to the Australian Aborigines and American Indians to see parallels – there are encouraging signs that the Moroccan government is beginning to pay attention to them. Berber is now recognised as an official language and is compulsory learning in schools.

The track hugged the steep hillside, so when I came upon a small clearing where a small mud-and-stone house stood, I walked over to the Berber family to ask if I could camp there. They insisted I stay in their home. I felt guilty for intruding because that was never my intention, but they appeared genuinely happy, and once I had shared out my biscuits and they served up tea, we were all more relaxed.

We sat on mats laid on the bare-earth floor with a small round wooden table in the middle. The wood-burning stove in the centre of the room kept the place warm, and in the corner was a pile of brightly coloured blankets, for use when the snow would start falling in a month or two. On three rickety wooden shelves, dented but shiny kettles and pots were neatly lined up with glasses and plastic containers for food and a spice rack – a fully functioning kitchen.

Dinner was only a few mouthfuls of goat meat and bread. It tasted delicious. But I would have rather gone without because there was barely enough for the children let alone three adults too. In spite of this, I was dished up the best pieces; they would not take no for an answer. I was all the more thankful because I didn't have any other food since I had expected to be in town by now.

It was an early night, as it is anywhere there is no electricity, because there is little to do but sleep once it is dark outside. Country folk the world over rise at dawn, and here that was at six o'clock when the children were packed off across the hills to school on a donkey. Soon after breakfast of tea with bread, when the mother was milking the cow and the father praying, I set off on my bike.

The cedar forests opened out on to sweeping vistas of green pastures and distant mountains with their tops covered in a light sprinkling of the season's first snow. As I descended, I passed three rugged men on horseback whose innocent smiles belied their bandit looks.

It was only a couple of days across the Middle Atlas, but the simplicity of the mountain life was so encapsulating, I was surprised to see satellite dishes on the mud-brick homes and a telegraph wire running along the valley that eventually met the tarmac road to take me into town.

It is easy to romanticise this life, unembellished and uncomplicated by modern technology. However, it is one thing to enjoy a few days of it when you know you can leave anytime you wish, and it is quite another when this is the only lifestyle you can afford and you must endure the harsh winters as well as the verdant summer, living only one day to the next. It is much harder to be poor in the mountains than it is in the tropics where food is plentiful and it is never so cold.

* * *

Down from the mountains, I pedalled through fertile valleys along the Gorges d'Aziz full with date palms, a complement to the rich, orange rock faces and *ksour*, the fortified villages built from the surrounding earth that blended like an architectural chameleon. Only the straight lines and tall minaret of the mosque gave the places prominence.

In a cafe in Rissani, in the heart of the Tafilalet oasis, regaining strength with a coffee, Mohammed, a shop owner began telling me about nearby Sijilmasa, the once great city at the western end of one of the trans-Saharan trade routes, where it profited from the flow of West African gold into the Muslim world.

In 1054, when the Almoravids took the city, the Arab author, al-Bakri, described Sijilmasa as a wealthy Islamic walled city with magnificent public buildings, beautiful houses with gardens, and a solidly built mosque. Yet, this was only a prelude to what the city would become as it prospered under the Berber dynasties and became part of their empire's larger economic network that spread from Spain to Timbuktu.

Just as great civilisations have risen to greatness only to come crumbling back down, so it is with cities. In 1393, a civil war led to Sijilmasa's downfall when the inhabitants killed the governor, destroyed the walls of the city and moved to the *ksour* in the surrounding area.

When Leo Africanus travelled there in the early sixteenth century, the city was on its way to being little more than ashes and dust, swamped by the desert and sands of time. While the famed Timbuktu in Mali is still a functioning town, albeit catering mainly for the tourist trade, Sijilmasa has largely been forgotten.

Mohammed took me to see Sijilmasa, but all that survives today are some rocky rubble remains. It was hard to imagine the thriving city as I walked over this fabled ruin amongst the scattered rubbish. So I went back to Rissani, and although it is only a provincial market town rather than a prosperous city of palaces, it is still there to be seen and the smell of spices from the market is more fragrant than the trash surrounding Sijilmasa's ruins.

Trans-Saharan trade peaked between the eighth and sixteenth centuries, from when the Ghana Empire rose to prominence until the first Portuguese ships arrived on the West African coast and opened new passages with Europe. The trade routes existed to meet the simple economies of supply and demand. The goods exchanged were primarily gold from West Africa that the Europeans desired, in return for salt that was taken from the mines.

Ibn Battuta was a Berber explorer who travelled extensively through the entire Arab world. In 1353, he went with one of the caravans that traversed the Sahara and described that the average caravan consisted of 1,000 camels although some had as many as 12,000. His journey took 25 days from Sijilmasa to the Taghaza salt mine in northern Mali. The mine was later raided and abandoned and the miners moved 150 kilometres south to Taoudenni. The route from here to Timbuktu is one of the shorter ones and is still used today. The camels are rarer now, instead replaced by trucks, which can transport much larger quantities of salt in a few days rather than weeks.

The Tuareg men in long flowing robes and indigo-blue dyed turbans strolled through the dusty streets of Timbuktu slowly and purposefully, as if each step were carefully considered to be worth the energy expended. It is a feature of desert life, in a hot and dry land, that everything happens slowly and even the simplest tasks are a colossal undertaking. In the exhausting oppressive heat, everything is considered whether it is worth doing at all and if it is, time is not a determining factor, but being able to finish it is.

He was tall, and his robes failed to hide his strong build. He spoke slowly and clearly, telling a story he had told many times before so that he had found the most concise way to tell it while telling only the most important parts, yet it still took a long time. And I knew it was only one of the stories he could tell, and I wished I could sit all day on the rug while drinking tea and listen to them all.

I met Shindouk at the Hotel Sahara Passion, which his Canadian wife runs, on the northern outskirts of Timbuktu where the town meets the desert.

He grew up working with the salt caravans and took his first journey at the age of thirteen. Boys usually start at sixteen, but Shindouk was strong for his age, which looking at him now I could well believe, and his grandfather was in charge of the caravan.

Tuareg society is traditionally hierarchical, and caravan life is no different. It is the youngest that gets up first to round up the camels and load them with the salt slabs, which are heavy for a young boy. Four greyish, marbled slabs each weighing 40 to 50 kilograms are loaded onto every camel. Once the slabs are secured with two on either side, the boy can then get a fire started for tea and only then when the tea is ready does he wake the other men.

When he was fifteen, Shindouk rebelled and refused to milk the female camels because he always had to milk them, but never got any to drink as it was reserved for those in charge. In the evening, he didn't bother to tie up the camels and the next morning they were gone, so his grandfather gave him a beating and sent him to find them.

Using stars for guidance, Shindouk walked and walked, following the camels' tracks until a storm blew up and erased them. He didn't dare return to camp without the camels and searched for three days until he found them. Twenty kilometres away, he chanced upon another caravan that gave him water, which probably saved him, and he returned to find his grandfather distraught with worry. His grandfather told Shindouk that he would have killed all his camels to have his grandson return safely.

Shindouk is a traveller. He has travelled many times across the Sahara, which the Tuareg call *Tinariwen*, 'The Deserts', because it is not one desert but many. Some are rolling dunes of our imaginations, dreamed up from pictures of Lawrence of Arabia, and others are flat and rocky, or mountainous and arid. He has travelled through Mauritania, Algeria and Niger, but to him the borders are meaningless because they are all desert and the desert of Mali is his backyard, and he loves it all. The hardships of desert life are a small price to pay for the freedom it gives to explore, not only wild lands, but also to delve into the desert of the mind because, ultimately, the desert is about discovery.

If I had met Shindouk in Rissani, I would have listened politely, but I could not have understood these things he said. Six months later, I was different. In that time, I too had made a trans-Saharan crossing. Although it pales in comparison with Shindouk's journeys, I learned many things on that long road, which is the twenty-first-century trade route with few gas stations.

Before I left Rissani, Mohammed gave me a gift: the *Croix d'Agadez*. Commonly called the Tuareg Cross, it is a silver diamond-shaped star to wear as a necklace. The centre represents God, and the four arms of the cross keep evil at bay. Considering the nomadic traditions of the Tuareg, it is apt that the four arms are also seen as pathways for spreading love to the four corners of the world.

'It will bring you good luck and help to show you the way. It is a compass and these show you north, south, east and west,' he said as he placed the cross in the palm of my hand and touched the four points.

'I don't know about that,' I smiled, 'but it will remind me of you and Rissani.'

Perhaps it did guide me because I made it to Cape Town, eventually. It is like many things, the cross can mean anything the wearer wants it to mean and will be as powerful as the wearer believes it to be. It now sits on my desk – it no longer has a chain, the southern tip is broken, the metal tarnished and the engraving worn like an old Roman coin dug from the ground, but it is my talisman.

4

Gateway to the Sahara

Western Sahara

'Are you Helen?' I turned around and saw a dishevelled-looking cyclist with heavily loaded bike walking towards me. *Who is that?*

'Yes,' I replied, confused.

'Hi, I'm Lars, nice to meet you.'

'Hi,' we leant over our bikes and shook hands. 'Sorry, how do you know my name?'

'I came across your website when I was planning my trip and looking at other blogs of people cycling in Africa. There aren't many women that cycle alone, especially here, so I guessed it might be you. I don't know why I remembered your name, but the website is Take On Africa, isn't it?'

'Yeah it is. Have you got a website too?'

'Yes, but I think you won't know it because I only write in Swedish. My English is not so good.'

'No, it's fine. So what's it called?'

'Lost Cyclist.'

We talked animatedly in the middle of Tiznit's street in southern Morocco, oblivious that we were blocking the way with our bikes.

'If we're both going south, we could cycle together through the Western Sahara. It might be more fun. What do you think?' Lars suggested.

I had been eager to tackle this road alone – it felt as though I had barely had a full day to myself since I left England. But there was still a whole continent of challenges to cycle through alone, and I already knew cycling across the Western Sahara would not be as hard as I had imagined at home. I had learnt that it is not so hard to travel anywhere. If you have food and water and time, and know the direction you wish to go, then you will eventually get to where you are going. All that is needed is patience.

'OK. That sounds good to me,' I said.

If I was patient, I would get the challenges and solitude I was looking for. As I had taken the lift with Radi and was privileged to see a part of Morocco I would not have otherwise, so opportunities opened by cycling with Lars. I just didn't know yet what they would be. They were like books hidden in the deep recesses of a library that you never knew existed, until one day by chance you stumble upon one, brush away the dusty cover and open the book to a new enchanted world.

'Have you just got here then?' Lars asked.

'No, I was about to leave. I've been procrastinating all morning by wandering through the streets of the walled medina, twice. I finally checked out of the hotel and had lunch. I was just on my way to the city gates to leave.'

'Oh, don't let me stop you. I do need a rest day soon though; my legs are tired.'

'I don't mind staying another day and then leave tomorrow,' I said. 'Which way were you planning on going to Guelmim? I was going to take the road via the coast.'

'Why don't you go that way now. I can rest here today and take the main road, which will be quicker, and meet you there in a few days.'

'Excellent plan.'

The 'Gateway to the Sahara' as Guelmim is known, was once an important trading post on an old caravan route. Today it holds little appeal for the traveller, except as a place to rest and refuel, which is all a traveller needs in the middle of the desert. No one goes to Guelmim; people only pass through it.

I rested and refuelled. It is debatable whether the extra food required to sustain a cyclist is cheaper than the cost of petrol required to power a car. I was eating at the rotisserie by the roundabout when Rachid, the owner, interrupted me, 'Your friend has arrived.'

I looked up but could not see anyone with a bike. 'Has he? Where?'

'I am not sure, but my brother has been looking out for him.'

A manhunt ensued to track Lars down and bring him to me. When making arrangements to meet someone, it is quite sufficient detail to give the name of a town with a population of 100,000 as the address when you are two white cyclists in West Africa. Within minutes, we were reacquainted.

Cycling on a quiet desert road is the perfect way to spend time with someone you don't know. You can cycle side-by-side and talk about the usual things that strangers talk about, and ask questions about each other until you find some mutual interests that you can continue the conversation with. If there is a lull in the conversation, when one line of questioning results in a dead end and there is a pause before the next topic commences, then all you do is drop behind the other cyclist, slip stream in the silence and savour the scenery until some curiosity sparks another flurry of questioning. This was made simple because we were two cyclists heading into the Sahara. Cycling, travel and deserts are three large topics of conversation. They were for Lars. I listened as he talked of escapades and misadventures. And he wondered how I had so much energy to cycle. Even talking was tiring in these temperatures.

Discernible features in the desert are few and far between. Distances become distorted – not everything you see is to be believed. A water tower in the distance defied logic and was nothing more than the back of a sign on the opposite side of the road. Shimmering heat hazes on the road ahead suggested that not all was as it seemed.

Later in Mauritania, I cycled alone across the flat sun-scorched stony *hammada*, bleached to baked shades of brown with only an occasional shrub standing alone in its fight to survive the unrelenting blaze. There, in the distance, I saw a shimmering lake surrounded by trees. I did not believe my eyes and said to myself, because there was no one else to say it to, that now I know what a mirage must look like, and I stared in disbelief that I could be deceived by something so beautiful. Even now, I look at the photograph I took of that lake and

I see it as clearly as I can imagine cycling to its shores where a group of brilliant white egrets and a grey heron takes flight to the safety of the far side, and removing my shoes and socks and dipping my hot, filthy feet in the ripples gently lapping at the shore and washing away the salt and sand, first from my legs, then face and arms, and enjoying the simple pleasure of feeling the cool water trickle down the back of my neck.

It was a beautiful lie, seductive and dangerous. I tore my eyes away, wiped the sweat running down my face with the sleeve of my shirt and told myself I must continue cycling, that only a fool would stop where there is no shade. As I cycled, I glanced sideways and the lake did not disappear. It spread until there was water on both sides of the road, and yet I never got closer to it.

I don't remember when the dunes emerged and hid the horizon, or when I came upon a town, but the water faded away. It was like a dream, except it remained clear in my mind. I was so unable to convince myself that there was not really a lake, a few days later I checked a guidebook and when I found no mention of lakes or wetlands, I turned to the Internet. In the end, I accepted defeat. I accepted that my eyes had fooled my mind, which until then I had considered infallible when faced with logic and reason.

After Guelmim the road followed the coast. We often stopped and wandered over to the cliff edge and looked down to see the waves crashing against the rock faces, forcing white spray skywards. The fine mist drifted with the wind and refreshed my exposed skin.

The ramshackle wooden shacks covered with tarpaulin that dotted the cliff-tops were noticeable as anglers' huts, not from the clothes hanging haphazardly or the blankets lying to air, but by the nets scattered on the surrounding rocks and the buoys and ropes lying in heaps. Most fishermen here don't own boats; instead, they fish with long rods from the tops of the cliffs.

Nearer Tarfaya, the cliffs receded and turned to vast windswept, sandy beaches with the force of the Atlantic waves forever pounding the shores. The beaches faded into the misty distance, and the air was damp and full of moisture.

This coastline, like the Skeleton Coast at the southern end of the continent, is renowned for strong winds and poor visibility, and many a ship has been wrecked close to its shores. I watched small fishing boats bobbing incongruously offshore, barely distinguishable in the vast ocean laid out to the horizon and far beyond.

Further south towards the Mauritanian border, where the road again nears the coast, I saw a ghostly ship stranded and rusting where it hit rocks long ago – an unerring warning through the morning mist.

In every other direction it was the same flat barren stony *hammada* as far as the eye could see – no hills or trees and only a continuous row of electricity pylons diminishing into the distance signalling the direction of the road, which turned inland to Laayoune, the largest city in the Western Sahara.

We had several days of rest in Laayoune, drinking coffee in the street where our hotel was, and playing pool in the evening as the locals did, and then walking to the upmarket end of town and through a hotel lobby to a bar where we sat and drank beer surrounded by images of the Green March demonstrations of 1975 when 350,000 Moroccans advanced into the Western Sahara in an effort by the government to get control of this disputed territory.

By the time we had eaten breakfast, packed panniers, checked emails, and checked out of the hotel in Laayoune, the morning had gone. By the time we had been to the cash machine, stocked up on food at a small kiosk, stopped again for unnecessary, luxury imported foods at a large supermarket on the outskirts of town simply because we could, had our passport details recorded at two police checkpoints, battled the 20 kilometres against a headwind blowing a fine layer of sand off the dunes and onto our sweat-laden faces and bare arms, and finally found somewhere to eat in El Marsa port and devoured a large platter of seafood, it was nearly four o'clock before we were on our way south. Even then I was distracted by the sight of two camels loaded in the back of a truck and had to stop to take photos.

I awoke in the night to water dripping on my face. A heavy layer of condensation had formed on the mesh of the tent and it was giving under its own weight, so I put up the tent outer, which hid the starry night sky. When I emerged early the next day, it was cool and the shore's defining features were enshrouded in a damp fog. The morning mist veiled the lunar-landscape, and the tops of the radio masts remained hidden from view. Occasionally the cloud cleared, and the sun brightened patches of ground, and when the chirping of the birds pierced the grey fog it was not such a desolate place. Soon enough we were cruising down the Saharan highway with the sun beating down on our already red faces.

Boujdour is a sizeable, modern, lively town and made a good stop for lunch. Lars was optimistic of finding an Internet cafe, which was of equal importance to him as beer is to me.

'Is there an Internet cafe here?' Lars asked the waiter.

'Yes, but it is Friday afternoon. It will be closed.'

'Unbelievable!' He said sharply to me. 'This always happens – I arrive in town on the day when everything is shut.'

'It's not long ago since we got online in Laayoune, and there'll be Internet in a few days' time once we get to Nouadhibou,' I said to calm him down. 'It's several weeks since I last had a beer and Mauritania is another dry country, so I'm going to have to wait until Senegal for my next one.'

'That is not the point!' he retorted. *OK, so that didn't help!* It was the first time I saw Lars annoyed, and it caught me by surprise. He was always so relaxed about everything. 'It is different. You know when you are in Islamic countries you can't get alcohol, but you do expect to be able to get online.'

Now that we had eaten, and knew there was no chance of Internet, there was no reason to linger longer. As the temperature cooled in the late afternoon, the cycling became enjoyable again with the moon rising in the darkening desert sky and the sun a golden orb hovering above the hazy horizon before it plunged into the sea.

The next two nights were restless as wild blasts of wind rocked the tents relentlessly, and the fine sand blew in on the damp air and encrusted everything like a coat of armour. We emerged tired-eyed. As we journeyed south, the days became hotter and the nights colder. The one constant was the wind, which continued unabated.

They were two slow, hard days for me. I was running low on energy. My focus was always on the next cafe or gas station where we could eat and rest. Our perseverance was rewarded with a change of fortune when, finally, we rounded a bend and got the tailwind we had been hoping for. The road ran close to the coast and on one occasion we got our hopes up that there was a town ahead in the distance, which might even have a small cafe, but it was nothing more than an unkempt agglomeration of fisherman's huts.

The amount of traffic on the roads diminished with every town we had passed after Laayoune. One afternoon though, we were passed by a series of motorbikes and their well-sponsored support vehicles taking part in an organised event. Apart from these teams, the traffic was mainly cars full of Moroccans or Mauritanians and their belongings squeezed into the remaining space with anything not fitting inside the car precariously strapped to the roof.

For dinner, we cooked pasta over an open fire because neither of us had a stove that worked. We devoured it in minutes. It was the fourth main meal of the day with snacks of biscuits and chocolate between. It was hard to believe I was not eating enough, except that I started fantasising about pizza and curry and Chinese takeaway and a juicy steak washed down with a full-bodied bottle of Merlot. I woke up in the middle of the night with a gnawing hunger that was only appeased by eating bread and jam, yoghurt, and more cakes.

Unable to sleep, I read for hours by torchlight, which was fine because it didn't matter what time I woke in the morning, although it would be when the sun rose and Lars would wish it were later. Lars was not a morning person although he could usually be coaxed out of bed by the suggestion of breakfast down the road. Until that first coffee, he cycled in silence. He was like the early morning sun when it is up but has no strength. When that no longer worked, I used my early-hours excess energy to make a fire to boil water for coffee. Lars was sure I clattered the pans on purpose to wake him, but really I was just clumsy.

By the fifth day after Laayoune, the road was quiet and we spent endless kilometres cycling side-by-side, spanning both sides of the road, only occasionally glancing behind to check for approaching trucks in case we hadn't heard the mechanical beasts of the desert rumbling over the horizon. Then we came to a towering sign for El Barbas, informing us of its facilities: a motel, cafe, restaurant, gas station, mechanic, parking, and Internet.

Lars shattered the peace with a booming, 'Oh! Wow!'

'What?' I exclaimed. It was the first time I had seen or heard Lars truly animated.

'There's Internet!'

'Well, that's what the sign says. But where, or what, is El Barbas?' Killjoy or realist, there was no denying the lack of anything nearby except sand and stone. This question occupied our thoughts for the rest of the day.

The next town, which lay off to the right of the road looked suspiciously quiet. We needed water anyway, so we took the side road. It was a ghost town – deserted. The blocks of houses that were neatly aligned into a network of streets had never been lived in, the metal gates rusting in the salty air creaked as I pushed them open, doors stood ajar revealing bare rooms with sand piling in the corners and rubbish that had blown in from the empty streets, the mosque's walls had never heard a prayer whispered and no muezzin had ever shouted through the loudspeaker atop the minaret, the phone lines had never connected distant relatives, and no men had sat in the shade or children played in the streets. The tax incentives offered by the Moroccan government were not enough to entice people to move to this desolate place.

There was no Internet here. Or water.

We cycled a few kilometres further and came to a functioning, open gas station. Time for coffee, coke, and three-egg omelettes washed down with a second three-sugar coffee, which was our staple second breakfast of the day. With my stomach temporarily satisfied, my mind soon turned to thoughts of what to have for lunch and dinner. The pasta from the night before had lacked salt. I decided to decant some from the large container on the table into my empty Nescafe packet ready for the evening's dinner.

The salt stuck to the shaker, the lid wouldn't unscrew, and then it fell off and large quantities of salt dispensed over my already sand-and-sweat-encrusted clothing. Eventually, I decanted some where I wanted and carefully placed the Nescafe packet on the table ready to pack away. No sooner had I done this than the waiter came along and cleared the table. Before I could react, the salt-in-Nescafe packet was in the bottom of the rubbish bin. *Sigh*. Lars laughed.

Later that day we approached another, identical sign for El Barbas. There was still no town, just a small derelict building, and no Internet. We stopped inside for the shade. Two concrete blocks were positioned around a flat stone like chairs at a table. We ate lunch and wondered about the many people who had stopped here before. The walls were covered in messages, a guest book for all that had visited, but it was all in Arabic and I couldn't read it, only admire the beauty of the script that flows from right to left, *tfel ot thgir*.

Cars occasionally stopped, and we were offered water we didn't need because we always carried too much, which was better than not enough. People asked us where we were going, which was obvious because there is only one road and we weren't going north, so we had to be going south, and they took photographs of us with our bikes, as I had photographed the camels in the truck because it was a novelty.

There is not much else to photograph when you are speeding along in a car. The drivers assume that because they have a photo of one view of the *hammada* then they have a photo of it all. In a car, you do not travel slowly enough to study every stone and see the subtle changes and realise that the desert is not barren, but a masquerade of beauty with many faces. Instead, they photographed our filthy, sweaty red faces with lines of salt dried white on our necks – there was nothing beautiful about that view.

There were plenty of road signs besides those for the elusive El Barbas. If the road changed direction by a few degrees, there was a sharp bend sign; where there was a slight undulation in the road, there was a sign for a hidden dip or a hill; occasionally there are signs warning of camels, but they roam free and were rarely where the signs were. The day before we had passed a sign for the tropic of Cancer. We made crossing the imaginary line a momentous occasion by taking a photo before continuing south towards the equator, which took me another nine months to reach – there was no sign on that dusty track through the equatorial forests of Gabon. Today though, it was a 'Danger - Mines' sign, so we camped close to the road and didn't walk far from the tents.

We enjoyed our next day's breakfast at the real 'El Barbas' complex, complete with a motel, cafe, restaurant, gas station, mechanic, and parking. In the long hours on the road, Lars must have resigned himself to the probability that Internet on the sign was more a hope than a reality. He didn't even ask about it when we got there; it was as if he had fallen just before the finish line. I took up his cause and asked at the motel.

There was no Internet.

No Man's Land was littered with the wrecks of burned-out cars. Several kilometres of unpaved piste wound through the desolate, dusty landscape to a police checkpoint on the Mauritanian side. Our passport details were laboriously typed onto an old computer by two guards – one read the details, the other typed using his middle finger only. The random sequence of letters bore no resemblance to our names, nationality, or place of birth, and rather than the usual questions, they asked Lars, 'Why you take woman with you?'

Momentarily taken aback, we looked at each other, stupefied. I wondered what Lars was going to say, and Lars hoped that whatever he said wouldn't offend me, who he had only known a short time, and wouldn't offend the officers, whose culture is so different to ours. Before he had chance to reply, another question shattered the silent interlude.

'How do you sleep?'

'In a tent,' Lars replied tactfully.

The officers looked at each other, grinned and looked back at us, 'Ah, you bring a woman to sleep with and keep you warm.'

'No, we have two tents,' Lars defended, and I suppressed a laugh.

'Sure,' and with that the police enthusiastically shook Lars' hand as though he had just won Olympic gold.

5

A Train Ride and Desert Solitude

Mauritania

I was catapulted into the Africa of my imagination.

Nouadhibou is the place where the Muslim North and black sub-Saharan Africa collide and unite – where wandering goats and dirty cyclists try to avoid colliding with battered cars weaving down the dusty roads and swerve to avoid an overloaded donkey cart, and drivers beep horns for any reason and no reason. The streets were lined with shops selling a delectable array of tinned food and cold cokes, *epiceries* were filled the meat carcasses hanging from hooks, plagued by flies even early in the morning, and the smell of freshly made baguettes in the *boulangeries* subtly wafted down the street, overcoming the stale odour of rotting vegetables piled into a rubbish heap. Slim young men in tattered clothes sat or strolled, never noticeably working, and buxom ladies in flowing print dresses and head-scarves that remain perfectly in place, regardless of the wind, purposefully walked home loaded with groceries.

It was the place where I rode into town unnoticed, another face in the crowd. Anonymity was assured, almost. Later that day, sat in a cafe, 'Bonjour Helen.'

Déjà vu - I had a perplexing Truman Show feeling where I was surrounded by strangers who already knew me, stage actors in my life play, and I was the unwitting star. But this was just the man who gave me directions when I was lost in town, and in return, I gave him my name when he enquired. I gave out my name as freely as Africans gave out their mobile number, and it was a cheap offering with little meaning.

The cafe was a little enclave of European taste, with French patisseries, espressos, electricity, and air-conditioning. It was an escape from the dust and heat and busy streets. It was a good thing they did not serve beer - cold beer with beads of moisture running down the glass - I might never have left.

Lars continued south to the capital, Nouakchott. He was running out of days on his visa and didn't feel the need for a detour. I took a train deeper into the desert.

The station, five kilometres out of town, was nothing more than a small whitewashed building that was easily overlooked, even with the words 'gare du voyageurs' written on the side. I pushed my bike over the sand and took a seat on the bench lining the wall along with the other passengers.

In the centre of the room several ladies sat listlessly, each by their own small table toppling with foodstuffs and fizzy drinks for sale. Nobody was interested in buying. Everybody sat in silence, staring blankly ahead, with the occasional sideways glance, always avoiding eye contact for fear that they might have to converse with the strange person staring back.

Train stations are the same the world over. Set a group of strangers in a train station and they become self-absorbed, self-conscious, introverted, and incapable of interaction. There is an unspoken rule that conversation must not be entered into. Put the same people anywhere else and they will find something to talk about – the weather is the default topic of conversation.

The train arrived almost on time – only one hour late – and I clambered aboard the passenger carriage. I preferred to pay a small premium for seating, rather than riding for free in one of the wagons carrying iron ore from the mines in Zouerat, where ending the 12-hour journey covered in a layer of ore dust was guaranteed.

The passenger carriage was little better. The seating was a bum-numbing, hip-crushing, hard-bottomed bench, and although the cushioning of the seat backs remained in place, they were fully faded and dust-encrusted. There were no doors and the windows were jammed open, and since the passenger carriage was at the tail end of one of the longest trains in the world, the sand and ore dust were lifted into the air by the two kilometres of wagons and entered the compartment where I sat.

The dust settled in my hair turning it grey and on my clothes, so my white kaftan was now smeared with sweaty filth. It irritated my lungs, so that I breathed heavily as though I had smoked since a teenager, and the back of my throat became so sore I coughed constantly unless I slowly sipped water to calm the burning. Worst of all, it settled thickly on my bike, which that morning I had spent hours in the hostel washing off the dirt, carefully degreasing, painstakingly scrubbing off rust from the chain, and oiling it until it was like new.

It was impossible to look out of the window; even with sunglasses on the blast of dust in my red inflamed eyes was too painful, and the thick cloud obscured the view anyway. Instead, I talked and drank tea with the local passengers and ticket inspector – they were used to the journey.

The elaborate method of rapidly pouring the sweet tea from pot to glass from unnecessarily high heights was skilfully done without a drop being spilled. Then I sat very still and slightly scared as the man next to me examined a sharp dagger while the train jolted forcefully and the wagons closed together and prised apart like a concertina.

Later, I lay with my eyes shut on the hard seats as the train rocked, vibrated, bounced, bumped, jerked, jolted, shook, swayed, creaked, and squeaked its way through the desert. Each time the train stopped, I peered out of the window to see where we were, but by then it was pitch black outside except for the stars, and there was nothing to see.

At official stops there were 4x4s waiting by the tracks to take the departing passengers to a nearby village, I presumed, because there were no roads or lights in the distance. For that reason, when the train stopped at Choum and I could not see any lights or buildings or roads in the three o'clock darkness, I put my gear on the back of a bush-taxi like everyone else, rather than attempt the 120 kilometres of desolate piste to Atar with no signs, villages, people, or water along the way.

The Toyota trucks were overloaded with whatever the passengers needed to transport. Safety of the baggage was top priority. Once all the main goods were secure with a large net holding everything in place, jerry cans were strapped to the netting, and my bike precariously placed on top. Only then could the passengers get in. Three sat with the driver in the cabin and four of us were perched on top of the pile. We wedged ourselves into any nook or cranny, and my feet dangled over the edge into the cool, night air. Hurtling along the web of pistes crossing the desert, wrapped in fleece against the cold, I drifted off to sleep, unable to keep my heavy eyelids from closing, even though I knew I should stay awake because when I did not hold tight, I was bounced towards the edge.

I woke with a sudden jerk and just enough time to grab the netting and pull myself back up. That was how the night passed until first light, when the sun slowly warmed us, and finally we arrived in Atar for breakfast.

Part of the reason I had made this uncomfortable journey was because I wanted to visit Chinguetti. It was once an important trade centre where caravans stopped to water their camels at the oasis. It was also a holy city and major meeting point for Sunni Muslims, who stopped here to gossip and trade and pray at the mosque on their pilgrimage to Mecca.

It was not destroyed at the hands of humans like Sijilmasa in Morocco. Instead, it is facing a slow decay into decrepitude. Soon it will be buried forever, another victim of the shifting sands of the Sahara, vast dunes on the constant move that swallow whole cities.

I could not reach Chinguetti. Heavy rain during a recent thunderstorm had destroyed the road there. It was going to take days to rebuild, I was told. I assumed, therefore, that it would take at least a week and probably more. Sometimes you have to accept defeat over events outside your control and move on. Mostly, my heart was not in it for a struggle. Ultimately, I had been more interested in the train journey than the town. Instead, I recuperated at a nearby oasis before taking the desert road to Nouakchott, Mauritania's capital.

The first day alone was difficult. I had become accustomed to company and was solemn with the solitude I had craved for so long. The monotony of the asphalt road, straight and unerring for hours at a time with nothing to look at except the endless sands and sporadic shrub was mind-numbing. All I could feel was a tiredness in my legs emanating slowly through my entire body, and all I could think about was getting to Nouakchott as fast as possible, so I cycled harder and that tired me more. I had to stop and rest, but I didn't want to lose any time even though I had all the time in the world. And the sun beat down relentlessly, ruthless in this unforgiving land. My thoughts turned to anger because I could not see the beauty beyond my own despondency.

In the distance a radio mast loomed and that was what I focussed on. It was a tall target in a featureless land. All my attention was on reaching this goal, which I had turned into the centre of my world – nothing else was important. I turned up the music on my iPod and pedalled harder and faster. I turned my pitiful anger into productive fury. It didn't matter that beyond the radio mast the road continued, never-ending to the unreachable horizon.

At the mast I met two cyclists travelling north. It was a brief meeting because it was too hot to stand still in the midday sun. We told each other what to expect on the road ahead. They said it was fascinating the way they had come; I said it was dull and monotonous. Of course, it was only our mindsets that were different, and not the road that changed here. I decided there and then to stop thinking about Nouakchott and friends and beer, and just enjoy the moment.

Gradually, my outlook brightened, and I realised there was still much to see in the desert. The shrubs were not all the same. Some had beautiful white flowers and large green leaves that seemed to defy the desert's natural selection, and there were vines that spread along the surface sand whose green and yellow fruits resembled melons, but were too bitter to eat. Shredded tyres scattered the roadside, a testimony of today's Saharan trade by truck. When something dies or outlives its usefulness here, it is discarded and left because the cost of removal from this inhospitable environment is too great. I saw a rusting oil tanker and burned wrecks of cars, and I wondered how there could be so many accidents where there was so little to crash into. Wooden frames where a village once stood lay like skeletons, a brightly painted corrugated hut stood alone with no apparent function, and an old shrine perishing atop a hillock was the only evidence that the place had meant something to someone once.

The landscape slowly morphed from a flat bed of rocks to a sandy plain, and then dunes began to rise in the distance and converge on the road. The only reason the road was not submerged was that it was regularly ploughed and the sand pushed aside into high-sided walls, so all I could see was the way ahead.

Villages appeared every 30 or 40 kilometres. The road enabled trucks to transport water, and where there was water, there could be life. Some villages existed at an oasis where deep wells had been dug and palm trees sprang up to provide shelter. Now villages can be anywhere – their main feature was a giant water bag that sustains the community until the next delivery of safe water from the capital.

I saw three trucks pulled over in the sand and a group of men sat on a rug, relaxing under the speckled shade of a tree. They watched me watching them, and when I waved, they called out for me to join them. When encounters are few and far between, you do not pass them up easily.

I wheeled my bike off the road, laid it down because it requires much effort to drag a bike through the sand, and walked over. They invited me to sit down. One man passed me a bowl of water to wash my hands. There was a large plate of noodles on the rug, and we each took a handful and moulded it into a mouth-sized ball in our right palm before placing it in our mouths, chewing laboriously on the lump of carbohydrate, and swallowing. There is a skill to eating like this and I had still not mastered it. The noodles stuck to my palm in a gooey mess that I couldn't get in my mouth without dripping the juicy vegetables on my shirt that was already filthy from wiping the sweat and dirt from my face onto it while cycling. Not one of the men noticed or cared. They were joking and telling stories of their own journeys, of places I had just travelled through and places I would soon see.

At first I was wary of walking over to this group of men, many miles from the nearest settlement, where it could be an hour before the next vehicle passed. But I considered that I had become a good judge of character and concluded that the casual air and lightheartedness of these men would lead me to no harm.

It is easy to be suspicious of everybody when you begin travelling, suspecting ulterior motives for every act of kindness. It is also easy, when you have been on the road for months, to become complacent and assume that everything is just as it seems because it has been so far. It is then, when you let your guard down, that things usually go wrong. These are the perennial problems of travelling alone. It is a fine line of suspicion and fear preventing full enjoyment of a journey, to one of ignorance and stupidity that will end in trouble.

I was no more likely to be robbed here than when cycling on the road or taking the Tube in London. But when one of the men walked over to my bike, for an instant I was concerned. The large jovial man, whose belly showed he was more adept at one-handed eating than I was, saw my anxious looks and patted me on the shoulder.

'Do not fear. One of the trucks must leave soon, and we don't want to accidentally drive over your bike.'

In the final hour before dark, when I was keeping a lookout for a place to camp, I passed a parked truck, and there was the jovial fat man who had calmed my fears at lunch.

'My truck has broken down,' he said.

'Is it a big problem? I don't suppose there is anything I can do.'

'Oh, no. I will wait until morning when another truck will bring new parts. I can sleep here.' The truck drivers must be used to breakdowns.

'Do you need any water or food?' I offered.

'No, thank you. I am fine,' he said. 'Why don't you camp here tonight? It is almost dark and company is good.'

While I was no longer suspicious, I was not stupid either. I knew that a single man away from home whom I do not know might have other intentions beyond a campfire and hot dinner. He was the kind of man who likes company more than time alone, which he must have plenty of as a long-distance truck-driver. I am sure he was harmless. But darkness is good at exacerbating small fears.

'Thanks, but I want to continue. I like to cycle when it is cool now the sun has gone, and it is easy with this wind behind my back.'

'As you wish. Good luck, and good night.'

Camped beneath a dune that night, I could not help thinking about that jovial man waving goodbye. *Is he silently sat staring into a campfire alone?* Separated by only a few kilometres of darkness, we were neighbours. For a brief moment, a pang of loneliness washed over me, and that almost never happened. Some people are larger than their self, and just as his cheerfulness was contagious, I think his loneliness radiated out touching those around him, and that night I was the only one near to feel it.

There was not a lot to do in Nouakchott, so I spent my time relaxing at Auberge Menata, camped on the roof terrace and reading under the trees, hiding from the sun and the rest of the world. I left the exploring of the city to the resident tortoises who have a network of tunnels beneath the streets. The tortoises and tunnels were here when Nouakchott was a small fishing village and have survived the rapid expansion during the sixties to the city of today. The tortoises travel in safety between connected gardens and safe enclaves where other tortoises live.

It was a surprise to find Lars at the auberge. We agreed to cycle together again. Pouring over our maps and guidebook, we made a plan for which way to travel. Now there were many options available, unlike when we had met in Tiznit.

The plan grew from an idea, much like the idea to cycle to Cape Town. A small seed was planted, and the more we nurtured it the faster it grew. From this one stem, more ideas formed like branches and spread and sprawled into a tangled confusion of possibilities and improbabilities. And when we could no longer see through the confusion, we pruned it back and then saw, clearly defined for the first time, a great new adventure: to paddle a locally-built *pirogue* down the Niger River.

Lars' original intention had been to paddle a river in Sierra Leone. As I didn't plan on going that direction, I looked on the map for another river that I could paddle instead. The Niger River was on my route, and it seemed feasible that I could either buy, or have made, a wooden boat in Faranah in the river's upper reaches and paddle it downstream to Kouroussa and on to Bamako in Mali.

'Would you mind if I joined you?' Lars asked when I suggested it.

'Of course not.' I liked the idea of undertaking this adventure alone though. I even tried to convince him that we should have our own boats. I had no idea then that it would be as tough as it was. Although we didn't know until we were well underway, neither of us could have done the trip alone. Sometimes two people are better than one.

'Let's agree now that whatever happens, even if we don't cycle together any more, we paddle the Niger River,' Lars looked at me seriously.

'Agreed, it's a deal.' I meant it and we shook hands. If we had been able to we would have consecrated the deal with beer, but we had to make do with a *shawarma* and coke.

6

Baobabs and Toubabs

Senegal and the Gambia

We left Nouakchott and cycled past the shanty town on the city's outskirts where nomads have come in search of jobs and a better life. Their temporary camps are now permanent fixtures with satellite dishes, which are what define a settled home here, although the display of wealth remains the number of goats owned that are kept beside the shack on a patch of dusty land fenced off with wooden slats and scraps of metal.

Beyond the market of mayhem with cattle, goats, trucks and traders, calm gradually resumed as we passed a gas station, another collection of camels, and a series of checkpoints.

Beyond a small wooden hut that had drinks for sale was the last police check point. Lars went to buy cokes, maybe even cold ones, at the shack. I walked over to the policemen with our passports to get the proceedings started.

'Where have you come from?' the guard asked.

'Nouakchott.'

'Where are you going to?'

'Senegal.'

'Are you married?' The older officer in charge spoke up, now holding our passports firmly in both hands behind his back. This is one of the top questions a female travelling alone in Africa is asked.

I looked towards the hut, but Lars was out of sight.

'No,' I replied.

'Why not?' *Sigh.* It is unusual for a woman of my age to be unmarried here. I considered which answer to give this time knowing that it would only lead to more questions. At least he didn't think I was so old as to be a widow.

'I am married to my bike.'

He laughed. 'Divorce your bike and marry me.'

'I can't. I'm very attached to my bike. We go everywhere together.'

'Marry me. I have a good job and can take good care of you.'

'I prefer to take care of myself.' The three guards standing a few feet away were closely watching this conversation. *How am I going to get our passports back without a wedding ceremony?*

Lars was now walking over with our empty water bottles. I changed the direction of the conversation, 'Can *mon amie* get some water?'

'Oh, he is your boyfriend?' I said nothing.

'Is there a problem?' Lars asked when he arrived.

'No problem,' and the officer brought the passports in front of him, looked down at them thoughtfully before handing them back while shaking his head. 'Bon voyage.'

Relieved, I turned around and walked back towards the bikes.

'Wait!' he called out. I stopped, dreading what might happen now. 'You need water.' He signalled to one of the guards to fill our bottles from the large plastic barrel that stood beside a pile of old tyres.

Now on the fringes of the desert, it was greener. Grassy tufts and shrubs appeared more frequently, and thorny bushes and acacia trees grew. Villages became more frequent. Sometimes the children called and waved. The men usually stood and stared. I saw one teenage girl carrying a mobile phone in her hand. It was not unusual though; it was only not what I had imagined.

Two young women were crouched under a small tree, staring at us cycle past. I watched their faces and tried to understand what they were thinking, but all I saw was fear. I smiled at them and waved, but they leapt to their feet, ran behind one of the buildings, and then sheepishly peered around the corner. I looked back at them, wondering what could be so frightful about us. 'Hey Lars, did you see …?'

Bump.

My front wheel caught the rear pannier of Lars' bike, which wobbled a little, and I swerved uncontrollably. My bike careered off the asphalt, hit the solid gravel, the wheel jammed, and I hurtled headfirst over the handlebars, sliding to a halt with my hands as brakes. *That hurt.* By the time I looked up, I was surrounded by twenty of the most curious villagers.

Lars was rummaging around in his front pannier. He looked over to me, 'Are you OK?'

'I'm fine,' I said, which considering I had just fallen off my bike in a most embarrassing and slightly painful way, and that I am a female of the species and never say exactly what I mean, meant of course that I was not fine. But my answer was sufficiently affirmative for Lars to take the camera from his pannier and photograph the remaining proceedings while I repaired my grazed, gravel-filled bleeding palms.

Bandaged-up and ego-bruised I got back on the bike. We continued down a corrugated dirt road that went directly towards the Diama Bridge border crossing to Senegal.

We approached one village in the hope of finding a shop because we had little food and were set upon by screaming, chasing pack-brats demanding sweets and money, of which we had none of one and little of the other. Their dirty fingers pulled at my panniers, and one succeeded in pulling off the rubbish bag.

It was just at that moment I realised I had a flat tyre. By the time I stopped, I was busy keeping the little hands from trying to open the panniers.

Lars looked back to me, 'Are you OK?'

'I'm fine,' I said, which considering I had got a flat tyre in the most inconvenient of places, and that I never say exactly what I mean, meant of course that I was not fine. But this was the answer Lars was hoping for. He rummaged around in his pannier for the camera and photographed the remaining proceedings while I fixed the flat and simultaneously fended off the children.

There were no swarms of screaming children in the Diawling National Park. Instead, warthogs raced along the tracks with tails erect, tusks menacing, and dust flying. Bordering the Senegal River, with a natural barrier of sand dunes, the park contains areas of fresh water and saltwater wetlands. It is home to 300,000 birds and over one million migratory ones. Flocks of flamingos, elegant slim-lined herons, wading birds, and pelicans all merge upon the myriad of lakes and waterways, saline flats, alluvial plains, and small mangrove swamps. There are lots of fish too. And fishermen. And tilapia and rice with peanut sauce – tasty.

Mauritania had been sepia shades of sand and dust – worn down by the wind and beaten by the sun. Senegal was awash with colour – cafes, signs, clothes, music, and buses painted bold. It had an upbeat atmosphere too. There was one town in particular that embodied this vibrant vitality. St Louis was not just surviving, fading, or dying, but living and thriving. And there was beer: Flag flying. That, alone, was a good reason to stay a few days.

St Louis was founded on Ndar Island in the mouth of the Senegal River by French colonists in 1659, and it was named after their king. The sea port, with its safe harbour, flourished with the slave trade. Over the decades, there were many marriages between freed slave girls and French merchants. The *Métis* community became characterised by the *signares*, wealthy women of the privileged elite. They lived in the colonial town houses with wooden balconies that still stand today (and reminded me of Old Havana in Cuba), and they were heavily involved in all aspects of the town's social life.

Although St Louis' role as a trade centre has diminished in favour of Dakar, now Senegal's capital, it has remained a centre for music and culture. I drank beer while listening to the soft, soulful music playing in the cafes, which are restful enclaves away from hawkers and tiresome artisanal traders. And between beers, I wandered aimlessly through the streets.

Across the bridge on the peninsula, I was immediately transported onto a bustling street, where Wolof tribesmen and Peul women wandered and traded along the dirt roads strewn with rubbish. Rusting cars, and broken black and yellow taxis were parked beside the river. I raised my camera to my eye to take a photo of the street, for no particular reason and of nothing in particular. As I did, a blinkered grey horse with bright coloured tassels on its bridle walked into my view.

Then chaos.

'Hey you! Stop! Stop!' shouted a man's voice.

I looked up from my camera to see what was going on because through the viewfinder all I could see was a horse and cart where I had expected a street.

'Lady. Stop! White Lady … Stop!' Since I could not see any other white people, I began to think that this faceless voice was talking to me. 'No photo! No photo!' By now my camera was already back in my bag.

The owner of the horse jumped off his cart and ran towards me shouting and waving. This attracted the attention of the locals nearby who came over too. Soon hundreds of men and a few women surrounded me. The owner was shouting loudly into my face.

'But I wasn't photographing your horse, only the street,' I explained. That was a mistake.

'You should have asked all of us before taking our photo,' someone replied.

The crowd of onlookers transformed into an unruly rabble as they jostled closer and shouted to be heard. It surprised me that it was the women shouting the loudest.

'Now you must pay us.'

Trapped amongst the chaos and concerned I might be lynched, I answered back when someone tried to grab my arm. 'What? Get off me! How dare you!' I yelled.

'Please calm down. Tell me, what is the problem?' When I turned round, I saw that he was a man of reason.

He listened to me and then spoke with authority to the crowd. Some quietened down, others shouted back at him.

'It is best you go. They do not understand.'

'I agree, but I can't get out.'

'You,' he pointed to some of the men stood silently, 'let this girl through.'

I made a sharp exit, disappeared down one of the narrow paths through the market crammed with small shops, and then took an alley towards the beach. *Phew. Glad I'm out of that mess.*

On the beach of golden sands were fishermen, who were really only boys, playing football at the end of a hard day's work. Goats nibbled on scraps of rubbish, and children played in the sand. Young men said hello and told me about their day. Everyone was relaxed and having a good time.

A young lad in football kit ran up to me. We talked meaningless talk until he got round to what he had come to speak about.

'Have you been taking lots of photographs of our town?'

'Well, yes, but …'.

'Then where is your camera?'

'Well …' I hesitated, in case he wanted to relieve me of it.

'Because I want you to take a photo of me,' he added.

'Err … sure, if you want,' I wondered if he were going to ask for money afterwards. But he didn't.

There are two kinds of people in Africa: those who utterly detest having their photograph taken, and those who love it. It is possible to photograph the first through bribery or deceit. If you have a camera, it is impossible to avoid photographing the second.

There is one everlasting image from Africa that will remain with me: the baobab tree. As we cycled from St. Louis towards the Gambia, we passed many impressive baobabs, whose trunks grow up to 25 metres in circumference. When I looked inside the hollow of one tree, I saw tens of little lizards scampering further into the dark hole, and two bats sleeping upside-down, which at night would pollinate the white flowers to produce the velvety green fruit.

There are many folk tales about the baobab. One says that it was among the first trees to appear on the land. Then came the slender palm tree, but when the baobab saw the palm it cried out that it wanted to be taller. Then the beautiful flame tree appeared with its red flower and the baobab was envious of the flower blossoms. When the baobab saw the magnificent fig tree, it prayed for fruit as well. The gods became angered by the baobab, so they pulled it up by its roots and, to keep it quiet, replanted it upside down.

Before I saw the first baobab tree with stunted, crooked branches that do look like roots, the arid landscape of dry, yellow grass was dotted with acacia trees and thorny bushes. Cattle were herded along paths with the sunlight hazily reflecting the dust clouds and vultures soared in the windless sky of midday. Women walked in twos and threes along the road, balancing baskets on their heads as only African women do and raising a hand to wave at us. Men drove donkey carts, occasionally using a stick to make them go faster and raising a hand or a smile as we cycled past.

We passed numerous villages too, where local men and women sat passively in the shade of a tree. That is how to survive the African sun. It's midday fury cannot be beaten, so surrender the battle, and if there are things to be done, do them when the sun is calm.

We were usually still camped when the sun was rising. That was when streets were swept with a *besom*, a bundle of twigs tied together. It was a never-ending task of dispersing the dust from the strip outside one shop or home onto the rest of the street. Dust, like the sun, cannot be defeated, so throughout the day we saw water being scantily thrown like confetti from a bowl, which subdued the dust and kept it firm to the ground.

We were usually already camped when the sun was setting. This was when the millet was ground. Two or three women stood around a large wooden mortar and took it in turns to pound the grain with a heavy pestle, and the dull rhythmic thud resounded across the Sahelian land. It was a comforting noise, familiar and homely, as I lay in my tent.

Sometimes though, when we had spent many days or weeks passing from one village to the next and were always being watched, I just wanted to hide from the world and I wished there was silence except for the sounds of nature emanating from the bush. And when I was woken in the night by the braying of donkeys and then in the darkest hours before sunrise by the crowing of cockerels and at first light when the call to prayer resonated from the mosque, the restless night made me all the more tired for the next day's cycling. It was on those days, when it seemed that there was not one piece of Africa where there were no people, and I was bombarded by the sound of children running out to see me, waving and shouting *Toubab! Toubab!* that I wished I could take each one of those children and plant them headfirst in the dusty earth like the baobab tree.

Toubab means 'white' and because the children didn't know our names they called us *Toubab* instead, even though Lars was a copper tan and I flushed pink. It was the one common feature of travel throughout Africa: everywhere, I was called 'White' – *toubab*, *oporto*, *obroni*, *branco*, *le blanc*, *mondelé*, *mutoké*, or *mzungu*.

It was here that the children shouted their demands for sweets and money and presents too, and sometimes for my bike. As we neared the Gambian border, a group of adolescent schoolgirls in matching blue pinafores and white shirts called to Lars, 'Give me *anything*!' and they giggled between themselves as though it were the funniest thing ever. It made us smile. After all, it was just a game, and we shouldn't take it to heart, especially when we were tired and short-tempered.

The Portuguese were the first Europeans to sail up the Gambia River in 1455, followed by the English, French, and Dutch. They came in search of rumoured gold, but they found a greater source of untapped wealth: slaves. The Gambia River became a major route into the interior of West Africa, and fortified trading stations were built and fought over for control.

In 1816, the British, who by then had banned slavery, acquired Banjul from the local King of Kombo. In return, they were to provide protection to the local population against the slavers of other European nations. Subsequently, when the African continent was divided up by European powers at the Berlin conference of 1884, the Gambia became a British colony. That is why people here spoke English rather than French like much of West Africa.

The only reason we came to Banjul was to get onward visas. It is a sleepy capital that has changed little since it was founded, except the colonial buildings are now collapsing and the shanty town has spread. Once we had found the embassies and were waiting for the stamps in our passports, there was little else to do. We drank Julbrew beer; the mosquitoes drank my blood. Unfortunately, it was not only malarial insects that were attracted to me – so, too, were many young Gambian men.

It started when walking down the street with an innocent, 'How is the morning?'

'The morning fine,' I replied, which was all the encouragement needed to be accompanied on my walk through town. Thoroughly fed up with the unwanted attention, the only tactic that succeeded in shaking off these young men was to be blunt and rude with rejection. It was the same tiresome hustle every day. Sadly, their chat-up tactics must work or they would not be so persistent.

Banjul was the first place in Africa I saw many white people – usually middle-aged, overweight, sunburned, and smoking. Either they were drinking in groups or one woman would be walking hand-in-hand down the street with a young black man.

Sex tourism in the Gambia is mainstream, which is fine for the middle-aged divorcee from England who wants sex, and it is fine for the Gambian man who, if he is lucky and the lady foolish to think she has fallen in love, may get the golden visa to Britain or at the least a few drinks and dinner; it is not fine for every other white girl who passes through Banjul with no interest in cavorting with the locals.

It was different when Lars was with me – fewer men called out and those who did usually spoke with him rather than hassling me. I was grateful for the protection, but it made me wonder what else travelling in company rather than having to fend for myself was shielding me from. It was intense spending 24 hours a day every day in each other's company, but we had become good friends and wanted to keep it that way.

It was time to experience West Africa alone. We promised again to meet up to paddle the Niger River together – we had a deal.

7

From Termites to the Fouta Djalon

Guinea and Guinea-Bissau

African countries, more than most, go through periods of instability. The current political situation of the countries was always a determining factor in choosing which route to travel. If I had avoided all the countries with internal disputes that the Foreign Office had recommended avoiding, or indeed listened to my doctor, I would not have gone to Africa at all. The truth is that the advice is conservative. The reality is that some of these countries are safe enough to travel as long as you avoid certain areas. It is also possible that a problem will arise while you are in one of the 'safe' countries. Situations change quickly. The only realistic thing to do is listen to the news and the locals, and make a judgement yourself. It is easy to say this now. The advice for Guinea at the time was to leave by whichever means available because the level of security had deteriorated steadily since the coup.

Following the death of the president, Captain Moussa Dadis Camara had seized control of Guinea as the head of the junta, simply by making his own announcement on television. He dissolved the government and said elections would be held in two years' time. It was a typical modern coup – bloodless and swift, and full of hollow promises that only help to extend the time the coup leaders can hold power.

Not everyone was content though. The following September, when I was in Morocco, there were protests against the junta. The presidential guard, known as the Red Berets, stormed the stadium where the protests were being held and opened fire. Soldiers shot, killed, looted, and raped in broad daylight, and after the atrocities, hundreds of the protesters were arrested and imprisoned without charge.

Camara set himself aside from the events, but he and the military were condemned internationally for the massacre. Arms embargoes and travel bans were imposed, and bank accounts frozen – Camara's days in office were numbered.

Then, while we were in Banjul, there was an assassination attempt. Camara was shot by the commander of the presidential guard, who was angry at being blamed for the killings, and was flown to Morocco for treatment. The country was without a leader, and looking at history, it was likely there would be a fight to fill the power vacuum.

I had no desire to be caught up in it, but I did want to visit Guinea. Lars agreed that we should watch how events unfolded and maybe meet up before the border to cycle through the country together.

The best thing about travel is that it rarely goes according to plan. Our paths crossed much sooner. He was waiting at the port in Guinea-Bissau's capital when I disembarked the ferry, returning from a weekend on the Bijagos Islands. We went straight to a bar and exchanged stories of the last week on our own.

I told him of my ride through the Casamance in southern Senegal, a region that has had a bad reputation in the press from the ongoing conflict between separatists and the military, and of car-jacking and banditry at roadblocks. The situation had calmed in recent years, and when I cycled through, the only sign of unrest was the military patrolling the main road, armed men stationed every few hundred metres. It was mildly disconcerting.

Military and police presence is high in much of West and Central Africa. Over time, I came to realise that these men were not to be feared. They were usually kind and considerate. Most were honest, despised the corrupt few, and would have helped me if I needed it. Later in the journey, I sometimes sought the police when looking for a safe place to stay. In Senegal, though, where I was only just getting to grips with travelling alone in sub-Saharan Africa, I didn't ask if I could stay at one of the military camps; instead, I cycled on and on until the patrols ended and with tired legs pushed my bike off the road through waist-deep grass and camped, safe in obscurity, surrounded by mosquito-infested swampy waters.

The next day I crossed into the little ex-Portuguese colony of Guinea-Bissau and cycled towards the capital. It had a small-town feel and was more jaded than Banjul although, fortunately, lacked the male wannabe-brides. Instead, young boys sold phone cards or newspapers, and some shined shoes. As I had no mobile, cannot read Portuguese, and was wearing flip-flops, these services were of no use.

I was tired and decided it was time for a peaceful, relaxing holiday. My plan was simple: take the Friday ferry to Bubaque, the main island of the Bijagos archipelago, find a quiet secluded beach and spend the weekend there.

In Bubaque, I filled my water bags, bought some food at the market and cycled the 14 kilometres across the island along a hardened dirt road, through the jungle of tall palm trees and old hanging lianas, knotted and untouched.

I put my bike against a tree where the forest ended and the white, sandy beach began, took off my shoes, walked to the water, and replaced the sweat on my face with salt from the sea. Then I sat in the shade on the beach, which for now was my beach, and I took a book from my bag and read. Occasionally I looked up to see gulls flying overhead, or a vulture hopping and lurching in the distance, or a fisherman wandering past who waved as he went and later returned. Some of the time I just lay back, closed my eyes and listened to the waves because apart from them there was no noise, and they filled my head and emptied it too. When the sun began to set over the horizon and fall into the sea, I started to feel a little cold and hungry. I put on my fleece, gathered some wood, and made a fire in a hollow I had dug in the sand, and the flames flickered and lapped the sides of my blackened pan. I devoured the pasta and then boiled water for hot chocolate, and I sipped it slowly as the stars emerged one by one through the darkening sky, and I could make out dim lights in the distance on a neighbouring island and the faint glow of lamps from small fishing boats dipping and dancing on the silver sea.

Whenever I camped in the bush, I slept with one ear alert and the smallest sounds would wake me if they were unknown. But here, from habit rather than fear, I could not sleep. I could hear nothing except the waves, which now sounded like huge, frothing monstrosities. Noises are amplified in the dead of night, and I could not hear trouble if it came upon me although I doubted it would.

At dawn, I unzipped the tent and heaped the remaining wood on the pile of ashes and started another fire for warmth and coffee. It was an overcast morning; the damp air was heavy. I knew that soon the sun would rise and gather strength to burn through the fog onto another bright, scorching day, but until then I could enjoy the pleasant calm and cool.

As I drank my coffee, the fisherman from the day before came by to collect water from the small stream nearby. We said hello and shook hands for the first time. He enquired if I'd had any problems in the night and hoped not – now we were friends and neighbours and no longer strangers to be nervous or fearful of. It was our beach, our shared secret. I wondered if I would have slept better if we had talked the day before. The old fisherman, whose name I never knew, was typical of many people I met in Guinea-Bissau, and Guinea too for there were many similarities with these two countries besides a common name. He was respectful of my privacy, but wanted to make sure I was safe. Privacy anywhere in Africa was rare and often unattainable, and it was one of the few things I craved for on my journey and cherished when I had it.

The ferry docked in Bissau, and as I wheeled my bike down the ramp, I saw Lars. He was leaning in the shade against a shipping crate. I smiled and waved to him. I was rested and ready for some off-road biking.

The following day, we took a boat across the Rio Geba into the south of the country. We were crammed into a small, motorised boat with 150 other people and their belongings. Thankful for the calm water and windless day, I still wore the life jacket that was handed to me. In rougher weather these boats sometimes upturn mid-crossing with fatal consequences for the passengers who can't all swim.

Now, on the other side of the river, progress was slow on the dusty tracks. Moving south through the humid tropical forests, we sweated our way towards Jemberem. The intensity of the sun in the bright blue sky with the orange earth and green palms and dense forest tired my eyes, which were already irritated by the fine dust.

When we reached the Rio Cumbija, we employed a local to take us in his *pirogue* to a track on the opposite bank. He stood at the back, and with a long paddle fixed in a rack, he weaved it from side-to-side through the water in fishtail figure-of-eights, his whole body behind the movement, leaning over the sides for leverage.

River travel by *pirogue* is the modus operandi in much of Africa. Many *pirogues* were dugouts, carved from one solid tree trunk, and most were old with the edges roughly weathered and battered.

The boatman sometimes sat and paddled it like a canoe, which is best for river crossings, or stood and punted, by pushing a long pole against the river bottom, which is most effective when travelling up or downstream and you can stay in the shallows close to the riverbank.

When the tracks leading to the river were wider and more regularly travelled, there was a rusting chain ferry in operation because cars and trucks needed to cross. The chain ferries were simply a floating, metal platform, attached to a heavy chain that spanned the river, although it could not be seen because the water was always a muddy brown or bright orange depending on the colour of the earth. Once, these chain ferries would have worked by motor, but now the locals used a crank to turn the wheel that slowly moved it.

It was a single-track path to Jemberem through head-high, yellow grass and then an arched corridor of thick jungle with palm tree fronds blocking the light. When the track opened up, there were mud huts with thatched roofs and a network of paths crisscrossing between them.

We were shown to a simple lodge with a restaurant, where an ecotourism initiative was being started. We put in our order for chicken and chips.

After three hours of waiting, I moaned to Lars again, 'How long can it take to catch, kill, and cook a chicken?'

'I think they're waiting for the chickens to hatch,' he joked.

'And the potato harvest. This had better be good,' I said.

'Don't bet on it.'

A table for us had been laid with a white cloth and real cutlery. The chef eventually arrived and placed our food in front of us, 'Enjoy your meal.'

We stared down at it in disbelief, looked up at each other, shrugged our shoulders, dug in and devoured it in minutes.

'Well, it tasted good for fish and rice,' Lars commented to break the silence.

'Yeah, but not for chicken and chips. It was so not worth the wait. And not enough either; I need three more of those to curb my hunger.'

'Shall we order another? It might arrive for breakfast.'

Still hungry, we stocked up on food from a snack-shack and left the village. Fatigued, we stopped shortly after, pushed our bikes into the undergrowth that grew over our heads and cleared a space for the tents. It was a peaceful night, and morning arrived late when the sun's rays broke through the leaves.

As I pushed my bike back onto the track, I trod on the end of a branch; it flipped up and hit the back of my leg. *Ouch.* A strange pain throbbed in my calf muscle. I looked down expecting to see a graze.

'Eugh! Lars!' I called out and dropped my bike to the floor, 'Lars!' I shouted urgently, clearly perturbed.

'Are you OK?' he turned around, unconcerned.

'No! Not fine,' I said, which considering there was a squirming insect embedded in me with its legs wriggling frantically trying to escape, and that I never say what I mean, so that when I say I am fine, I'm really not, and when I say I'm not fine, then something must be very definitely wrong.

What the hell is that? I wonder how long it is. Could it be some horrid poisonous insect? What will happen to my leg if it is? Could a thing so small really do me much harm? In an instant, images of swollen limbs, necrotised flesh and gangrenous sores streamed to mind. *Get real.*

Before Lars had a chance to dig out his camera, I told him to bring his first aid kit instead. He crouched on the ground looking at my leg, peering at the foreign body twisting and jerking.

'What is it?' Lars said to me with a childlike curiosity.

'I dunno. Just get it out of me – all of it. Don't leave any in.'

With a pair of tweezers, Lars pulled at the body and held the tweezers up for a closer look at what appeared to be a six-legged abdomen.

'You missed the head.' I knew even though I hadn't looked closely – I could feel it in my leg.

'I can see that.'

'Well, you'd better get it.'

He attacked my leg with the tweezers and after more digging, extracted the other half. We laid the parts on a piece of wood and bent over closely to identify what it was: a termite. Now terminated.

I had never seen termites before. Ants, yes, but they are not the same. Termites are, genetically, more closely related to cockroaches, although their social behaviour is similar to ants.

Each termite nest has a queen and king. The other termites are all blind and are either workers or soldiers. The soldiers, like the one in my leg, are easy to distinguish by their large heads and big mandibles. Their sole function is to protect the nest from invasion, and they do so in kamikaze style. If the entrance through which an invasion is coming is larger than a single termite, the soldiers make formation and fill the entrance, all facing headfirst to the oncoming attack to block the hole. The problem is that once they are in formation, it is impossible for them to retract. They die on the battleground. It would also seem that when an invasion comes from a person who is, of course, much larger than a single termite, the soldier's self-sacrificial manoeuvre is to plant itself headfirst into the intruder.

I did not see many termites in Africa, not compared to ants. This is surprising when I considered that there are over 2,000 species and, according to one estimate, half a tonne of termites for every person on earth. One reason for this is that termites live underground and build shelter tubes of soil to travel through. It protects them from the environment and predators because they do not have exoskeleton armour like ants.

Termite mounds, however, are easy to see. In the Congo, I saw fields of termite citadels rising above me, pillars of earth dug from the depths and formed by the mass action of a colony working as one. In Botswana, single pyramids of whitish clay rose up through the bush-covered savannah. In Guinea, low-lying mushroom-shaped mounds stood like headstones covering the bare landscape where whole fields of yellow grass had been burned and the earth was blackened and sprinkled with ash.

Ants, however, are everywhere, and they are the bane of the bush-camper. They hunt down your food like mini heat-seeking missiles. A few dropped crumbs in the tent are enough to encourage the ants to eat through the ground sheet to reach them. The tiny circular holes they leave ensure the tent is not watertight until you make repairs with duct tape. Once the ants are inside, they run over you back and forth through the night. If you have pitched your tent on an ant run in the undergrowth, every time you turn over in the night, the ants, perceiving a threat, vibrate their tail segments against the surrounding leaves, so the earth sounds alive in your ear.

As I pushed my bike along forest trails in the Congo, I had to step over a thick black writhing line across the track. It was a marching column of siafu ants crawling over one another. These ant armies can be over 20 million strong, and they roam the forests and devour anything in their path, smothering animals that cannot escape like chickens or a tied-up goat. They crawl into any orifice available and cause death by asphyxiation. Smaller prey like grasshoppers usually die by envenomation from the ant sting and sometimes dismemberment by the ants' large mandibles.

Ants were one of the many animals that encouraged me to sleep inside my tent with the zip done up, even on the hottest nights. The others were mosquitoes, sandflies, spiders, scorpions, and snakes – but those stories come later.

The single-track paths weaved through tall grasses, separated and rejoined. It was unclear which were the best paths, or the correct ones, to take. With no way of knowing, I took the lead and picked one. It started to rise up out of the shallow valley, and gradually we found ourselves cycling with the sun on our faces. If our map were to be believed, we should have been travelling north-east.

'Are we going the right way?' Lars called out from behind. 'I think we're going south. If we're not careful we could end up in Guinea.'

'The same thing just crossed my mind. I'll check the GPS.' There was no fence or barrier where we crossed the border there. It was the same dry land littered with termite mounds. We backtracked the way we had come and chose another path.

Some days are perfect; they don't come around very often. We need the imperfections to make us realise when we've got something really good. I'm not talking of those halcyon days of our youth that we remember through rose-tinted glasses, happily erasing any troubles from our minds. I'm talking of simple days when at any moment you may find yourself thinking how lucky you are and how wonderful life is. Those are the days that if you could choose any to relive, it would be one of them.

That day of off-road cycling down winding trails, never quite knowing if we were going the right way, but it didn't matter because we had food and water and just to be moving and seeing was enough; that day, which started slowly by collecting some wood for a small fire where we had camped, so I could make coffee for our breakfast, even though our breakfast was only some slightly stale bread; that day when we had done enough cycling, we stopped to camp exactly where we were because we were in the wild, and there was no one else around, and it is always best to stop cycling for the day when you still want to cycle more because then you wake the following morning eager to pedal again; that day when we pitched our tents early, but then sat outside on the ground under the dying sun and felt the warmth on our bare skin, and when the sun set, we lit a fire with the wood we had collected and watched the flames jump and leap into the darkness as the stars shone down. That day I was truly happy, and it was perfect.

The night was also memorable. I was wrenched from sleep by a wild, piercing scream. The cicadas had stopped their rhythmic chirp, and there was silence as I held my breath with haunted thoughts. The animal howled again.

'Did you hear that?' I called out to Lars.

There was no response, only rhythmic snoring.

I dismissed thoughts of danger and tried to sleep. That was when my legs started itching. I tried to ignore the urge to scratch, but the more I resisted the more intense the sensation. *Don't scratch! … But the itch!* When I could resist no longer, I gently scratched just one bite. *Ah, that feels good.* I scratched another bite, and then I scratched a little harder until I was frantically running my nails up and down my legs from knee to ankle. *Stop. You'll only make it worse.* I lowered my legs, which had been waving in the air as I had lain on my back like an upturned beetle, rolled over, and tried to sleep. *But the itching!* Oh, I just had to scratch those bites. Antihistamine brought enough light relief to drift off to sleep, but I woke up repeatedly in frenzied fits, manically attacking my bitten legs. That night was far from perfect, and by the time dawn came, I was exhausted.

After a week of hard cycling and camping on the trails, we treated ourselves to a hotel. Our choice, one attached to a discotheque, was unwise. The seven beers we each consumed that evening were insufficient to send us to sleep, even after the club closed in the early hours due to the snoring night watchman lying outside, the baying donkey across the street, and the incessant itching of my bite-infested legs.

At light, exhausted and red-eyed, we drank coffee, packed up our bikes, and hit the road again for Guinea (intentionally this time).

The locals and military near the border said Guinea was safe. So we went. The Foreign Office advice was unchanged even though there had been no new developments since the assassination attempt two weeks earlier.

Across the border, imposing cliffs towered above the grassland. We cycled further into the Fouta Djalon hills, winding up and round, and up and down. Unfortunately, it is difficult to appreciate the beauty of the surroundings from the saddle of a bike when the rough tracks require both eyes on the ground in order to avoid the potholes, divots, rocks, and sand that will lead to a crash if your attention momentarily lapses.

It was loose gravel and sand that resulted in Lars exiting the left side of his bike.

'Are you OK?' I called out.

'I'm fine,' he said, which judging by the tone meant he was not fine, so I had the good sense to leave my camera in my bag.

On Christmas Day, we levelled out onto a windswept plateau and fought the headwind. Blue rags roped across the road barred entry. Once past the checkpoint, we were allowed into this Wild-West frontier town with the wind blowing down the wide dusty street lined with low wooden buildings.

We could have chosen any of the small cafes along the roadside – they were all the same just like every village. On a wooden table covered with a plastic cloth were thermos flasks of hot water, tins of sweetened condensed milk, a small metal can of Nescafe, a jar of sugar, and industrial-sized containers of mayonnaise. The baguettes were wrapped in large clear plastic bags with flies trapped inside.

'What do you want?' I asked Lars, as if there were a choice.

'Coffee and bread-mayo.' Bread-mayo was what we called the bread spread with mayonnaise that came as standard with morning coffee. It was a tiresome feat to get coffee without bread until we learnt that the phrase to use was '*café simple*', and then it was simple.

We always bought extra bread-mayo for our lunch, not because we liked it, but because there was no alternative. We embellished it by calling it a mayo sandwich. Sometimes we spiced it up with slices of onion, chilli and a sprinkling of Maggi stock cube – the other readily available items in a Guinean village market. When you are hungry, it is surprising what foods become appetising.

Our Christmas lunch of mayo sandwiches was reminiscent of roast turkey at home where you have eaten so much turkey at Christmas dinners with friends and work colleagues in the weeks running up, so that when Christmas Day arrives you are truly sick of the sight of it. When we arrived in Labé, the main town in the Fouta Djalon, on Boxing Day, we treated ourselves to pizza and beer.

A passer-by insisted that the dim and dirty shack was a restaurant. A few locals were eating, and between mouthfuls, they stopped to kick a squawking chicken out from under the table and swipe at the festering flies. Our last meal in Labé was rice and peanut sauce. Somehow, the cook had succeeded in turning a typically tasty dish into a bland bowlful of brown sludge, so I took a large helping of crushed chillies from the pot on the table. It might have been a cheap meal, but I paid a high price.

I barely managed to cycle 20 kilometres out of town with a fit-to-burst bloated stomach. We camped early in the long, golden grasses beneath a black rocky outcrop overlooking the rolling hills and valleys. We had left Labé well prepared, and the numerous sachets of Youpi-Choco chocolate spread and red wine for dinner temporarily had the right effect on my stomach.

The next morning we made a pit stop to refuel; my legs were still very tired from the previous weeks' exertions.

'You should eat one. You need the energy,' said Lars through a mouthful of egg and bread-mayo.

'I know. But my stomach doesn't feel good, and it's so bloated again I can hardly cycle. I definitely can't eat anything.' I drank a coke instead, which didn't help either. We each bought bread-mayo for lunch, and then turned off the tarmac and back onto the familiar dusty tracks.

At some point in the network of paths we took the wrong one and inadvertently backtracked towards Labé. It was a long scenic detour. On any other day, I would have loved winding along hedgerows between grassy fields with the cows grazing among the violet wildflowers and over small bridges spanning gently trickling streams.

It was late afternoon when we rejoined the right track. 'Lars, I'm running out of energy, do you want to go much further?' We stopped to eat a few peanuts, shared an orange, and then carried on. My legs had nothing left to give. I needed to rest.

I was ahead on the dusty track having left Lars to close his panniers. I called back over my shoulder, 'I've still got no energy. I need to stop soon.'

'You should have eaten that sandwich. I told you so,' he called out. *Did he really just say that? He did. I can't believe it. … Don't respond. Just keep pedalling and ignore him. Such a typical, insensitive guy. … And he's wrong. What I should have done was rest longer in* Labé, *and I've no one to blame but myself for setting off too soon. Don't tell him that though. He didn't have to say, 'I told you so'.*

Lars caught me up and overtook as we climbed another hill, and I got slower and slower and was left further behind. I must have been ill – Lars was never ahead when we cycled the dirt tracks. Struggling to keep up, at every turn I saw what could be the perfect camping spot. I just wanted to crawl into my tent and sleep. By this stage, a bed of thorny scrub would have been perfectly satisfactory.

Eventually, I gave in and stopped. 'I just can't go any further,' I slumped over the handlebars and waited to see what Lars would do.

'OK, let's find somewhere to camp.' Lars put down his bike, climbed the bank, and walked off into the trees. He seemed oblivious to my anger and exhaustion. He wasn't. We laughed about it later when we were less tired, not ill, and not cycling. I still can't believe he said, 'I told you so'.

It was New Year's Eve, and we were well prepared having learnt from our dismal Christmas dinner. That I could only force down one small cup of wine was a clear symptom I was ill. The second symptom was that I was still asleep when Lars got up the next morning. It was the only time he made the morning coffee.

It was a scenic day winding downhill through the green, forested hills with the granite escarpment rising formidably skywards. By sunset we were camped in pastures where the road flattened out near a small village. The sounds from the houses were amplified in the night and I could hear a TV. The national power network had not reached this region, so people who could afford it have a noisy diesel generator, and satellite dish.

Guinea is one of the poorest countries in West Africa and even in towns power was not guaranteed and blackouts were common. Even in Kindia, Guinea's second 'city' to the capital, the hotel I stayed at had electricity only between the hours of midnight and six in the morning. The rest of the time, the room was lit by a lone candle and trips to the toilet were taken by torchlight. Once the power came on, men started to work and the sound of drilling and machinery came through the slatted window of my bare room.

Still in the Fouta Djalon, we continued downhill staring out across endless vistas of hills rising and falling, fading to the hazy horizon. It was a *Lost World* of untouched forest filled by tall plants, vines, creepers and palms; cliffs and car-wrecks and colourful flora; rivers and ravines and bright-red fruit on leafless trees.

At a junction we saw some men sat around a table with three large Thermos flasks – the telltale sign that we could get our morning coffee fix.

'Good morning. Do you have coffee?'

'Yes,' came the definitive response.

'Two coffees with milk, please.'

'Do you want Nescafe?' he asked

'Yes.' *Of course, an espresso or cappuccino would be preferable, but we can't always have the things we want.*

'Do you want milk in the coffee?'

'Yes.' *Didn't I already say that?*

'OK, is that sweetened condensed milk or powdered milk?'

Really, I don't care. Whichever milk we wanted, we had to go to the shop next door and buy it ourselves. A morning coffee should not be this complicated. We told the owner to buy the milk himself. He returned with a tin of the condensed, sweetened variety.

He then realised that he didn't have any Nescafe. *Now, what exactly did you mean when you said you had coffee? That if we waited long enough, you could buy everything you needed, by which time the hot water in the Thermos would be cold, to make an average, under strength, overly sweet, dark-coloured drink?*

We sat silently on the bench, outwardly patient and inwardly fuming. The owner sent a younger man to buy the Nescafe, who came back five minutes later with one sachet. *Sigh.*

'That's not enough for two coffees. We need two sachets, each,' I told the old man.

Another five minutes passed while the young man went back to the shop.

'I am sorry. That is the last sachet.' *Help me, please!* With this, the old man left the table, got on his motorbike, and with dust rising, disappeared in the direction of town, 15 kilometres away.

'Let's go,' said Lars. With this, we left the table, got on our bikes, and with dust rising, disappeared in the opposite direction.

'We can get our morning coffee in the next village,' he said.

'I won't hold my breath.' We got an afternoon coffee.

That evening when cooking dinner where we were camped in the bush, we heard crackling nearby.

'What is that?' I asked Lars.

'I'm not sure. It sounds like a bush fire,' he replied half-jokingly as he disappeared through the undergrowth. I followed his track and caught up with him.

'Yep. It's a bush fire,' I said, observing the smoke and flames.

'Do you think we should move?'

'Let's keep an eye on it and see if it spreads.'

With the decision made, Lars went back to the cooking pasta, which he clearly considered the most pressing issue. I listened to the grass crackling and popping.

'It's definitely getting closer,' I called to Lars. 'Perhaps we should move.'

'There must be time to eat first.'

'Hmm, I'm not sure.' For once, food wasn't my top priority. 'OK, but let's pack everything up now, just in case we need to make a dash for the road.'

There was barely enough time to finish cooking the dinner before I called the evacuation. With bowl of pasta in one hand, I pushed my bike to the road, with Lars following reluctantly. By now it was dark except for the fiery orange flames that lit the immediate area and enabled us to push our bikes without the need for torches until we found a safe fire-free place to camp on blackened, ash-laden land on the other side of a village.

8

Rebels and Spiders on the Road to Freetown

Guinea and Sierra Leone

Two days in Kindia was not enough rest for me, so I stayed another night while Lars rode out of town to relax in the peace of the bush. We promised again to meet up later for paddling the Niger River together – we had a deal.

I liked Kindia; it was just another dusty, noisy, chaotic African town, but I found my place in it and was content. I got a morning *café au lait* around the corner from the hotel, the Senegalese restaurant down the potholed road served good food, and there were two Internet cafes separated by a bar that served big bottles of Guiluxe beer. I had to watch out for all the speeding motorbikes still covered in bubble wrap in futile attempts to keep the dust off, it was difficult to wander around after dark because there were no lights and lots of potholes, the power only came on after midnight if lucky, and the variety of food in the market was limited. None of that mattered though because the people who lived there were kind and made me feel welcome.

At the Senegalese restaurant, the owner's son was doing his homework at one of the tables. When the film Rocky started on the TV, he was quickly distracted, and it wasn't long before the doorway was full of small heads peering in. It was one of the few places in town with a generator. Otherwise, it looked like many other restaurants – the tables were covered in bright plastic making them easy to clean, the chairs were the white plastic garden variety that you see everywhere in West Africa and are always breaking, and the walls were covered in gaudy posters of fruit bowls and plates of burgers and chips and bottles of coke. At least it was a change from the posters, which were popular in Morocco and Mauritania, of two girls praying with a photo of Mecca in the background. Importantly though, they cooked other food besides rice and peanut sauce at this restaurant.

It was there I met Ward, a Belgian NGO worker who had been working in Kindia for a few years. He told me that cycling over the border into Sierra Leone alone was very dangerous given the current political situation. Tensions might have been running high in Conakry, the capital, but it seemed to me that elsewhere the local people were completely unconcerned by recent events.

'There are reports of rebels from Sierra Leone and Liberia amassing at the border. And it's common knowledge that mercenaries from South Africa have taken over one of the hotels outside Conakry and are waiting for a *coup d'etat.* I really don't think it's a good idea to cycle alone. Do you even know the road to Makeni?'

'No, why?'

'It's in a very bad condition and dangerous to travel. It is very narrow in places with big rocks too. I went down it on a motorbike once, and fell off and broke my arm.'

Rough roads and rocks I was happy to ride over, but rebels I was less eager to bump into. At the back of my mind, I was sure there would be no problems – I was used to scare-stories from people who either didn't have all the facts or liked to embellish them. Even so, by the time I had finished my lunch, I was wary about the road to Sierra Leone. It was probably for no other reason than for the first time in weeks, I was by myself again.

Travelling with someone else often feels safer. The reality is that in most situations, including bumping into rebels with guns, I am no safer with company – it would only mean that two of us would be in trouble, not one. I told myself to man-up and go.

The next morning, I packed up my gear and went for breakfast at the cafe that was a single room with mint green and blue painted walls lined with wooden benches and low tables. The posters were of smiling men eating a feast of fruit and pastries at Ramadan, thereby successfully combining food with religion. The flasks of hot water lined the work surface at the back and the soft drinks in the fridge were not cold because there was no power.

I asked the men at the next table if they knew anything about the road to Sierra Leone and whether there had been problems locally regarding the political situation. They looked at me as if I were crazy. Instead, I asked if I could buy a newspaper somewhere. I had seen some men reading one the previous day. One young guy said, if I waited ten minutes, he would go and get me one.

He did as promised and soon enough, although longer than ten minutes later, I was looking at the advertisements section of a crumpled paper that was now two months old. *Sigh*.

The busy streets gave way to small houses and people who waved as I passed. I took a deep breath and felt my worries floating away as the mayhem became a distant memory. There is something restorative about the freedom of cycling with everything you need to be self-sufficient packed on the back of the bike – life is simple and carefree.

I turned onto the road to the border, which was the smoothest gravel road I had cycled on so far. I have no idea how Ward had managed to fall off his bike; there was barely a rock bigger than my thumbnail to hit.

At the border, I cycled straight through to the barrier and stopped outside a building that some men were pointing to. I knocked on the open door and waited – there was no response. I went in. The room was empty except for a desk stacked with papers. I went out and looked for someone official.

A policeman jogged over and ushered me back into the room, where we went through the usual formalities. He finally understood that I wanted to leave Guinea, not enter, so he took me back to the other side of the barrier and into a room where a stern-faced military man sat. Another confusing conversation ensued as I tried to explain I was wanting to leave Guinea and not just arriving from Sierra Leone as it looked since I was on the other side of the barrier with my bike facing in the wrong direction.

He asked if I was carrying cocaine or guns in my bag, which I denied, of course. Then he stamped my passport and said, 'You pay now.'

'I'm not paying anything,' I exclaimed standing over the desk.

'But you must pay me. Then there will be no problems,' he explained, firmly gripping my passport.

'I'm not giving you any money,' I repeated forcefully and sat back down in defiance on the bench against the back wall, ready for a long wait.

We stared at each other in a silent standoff until he gave in, 'Fine, I must check your bags then; it could be serious. Or you can pay me and then you have no problem.'

'Fine,' I said and went to get my bike.

The next ten minutes was spent slowly opening one pannier at a time. With every item I removed he demanded loudly, 'What's this?' and, 'What is it for?'

I played along, 'This? It's a book for reading. This is my tent; I sleep in it. And this is a water bottle with water in it for drinking.' And so it went on.

I was saved by his heavily built superior who arrived and demanded, 'What is the problem here?'

'He's searching my bags for cocaine and guns,' I said. It was a farcical situation and deserved a ludicrous response.

'Well, are you carrying cocaine?'

I tried not to laugh, 'Of course not.'

'And do you have any weapons in your bags?'

'No.'

'And you have told him this?'

'Yes.'

'Then what is the problem?'

'He won't give me my passport.'

He turned and shouted at the man, took the passport from him, handed it straight to me, paused for breath and then said sincerely, 'I'm very sorry for his behaviour but I suggest you go now. Have a safe journey.'

'Thank you,' I said and pedalled around the barrier with shouts from the superior at the corrupt official slowly fading away as I ventured into No Man's Land.

With ten kilometres to the Sierra Leone border post and the light quickly fading, I found a place to camp where I would not be found by any rebels.

I consider myself a rational, logical person, except when confronted with spiders. So when I folded up my tent and saw a fat body and eight hairy legs lying on the groundsheet, I leaped back and my heart skipped a beat and then raced at the double. I stood sweating, fixated on the huge arachnid. It looked dead, probably trampled when I had erected the tent.

I reached for a long stick and flicked it off. The carcass sprang into life with the eight hairy legs in a crouched, ready to leap stance.

'Oh, crap!' I shouted loudly. 'It's alive!' With only the surrounding trees to hear me, I whined, 'I hate spiders,' when I realised I had to deal with this myself without the aid of a vacuum cleaner, which is my preferred method of removal back home.

I dug out my camera for a photo, and then I went to find a five-foot-long branch to poke it with, which gave enough distance between us. When I returned, the spider was gone. Out of sight, out of mind? – not likely. I was going to pick up my flip-flops when it occurred to me that the spider might have crawled underneath them, so I flipped them over and found the spider clinging tightly to one. *I really hate spiders.*

With an urge of annoyance that I was letting a spider take up so much time, and with my fear turning into hatred, I poked the spider. It jumped away. I poked again and it leapt in response, scurried a few feet, and stopped. Poke. Leap. Poke. Leap. Eventually, I lost sight of it in the undergrowth of fallen leaves. I wasted no time after that packing up my bags and getting back to the relative safety of the dirt road. I would rather have encountered a rebel than another arachnid.

I dealt with my next arachnid close encounter more calmly – months later when cycling on northern Ghana's tracks, covered in orange dust from passing minibus *tro-tros* and taxis, I felt a sharp stone in my shoe. I tried to ignore it, but it hurt. So I braked, dismounted, removed my shoe and bashed it upside-down against my hand. There was nothing – no rock, no sharp object. *That's strange.* I shook harder.

'Eugh!' A huge, pale green spider fell to the floor and escaped as fast as its eight legs allowed. *Will I ever learn? Always shake out yours shoes before putting them on.* My sock now had a hole in it although the big toe appeared whole, which was something.

By the time I reached the Congo and discovered a giant spider above me in the shower – a brown monstrosity with an eight-inch leg-span, bigger than my hand – I had the composure to grab a towel and cover my tits before rushing out into the yard naked, wet, and covered in shampoo. Imagine how horrified the other guests would have been if I had completely lost control (or would have been if it weren't an establishment where the men pay women an hourly rate to stay).

When I told the locals of that arachnid encounter, all they said was, 'Oh yeah, we see lots of those at this time of year when the rains begin. They are only rain spiders,' or something equally dismissive.

'That's all very well for you, but we don't get spiders like that in England, and it rains all year there,' I replied.

By the time I reached South Africa, I had learnt the lesson about shaking out my shoes, and that was lucky because I shook out a large black scorpion instead.

* * *

The track was in a worse state than the Guinea side. It was narrow with protruding rocks and slick slabs of stone. *I guess this is where Ward broke his arm.* It was always either up or down. Eventually, I came to a sign for the Otamba–Kilimi National Park.

Lars and I had originally planned to visit the park, but our enthusiasm for the detour had dwindled when we heard that the last remaining elephant herd had been wiped out by poachers only a month or two earlier. There would be plenty of other wildlife though.

I was tired, had no local currency and almost no food, so had decided I would skip the National Park and continue to Kamakwe the next village. According to the locals I passed, Lars was ahead of me by a couple of hours.

As I came to the sign for the park, I saw on a scrap of notepaper saying, 'HELEN!!!' I slammed on the brakes and screeched to a halt. The note was from Lars – I recognised the paper and handwriting. *Is that supposed to mean he's gone to the park, or not?* Since it was next to the arrow pointing to the park headquarters, he must have made the detour. He would not be visiting without money and food. Extremely fatigued, I set off on the ever smaller, bumpier track with hills so steep vehicles cannot get up them. In a forest clearing was the park headquarters, rustic and rundown. It looked eerily devoid of people, and bikes.

'Is there another cyclist here?' I asked the warden when he came to welcome me. Bemused, he only stared. 'A man with a bike, a *toubab* like me?' I explained.

'No.'

'Are there any other tourists?'

'No.'

'No one?'

'Only you, me and a guide. Would you like to stay in one of the huts?' *Yes.*

'Can I pay with Guinea francs?'

'No.'

'Is it possible to get food here?'

'No, the cook is not here.'

'You don't have any food?'

'No.'

I found a chair, sank down into it, and laid my head on my hands. I hoped that when I looked up I would be sitting in a cafe in Kamakwe and not next to a small circular thatched hut overlooking a river in the arse-end of nowhere.

I ate the last remnants of my food and set off back along the track I had just come. At the bottom of the steepest hill I got off my bike and just stood there, devoid of energy. With no strength left to push, I was going to have to unload the panniers and relay my gear. A teenager carrying a large load on his head came along and waited.

'After you,' I said. He didn't move.

With all the force I could muster, I started to push the bike upwards. It was easy. The boy, with one hand holding the carefully balanced load on his head and the other hand firmly gripping the back of my bike, was pushing equally hard. Never was a helping hand so welcome.

Three hours after seeing Lars' note and a pointless detour later, I finally returned to the road and set off towards Kamakwe.

Why didn't the idiot write a message rather than leave that cryptic exclamation? It then occurred to me, he might have written on the back of the note. *Why didn't I think to check earlier?* I returned to the sign and looked closer – there appeared to be something showing through from the underside of the note. I peeled up the corner and saw more writing. I tore it off:

> Helen! I made it here – I got arrested at the border but they let me go after 10 mins! NOT going to the park. Cycling down to the ferry and on to Kamakwe. Lars.

Who's the idiot! I raged against my own stupidity and ripped the note into little pieces, threw them at the floor, and kicked the sign for good measure. Surprised at my own outburst, I looked up to see a woman watching me.

'Are you Helen?' she asked sheepishly.

Once I had exchanged some money in Kamakwe, I bought too much food because I could – bread and cheese triangles, biscuits, nuts, oranges, and coke and fake Fanta – everything except mayonnaise. Then I left town and pitched my tent in darkness in the midst of the thick undergrowth. I crawled in, lay down and stared up at the stars, too tired to eat anything.

The next morning I awoke feeling exhausted still. There was no shade, so I got dressed into my biking clothes that were still drenched with sweat because of the humidity, and packed up. Then I discovered the flat tyre. *Sigh.* What should have been a simple process was complicated because the valves of the spare tubes I had bought recently did not fit through the rim and the patches would not stick. *Typical.*

Once I got on the road and began cycling, I tried to shake off my grumpy mood. I couldn't wait to reach Freetown, where I could rest for longer.

'Helen!' I braked and looked around. *Who's that?*

Lars' face peered out of a nearby wooden shack, 'I'm just having breakfast,' he called out. *Coffee, good idea.*

While I had camped wet, hungry and tired, he had been invited to stay with a missionary where he ate a belated Christmas dinner of roast chicken (not mayo sandwiches), washed his clothes, and slept on a mattress.

Fortunately, it got easier from there. The road was smoother and less hilly, and once we reached Makeni it was a tarmac road to Freetown.

We passed from the dry north, through the lush green lowlands to the Freetown peninsula with the historical English-named towns of Wellington, Hastings, and Waterloo, and where blue taxis and minibuses packed with people crammed the roads and sped towards the sprawling capital. It was a stark contrast to Guinea's peaceful hills.

From the bustling streets of Kissy Road in the East End with stalls selling everything from second-hand shoes to fake Sony radios, we navigated our way through the commercial district centred around the towering cotton tree, down along Congo Road, across the poor shanty district of Kroo Bay where fishermen from Liberia reside, and onto the prosperous Aberdeen West End with its large Lebanese-run supermarkets selling expensive imported foods, and where numerous white Toyota Land Cruisers, owned by the multitude of aid agencies, sped down Wilkinson Road.

Resident in Freetown for two weeks, we rested, repaired bikes, and wrote blogs. We had a regular routine dictated by the heat and unpredictable power supply. There was a TV in the hotel room, which I was addicted to after so long without. I spent hours watching CNN with the same news stories on endless repeat until the power was cut. Without the fan working, it was too hot to stay festering in the room, so we went for lunch and spent hours in an air-conditioned cafe with Celine Dion playing on endless repeat. When we could bear the Titanic theme tune no longer, we returned to the hotel via the Internet cafe if it were open, walked past the young men in wheelchairs, and then risked our own life and limbs crossing the busy road.

It was a common sight to see men with a missing arm or leg – a reminder of the civil war that had ravaged Sierra Leone less than a decade ago. The effects of war linger on long after peace treaties are signed, and the war will be with these men for the rest of their lives.

We drank beer or cheap wine in the early evening and ate chocolate bought from the supermarket. Sometimes we ate at one of the many smart restaurants, which involved navigating the city at night – always a hazardous affair. The pavements had wide, open drainage channels, which would be easy to fall into up to the waist if not watching where you stepped in the dark. The taxis were expensive, but a far safer bet than squeezing into one of the poda-poda minibuses with names like 'Allah is the Greatest' and 'God's Time is the Best Time' that screamed down the streets.

It would have been easy to stay longer, but we were conscious that the dry season was well under way, and there was a river we wanted to paddle.

Before we left Freetown, however, we needed money. Gone are the days of carrying travellers cheques and having money transferred from home. All you need is a Visa card, but it is no use without a cash machine. Even in Africa they are in every major city. The only problem was that we didn't go through many.

The other problem was that in some countries the cash machines dispense only very small amounts in one go, so you have to withdraw cash several days in a row, and often the machine is not working because the power is off or the machine is out of order or there is no money left to dispense. It was simpler to go into the bank, when it was open, and get cash from the teller.

We joined the queue and watched as people walked out one-by-one grasping large brown paper bags or briefcases full of cash because the largest denomination notes are worth so little. Briefly, I was a millionaire.

Rather than retracing our ride to Freetown, we took a taxi back north and covered the three-day cycle in just three hours. From there we cycled to Faranah in Guinea. It was a shock after the two-week break. That night, camping in the bush, I woke up to rustling in the grass nearby.

Bleary-eyed, I looked out through my tent, but I could not see anyone. Silence. I checked the time; it was midnight. I rolled over and was drifting off to sleep when I heard the rustling sound again. Closer. Louder. Then silence. Fully awake now, I held my breath and listened for the sound. *There it is.* It sounded too loud to be a rodent or bird. Whatever it was, it sounded as though it was taking a few steps closer, stopping and then a few more steps. Lying in the darkness, my imagination took over and my heart beat faster. *Could it be a wild animal? It couldn't be a lion, could it?*

'Lars, did you hear that?' I whispered.

There was no response, only rhythmic snoring. I tried to sleep.

The crack of a rifle in the distance ripped me from my dreams, and I listened to a series of shots. Wide awake, mind alert again. *What was that?* A single gunshot would be a hunter, but because ammunition is expensive they don't fire multiple rounds. With a second series of shots, closer this time, my mind wandered back to the warnings by Ward about rebels in the border areas and a possible civil war brewing in Guinea. *We're near the border, but surely we would have heard news in town?* More shots came from down the road, amplified in the ensuing silence. *Am I going crazy?* And then I heard more shots from the other side of the road.

'Lars, did you hear that?' I asked louder this time

There was no response, only rhythmic snoring. *I must be going crazy. If Lars can sleep through the night in blissful ignorance, then I shall do the same.* I rolled over and tried not to listen. Then I heard the faint sound of a cockerel crowing and knew it was four in the morning. When the sun rose at six, I moved outside and lay on the flat rock and read until Lars emerged a couple of hours later looking well rested and wide awake.

The border at Gberia Fotombu on the Sierra Leone side was a hive of activity, but over in Guinea the calm returned. Almost immediately I caught a faint whiff of the familiar smell of burning. Instead of tall grasses blocking the view from the road, I could see beyond into the fields with grazing cattle and rickety fencing marking property boundaries. The first village was Heremankono, which means 'Home Sweet Home' – we were back in familiar Guinea with its quiet, kind people and fewer screaming children.

The Niger River

9

The Birth of Joliba II

Niger River

Three months had passed since our idea to paddle the Niger River. In that time the dream had been kept alive in our imaginations during the long hours in the saddle and dark nights in our tents. Now we were in Faranah, the dream was real.

Staring downstream from the bridge at the entrance to town, only 100 kilometres from the river's source, I said to Lars, 'Yeah, we can paddle this. We just need to find a boat.' How far we would get down the 4,100 kilometres of Africa's third longest river, we would find out soon enough.

We enquired in town about where to buy a *pirogue* or speak with someone who could build one. Boh, the manager of the hotel by the river, said he would arrange a meeting with a local fisherman for the following morning.

Daman, the fisherman, agreed to build our boat. The wooden pirogue would be similar in style to those used locally, six metres in length, and flat-bottomed, made from joined planks of wood since this is more stable than the dugout variety. He assured us this would be big enough for two people, two bikes, our bags, and food. Paddles and a long pole would also be provided and to ensure we didn't get stranded, we asked for spares. Long negotiations ensued until we agreed a price, and importantly, a date that the boat would be completed. For 1,200,000 Guinea francs (about 230 US dollars) it would be ready in five days' time. Now we needed provisions.

We had read that it should take 10 to 14 days to reach Kouroussa, 350 kilometres downstream. We assumed, since we were both fit and willing to paddle hard for long hours, it would take nearer ten. The locals at the hotel said it would take one and a half days, maybe two. Boh was more conservative and thought if we took time to enjoy the scenery and take photographs, it might take four. Basically, we had no idea.

To be on the safe side, we bought food for 15 days plus extra pasta for good measure. We made a shopping list, based loosely on what we wanted and refined considerably to what we could actually purchase in this part of Guinea, and then we delved into the market.

For five days, time trundled on steadily and unstoppable like a tanker on the horizon at sea. With ample time, we moved unhurried like the locals. Even Lars didn't get bored or frustrated with the wait – Africa affects us all, eventually.

We visited Daman's home where the boat was being made, which was a modest group of round thatched huts situated between the river and the town centre. There were shaped planks of wood nailed together on the ground. Two of Daman's helpers, one significantly more skilful and careful than the other, were slowly carving out the shape for the side panelling. We inspected the work, clueless about whether it was going well.

What we lacked for in knowledge we made up for in interest and returned the next day to see the progress. The men were busy inspecting and repairing the nets strewn about the compound. They were preparing for a big fishing trip. We were surprised to see that the pile of wooden planks had been transformed into a boat-looking structure. There didn't appear to be much more work needed.

The next day we were told that it was finished. I was excited and eager with anticipation to see it. Led by the children, we walked in single-file along a well-worn footpath to the river with Daman bringing up the rear. We peered down the steep bank and saw, for the first time, our boat afloat on the Niger River.

That's it? I was overwhelmed with disappointment. It was roughly built, and being clambered upon by the bathing kids, and there was a significant quantity of water sloshing around in its breeches. *That unassuming, unimposing, pathetic-looking child's toy is supposed to get us down the mighty Niger River? Help us!*

Daman shouted at the children and within moments they were scarpering except for one girl who was left to empty the boat of water using a plastic scoop.

We followed Boh's lead and clambered aboard. Daman then paddled us proficiently upstream towards the hotel. *Well, it seems to do what it was made for, I guess.*

'Can we try paddling? We have to try some time and you're here now if we have any difficulty,' I said.

With careful manoeuvring within the wobbling boat, Lars crawled to the back and took control. He cautiously placed the paddle and slowly dragged it through the calm water as if he were stroking a cat. Nothing happened. He repeated this manoeuvre several times, and we moved in a crooked circle, drifting downstream with the current when we were trying to get upstream. Lars was smiling, oblivious, like a child with a new toy. I sat at the front facing him trying to conceal my concerns. *What have I got myself into?* We had what appeared to be a leaking boat that we couldn't steer let alone propel forward.

Before Lars had completed an unintended 360-degree turn, Boh took over and paddled us back to the bank. It was time now to put aside any facade that I was the subservient female. If it were really so hard to paddle, we needed to start learning soon.

Cautiously, I took the paddle from Boh and made a determined stroke, and then another. The boat crept forward slowly, and with each stroke, it picked up speed until it was gliding effortlessly over the water. I turned the boat around and paddled back up to the hotel. The minimal experience I had from the occasional day out canoeing when younger, together with punting and rowing during my inebriated university years had paid off.

My attention then turned to the increasing volume of water inside the boat. Boh dismissed my concerns and explained that it was normal. I insisted that something needed to be done about it. He listened patiently, like the hotel manager he was, used to pandering to the whims of ignorant tourists. He scooped the water out of the boat and inspected the seams.

'It is normal, I promise,' he said.

I let the issue rest; we could check that the boat was still floating the next day. We retired to the hotel for a celebratory beer – we had our boat. It was the first major step on our journey downstream.

When we returned to the river the next day the boat was nowhere to be seen. *It can't have sunk overnight, can it?* Boh was not at the hotel. Daman's house was deserted except for the youngest children and women. The men were gone, the older boys absent, the fishing nets had disappeared. We walked down to the riverbank, but the boat was not there either. *Where is it? A leaking boat is better than no boat at all!*

When we returned to our hotel that evening, Boh came out to meet us, 'You are back. Come. The fisherman is here.' Daman was waiting with the finished paddles and poles.

'Boh, where is our boat?' I asked.

'I moved it upstream away from the children. I'll bring it back in the morning.' I felt bad for wondering if someone had stolen it.

Once we had packed our belongings and wrapped them in numerous plastic bags in an attempt to waterproof them, there was only one thing left to do: name our boat.

Mungo Park, a Scottish physician, was one of the early European explorers to the continent. He offered his services to the African Association, which was looking for someone to discover the course of the Niger River. On his second expedition, in 1805, he set sail from Segou in present-day Mali in a 40-foot-long boat converted from two canoes. He christened the boat after the local name for the Niger River: *Joliba*. Since it was his story that had, in part, inspired my interest in the Niger River, we christened our boat after his.

Joliba II was born.

10

Two Weeks Paddling a Pirogue

Niger River

Day 1

Departure — 3 beers — Will we make it?

The large sacks with our gear were heavy and we struggled to carry them down to the river. Boh ordered the straggle of children following to help and we were left to wheel the bikes. A small crowd had gathered on the bank, looking on curiously as we secured everything in the boat.

'Oh no, we forgot to buy beer!' I exclaimed. *This situation must be rectified.* My birthday was in a week – I did not want to celebrate without an alcoholic beverage.

'Boh, can we buy some beer from the hotel?'

'Of course. But there are only three bottles left.' *Disaster.* It would take too long to go back into town now – three would have to do.

During the short wait as one of the staff ran back to fetch them, Boh told us, 'I will come with you for the start.'

'Really, that's not necessary,' I said, 'or is it?'

'Around the first two bends where it is difficult I can help you paddle or steer,' he explained. 'After that it is calm.'

Once the three beers were safely stored in the boat, we waved goodbye, clambered aboard Joliba II, and with a small degree of trepidation, pushed off the bank.

The paddle on the Niger River begins!

In the first 'tricky' section, we got stuck and had to get out and push to release the boat. Boh and I guided it in the waist-deep water between the exposed rocks while Lars concerned himself with his flip-flop that had come off.

'Lars!' I called out abruptly as I saw him getting left behind. He came splashing and crashing, reached out for the boat, and grasped it. He was dragged inelegantly until the rocks disappeared, the river widened, and the flow slowed enough, so we could all climb aboard.

No sooner were we in the boat than more rocks appeared. The bow rose over one and got stuck again, and the stern with me in it swung round until I was at the front and Boh at the back. Boh now steered and took the next section in his stride. Then he directed the boat over to the side, jumped out, and walked up the bank. *He's leaving us? Don't go – we're not ready!*

'Thanks!' we both called out quickly because without Boh we would never have made it this far and he was about to disappear from our lives forever.

'Do you think we'll make it to Bamako?' I called, trying to delay the moment when he was gone.

'No!' came his definitive response that was echoed by the trees and resounded downstream. *He could have lied.*

And then we were alone.

It was already mid-afternoon, so we pulled up on the next sandy bank. We had not eaten since breakfast, so we ravenously devoured a mayo sandwich and shared one of the three beers while it was still cold.

For two more hours we paddled on the peaceful river with only the birds for company. I had not seen so many since Senegal. When we stopped for a break, I was targeted by innocuous-looking little black flies. These sandflies, however, feasted on my exposed skin until I was covered in tiny red pin-pricks of blood.

After a couple more hours paddling, we pulled over to the shore where there was a clearing behind some bushes and manoeuvred the boat back onto a muddy bank to secure it. We untied the bags and set up camp.

'A beer would be great right now,' I said to Lars.

'We could have them.' *So tempting.*

'No. They'll taste much better in a week.'

'I wonder how far we went today,' Lars pondered between mouthfuls of pasta. I turned on the GPS to check.

'Hmm … not far. It's going to take more than one and half days.'

'How long do you think it will take?'

Our progress had barely registered, and I was doubtful if even two weeks were enough. 'It's too early to tell,' I said.

We retreated to our tents, and I lay awake for hours as the sandfly bites itched to distraction. Later I heard voices and the rhythmic splashes of paddles in the water that were so slow and gentle as if the fishermen did not want to disturb the sleeping night, and when I peered out from my tent, I saw through the trees a greenish glow of torchlight reflecting on the river moving steadily upstream. My first thoughts were whether they would see us and what they would do and whether our gear in the boat down on the shore was safe. I always had to remind myself that people were just going about their lives, and mostly they were unaware of us and certainly meant no harm. I looked forward to the nights when I would sleep as peacefully and assured of my safety as Lars.

Day 2

Use of a plastic kettle — Aussie encounter — Beer surprise

Not long into the day's paddle, we came to some minor rapids. They would not be noteworthy if we had been in an inflatable raft, or modern kayak or canoe; but we were in a heavy, fully laden, locally-built wooden pirogue that was for navigating and fishing on calm waters.

The pirogue picked up speed, and I used all my strength to steer, but it was not enough and on the final sharp bend, the front jammed against a rock and the back end swung around in the white water. The boat, now wedged between rocks, was leaning at an angle and water was coming in over the side. I leapt out of the boat and screamed, 'Lars, get out!' Startled by my outburst as he turned to face me, he fell out. Now we were both in the river, the boat rose and the inflow ceased.

Later, when we were enjoying some quiet, uneventful paddling, we heard laughter from downriver and saw three figures on the riverside. I had seen only three white people in Guinea in over a month and now, unexpectedly, we saw three more. Intrigued, we paddled over.

They were ex-pats working at the nearby mines and had come here for their weekend break. They were equally surprised to see us and quick to hand us their last two beers, which we thirstily gulped down.

'Sorry we don't have more.'

'Yeah, me too,' I replied. *Only two beers left for two weeks.*

Day 3

Sandflies — Following the flotilla

While Lars slept peacefully, I collected wood for a fire to make coffee in the cool dawn when thin layers of mist snaked over the river and little whirls rose eerily upwards. By the time Lars woke, the sun has risen and the sky was clear.

An eagle watched over us as we paddled along the silky smooth water. The river widened, and the forest grew thicker and wilder – huge trees loomed up to the sky that blocked the sun and thick vines trailed down to the ground.

The tall riverbanks were vertical from when the rains came and the bloated river carved the earth away. Weeds were knotted around tree roots that protruded from the bank, and occasionally I saw a plastic bag or piece of ragged clothing hanging to a branch way above us.

We stood up to get a better view as we struggled through a maze of rocks, but we still hit shallow water and had to get out and push or drag the boat until a deeper section. We would have barely got in and caught our breath again when we would grind to a halt in what was beginning to seem an unnavigable river. *Have we left our departure too late in the dry season? There's simply not enough water.*

Just then, we were overtaken by a local fisherman proficiently poling his way through the rocky labyrinth. He knew the river and where the deepest channels were; he never got stuck. Soon, another pirogue passed us, and another. We looked upstream and saw a flotilla of fishing pirogues heading towards us.

I was envious of the way they moved through the water with such ease. One man stood at the back of each pirogue, and using a long pole, two to three times his height, placed it on the riverbed and pushed backwards to propel the boat forward in a long burst of speed. My punting experiences were insufficient against these professionals. Instead, we paddled as though in a canoe. Eager to keep up with them, we paddled hard for as long as possible, and that afternoon we covered a good distance and rarely ran aground.

After three days on the river, I thought we were getting the hang of river travel and it would be easier from here.

Day 4

Shallow maze — Near disaster — Crocodile Island

How wrong I was.

Progress was steady until the afternoon. The river was still with barely a ripple on the surface except for the wake of our boat and the circular splashes from our paddles. We glided with serene ease, and there was silence between the walls of the deep-green tree-lined banks.

It did not last.

We heard a faint rumble. *Wind? A distant bush-fire?* The sun was scorching, but the air was motionless, and there was no smoke over the horizon. The river was straight and calm. As we paddled on, the rumbling sound grew and our nerves engulfed the boat. *Rapids?*

Urged on by the sound that drowned out all thoughts, we pulled over at the wall of rocks and clambered up to take a closer look. There was only one passable route, so we pushed the boat back out into the middle of the river and paddled towards uncertainty.

The boat sped up in the current. I stopped paddling and put all my strength and determination into steering to avoid the boulders we shot past. One boulder ... two ... three ... and the water slowed, so we could pull into the side and rest before attempting the next part. My heart was pounding and my body full of adrenalin. *That wasn't so bad!*

We walked over the rocks and led the boat down the next part with ropes. While Lars guided the front end, I pulled back as hard as I could from behind to slow it down. But the boat was at an angle to the flow, and the flow was too fast. I pulled and strained, but the rope burned through my hands. The front end jammed. And the back end swung round until it was pinned – water flooded in.

We leapt into the river and lifted the sinking side up just enough to stop the flow, and then, without a word, we rapidly untied our 'valuables' bags – the ones we were to save first in the event of a capsize.

We pulled the stern backwards and hoped to free the front end, but it only became wedged on another rock and stuck solidly. Now water gushed over the side, rushed through the boat, and exited over the bows like a flume. We leapt and grasped at loose items as one paddle disappeared out of sight downstream. We untied bags and bikes and carried them dripping to the safety of the shore as the water continued to flow through the boat.

Once we righted it enough to stop the inflow and had scooped out the water, with one final show of adrenalin-fuelled strength, we slowly heaved the boat forward – it cleared the rocks and rushed down and around the bend with loose ropes trailing in the water.

I ran over the sandy island covered in crocodile tracks to see its fate. It had come to a standstill, still floating, in the bay below. Putting thoughts of reptiles out of my mind, I waded into the river up to my neck and retrieved it.

With the sun setting, I rushed to put up tents as far from the shore as possible while Lars laid out the sodden food, and we cooked dinner and retired to bed as darkness fell upon us. We didn't want a crocodile encounter after that day.

Day 5

Aches and pains — Machete — Wrong way — Rapids

The boat was still parked and afloat where we had left it, the food drying in the morning sun hadn't been eaten by any wildlife, and the rest of our gear had survived intact and dry. The only things lost were a towel, a water bottle, and the plastic scoop (we found the paddle again).

I didn't feel so lucky. My whole body ached from using muscles it was not used to and my hands were stiff from grasping the paddle. Now I had rope-burned fingers, and a bruised ankle and shin from when I had slipped on a rock, too.

We had still not seen any large animals except a floating bloated dead cow two days ago, which was a vivid reminder to purify the water we took from the river to drink. Other wildlife, however, was abundant, and I loved watching the birds of prey circling in the thermals and the kingfishers that swooped low over the water and little bright blue birds whose feathers shimmered in the sun. Herons stood as tall statues and wading birds pecked at the bugs that hovered over the water and egrets congregated on a black rock in midstream or a riverbank bush. Delicate dragonflies of blues and pinks and reds hovered and darted, and there were always spiders in our boat that when I shooed them out they skated across the surface, and we even saw a snake swimming with its periscope head clear of the water.

When we came to a fast flowing channel, neither of us was keen to take it, so we scouted for an alternative.

'Lars!' I called out since he was clambering between rocks on the other side of the river, 'I think we can get through here.'

There was a narrow passage that flanked the right bank. It was partially blocked by low-lying branches, so we waded alongside the boat and Lars hacked a clear route using the machete. When we were finally clear and had dragged the boat over more rocks, we paddled round the bend into calmer waters and stopped.

Shit. It's a dead end.' My heart sank with what this meant. 'I'm really sorry. I honestly thought it was clear this way.'

'What shall we do?' was all Lars asked.

With considerable effort, we pushed the boat back upstream and reassessed the situation. After walking over all the rocks, we finally concluded that we would have to attempt the gauntlet.

We set off and sped downriver, jettisoned through the flume and soon emerged at the other end unscathed. *Phew! What an adrenalin rush! Now that was fun!*

'We should have just done that in the first place,' I said. It would have saved us an hour of hard work.

Day 6

More rapids — Woman overboard

We followed our new rule of checking the entirety of any route before we proceeded, so we rarely got stuck. Instead, we spent most of the morning out of the boat checking routes rather than just paddling and hoping and pushing if needed.

At the next rapids, we assessed all viable routes based on our rapidly increasing experience of them and opted for the fastest, direct one. It was the same scenario – paddle nervously, speed up, steer aggressively, adrenalin rush, a couple of close shaves, and pop out into calmer water – except this time I didn't manage to turn sharp enough around the last bend.

The current took us side-on into the bushes. I grabbed a branch as I was catapulted from the stern and instantly submerged in the torrent. Clinging to my left flip-flop with the end of my toes, I tried to reach it with my spare hand before it was lost to the undercurrent. I was about to lose the sunglasses from my head too, but I didn't dare let go of the branch. At some point in the decision-making process inside my submerged head about whether to save the flip-flop or the sunglasses – a flip is no use without its flop, but I had lost too many sunglasses to rivers in previous water-related escapades to lose yet another pair – it dawned on me that I should save myself first. Only my right forearm to fingertips was clear of the water, saving me from being dragged downstream. With sudden clarity of mind,

I abandoned the flip-flop-or-shades debate and reached my left arm out of the water to grab another branch. I heaved myself up and took a much needed gasp of air. My flip-flop and sunglasses were gone though.

Day 7

Where are you going like that? — Bee Island — Frogs

About 100 kilometres downstream of Faranah, we were getting close to the Haut Niger National Park. We saw fewer people with each passing day, and now there was just the occasional onlooker from the riverbank or a lone fishing boat. We always exchanged the bare essential greetings. People here knew no other French, and we knew no Mandinka or Fula, so after that we passed in silence. One young man today, however, did shout, '*Où tu vas comme ça?*' A fair question.

'We're going to Bamako,' I replied. We hoped. Progress was painfully slow, and neither of us was sure if we would make it.

'Let's reach Kouroussa first,' Lars said. That was still far away.

The day passed uneventfully, which made a change, and consequently we covered our longest daily distance yet. As the evening drew in, we spotted a small grassy island isolated in the river. There had been no clearings on the banks or rocks for miles, so we decided to camp there.

It was not as idyllic or peaceful as it appeared from a distance; it was surrounded by a buzzing swarm of bees. We lit a fire to cook on and the smoke kept most of the bees away, and then we retreated into our tents. The bees left as the sun went down, and I watched the stars appear in the sky as the darkness and silence deepened.

Then a frog croaked near our island. It was followed shortly after by another croak in another key and then many more frogs joined in, and their song rallied upstream and echoed back down. As suddenly as the cacophony of croaking erupted, the frog-orchestra sounded its final note and the silence was filled with the background chirping of cicadas. The prelude was over. Then, the main ensemble began. The croaking filled the darkness and in the pauses loud splashes resounded like an applause. I hoped they were just fish and not a crocodile.

And it was with this music of the river that I drifted off to sleep each evening.

Day 8

Monkey Rock coffee – Hippo tracks – Fishermen's warning – Fish supper

The bees returned with the sun, so we made a hasty departure and stopped for morning coffee further downstream, where a troupe of vervet monkeys scampered over slabs of rock.

Later, where the river divided around two large islands of sand and boulders, we went left. It was another dead end. The sky had clouded over, and the air was oppressive. All was eerily silent.

'It's like the calm before the storm,' I commented to Lars.

'Do you think it's going to rain?'

'I don't know, but it feels as though something is about to happen.' I was tense and not sure why. 'Shall we check out the route?'

Lars stepped over the rocks towards the island. I was getting my camera out when he called back, 'Oh, wow! Have a look at these footprints – they're huge!'

'What are they?'

'I don't know. Hippo, I guess.'

'Wow. Yeah, I think you're right. Let's be careful.' I had joined him, and now I was scanning our surroundings for more signs. 'They are boulders over there, aren't they?'

For once, there was no storm, or hippos. I was mildly disappointed. Although hippos are known to kill more people in Africa each year than any other large animal, I still wanted to see one (from a safe distance).

As was so often the case when cycling, at the point we wanted to camp, people appeared. We had pulled over to some flat rocks and while Lars was exploring, two men from the fishing camp we had passed earlier paddled towards us. They asked where we were going and said that downriver it was difficult to pass. In sparse French and hand-signalling, they explained that we needed to push the boat through or carry our gear over land, but they could accompany us and help. *So much for camping early.*

The young men were less concerned about helping than having a cigarette. They reluctantly took some rope when I passed it to them, but we hadn't walked far with the boat before they were explaining that they had to return to fish. They handed back the ropes, retreated to a safe distance, and watched us struggle on alone through the rapids.

On the other side, we could finally camp and cook the fish we had bought from a fisherman earlier. Our own attempts with a hook and line had been unsuccessful, so now we just dropped crumbs in the shimmering pools between the rocks and watched as the little fish, black ones with yellow spots and pale ones with red arrow tails, darted in and out of the shadows.

Day 9

Half day – Snake escape – Stock check – Beer

It was business as usual: morning coffee followed by a good morning paddle. We covered plenty of ground and agreed to take the afternoon off to rest – it was our first break since we left Faranah and I, at least, needed it.

I slept under the shade of some trees inside my tent, safe from sandflies and tsetse flies. When I woke, I collected some wood ready for a fire later and then retreated back into my tent. I set to work on the tsetse fly that had invaded, but they are more resilient than sandflies. I was well into round three of giving this bothersome one a pounding when I heard Lars shout, 'Helen! Look out! Snake!'

Distracted from the fly, which was now leaving a thick trail of blood on my tent floor, I looked up to see a snake slithering with exceptional speed towards me; the rustling as it moved through the dead leaves reached my ears a split second later. I focussed intensely on trying to zip up my tent before the snake reached me, but as I grabbed at the zip, the snake slithered under the ground sheet.

'Helen! Don't move!' Lars screamed. I froze, pinned to the spot like the sandfly remains on my tent roof. Fortunately, the snake left as quickly as it had arrived and disappeared into the forest behind. I don't know who was more scared: me, Lars or the snake. I do know that my heart was pounding double-time from some new location in my chest cavity to where it had jumped.

When we were sure there were no more snakes hiding in our food sack we did a food stock check. Some of the pasta had got wet when the boat had flooded and was now mouldy. We had just enough food for another six dinners if we ate less; then we needed to be in Kouroussa. It would be close.

At the end of the day, we sat by the fire and opened the two beers we had saved.

'Happy Birthday,' Lars said.

'Cheers!'

Warm beer never tasted so good.

Day 10

Chimpanzee Rehabilitation Centre

Today we saw the first man-made structures besides pirogues and one bridge since leaving Faranah. We paddled over to investigate the large corrugated-roof buildings, which were not typical of houses in rural Guinean villages. After nine days of Lars asking, 'Do you think we'll reach the National Park today?' we were here, at the Chimpanzee Rehabilitation Centre.

Estelle had been running the centre for ten years. 'We don't usually have visitors because most of the chimpanzees have been traumatised before they come to us and it upsets them. But as you are here, if you wait until noon, you can see them being fed.'

'Where have they come from?'

'Some have been caught illegally for bush meat or as pets, and some are brought as young orphans, and we try to rehabilitate them.

We recently made the first group release of chimpanzees back into the wild. It has gone better than we expected. They are adapting well to their new environment,' Estelle said proudly.

At feeding time, the dinner bell rang and the local workers carried the lunch round in wheelbarrows. The chimps knew the bell and were causing an expectant racket. We observed from a distance as Estelle and the other workers handed the food through the cage bars. But the chimps were aware of our unfamiliar presence – the males aggressively beat the bars, which shook under the force. *I hope we don't encounter one with a temper like that in the wild. I can't believe how much bigger than me they are.*

Before we left, Estelle provided us with some useful advice. 'You should look out for hippos. It's probably best if you paddle down the middle of the river where it is deep, so they can't rear up and trample you or the boat. Also be careful where you camp because water is where hippos feel safe and if you get between them, they may charge you and try to reach it.' *Great.*

Yet again we were confined to our tents as soon as we set up camp because of the sandflies and mosquitoes. We didn't even bother to get out and cook; instead, we ate mayo sandwiches as we had been given some bread at the Centre.

Day 11

Broken boat — Hippo encounter — Bat exodus – Poachers

Now in the National Park, we saw more wildlife. It was always startled when it saw us. Antelope fled from where they had been drinking, and stampeded with deafening splashes until they were clear of the water. A warthog family darted through the bush and guinea-fowl waddled away. A small duiker stood with a frozen stare and then, in a flash, was gone. I spotted something jutting out of the water.

'That's just a rock, isn't it?' The rock's ears twitched. 'Hah, it's a hippo! Brilliant!' And once my excitement wore off I asked Lars, 'Which side should we pass?'

'The side furthest from it,' was his matter-of-fact reply.

I steered sharply towards the left bank. The hippo's head sank below the river surface, and that made us nervous. We passed the point we had seen the hippo and when it resurfaced, it was exactly where we had been when it first disappeared. *Is it trying to catch us?* It let out a resounding snort and disappeared underwater again. I repeatedly looked back for signs of the hippo, but was soon distracted by the drama unfolding downstream.

Hundreds of winged creatures were swarming in erratic frenzied circles above the water and their high-pitched screeching was unnerving. *Are they bats? What the hell are they doing in the daytime?*

Smoke was rising above the trees. *Maybe the bushfire has got too close.* The bushes looked as though they were draped in tattered black plastic bags – the bats that had not yet fled to the sky.

We changed our course for the other bank, and then we saw another hippo. We agreed we would rather deal with rabid bats than an angry hippo, so we paddled back to the left bank where the black horde was now making a mass exodus upstream. We were so close I could see each individual mouse-like face with big ears and sharp teeth, and I wondered if fending off a bat attack with wild swings of my paddle to send them flying over the riverbank for a home run would be more successful than pitching my strength against a mighty hippo, whose jaws could surely crush my wooden paddle like a toothpick.

'Is that *another* hippo?' Lars asked.

I tore my eyes away from the bats, 'Yeah.' *Shit.*

We crossed the river a third time and when we reached the far side, we heard a loud rustling from the trees. We both swung our heads round, and there it was: a huge male chimpanzee. He had peeled back the leafy branches to get a better look at the passing peculiarity: two white people in a pirogue. For a few moments, he stared at us with intelligent curiosity and we smiled right back in stupid wonder. His calm reaction was in stark contrast to the destructive violence of the chimpanzees at the sanctuary. We would have loved to sit and observe our passive cousin longer, but we were more concerned by the hippos, whose attention we continued to attract.

We pushed on downstream until, finally, the wildlife of the Niger River gave us some respite and we could safely stop. That was when we heard an engine and then saw a military officer approaching us in a motorised dinghy. He interrogated us via his local guide translator about what we were doing.

'No, we are not poachers. We're just tourists,' we explained again. Even I knew that most poachers of antelope were none other than locals with a gun trying the only way they knew to feed their family. They are definitely not white English-speaking novices paddling slowly down the river with bicycles strapped in their boat.

Unconvinced by our story, the officer spent an inordinate amount of time staring at the front cover of our passports, which he had demanded, and then asked, 'Are you American?' as he handed them back. *Can you not read? Probably not.*

Day 12

Sounds in the night — Sandflies — Joliba II suffering

I was woken in the night by a strange call. We were camped up on the riverbank in the bush. *It's not a lion, is it?* I was thinking about Estelle's comment that the guards had heard one recently while on patrol.

Now alert, I opened my eyes and, to my horror, realised that I had fallen asleep without putting up the outer cover of my tent. If there were a predatory animal on the prowl, it could easily see me lying on the forest floor. *Oh crap!* I lay there motionless, glancing from left to right, looking for any movement in the shadows. I remained frozen, feeling my heart pounding in my chest.

I heard more rustling, then silence. I didn't even ask Lars if he had heard something and only lay there quietly until a peaceful period had passed. Then I unzipped the tent, hastily put on the outer cover and retreated inside. *I'm such a wimp!*

'Hey Lars,' I said the next morning, 'did you hear that noise in the night?'

'What noise?'

'Did you even hear me get out and put up my outer sheet?'

'No.' *Unbelievable.*

'I did hear you scratching your bites again though.'

I was still plagued by sandflies daily. My attempts to thwart their attacks on my legs by wearing trousers resulted in them attacking my arms. In wearing long sleeves, they mercilessly feasted on the backs of my hands and neck until they bled. To make it worse, the bites then itched for a week and gave me countless restless nights. Why is it the smallest creatures cause the most misery and discomfort?

'I'm sick of them. Mosquito bites are nothing on these.'

'At least you can't get malaria from sandflies,' Lars said.

'I'd happily take that risk right now.'

'I don't know. I've got one that's itching a bit, but it's not that bad.'

'One!' I exclaimed. 'I wouldn't be complaining if I only had one!'

'I have a few others, but they don't itch much.'

'You don't get a say until you have several hundred of them. It's so not fair!'

'I'm glad you're here,' Lars said with a touch of sarcasm, patting me on the shoulder. 'You make me coffee in the morning and you make a good insect repellant too. Good on ya.'

'Oh, shut up,' I said in jest and we laughed. 'Want another coffee?'

It was another tough day with more time spent pushing and dragging the boat than paddling. Poor Joliba II was suffering badly from the continuous pounding against the rocks. Long pieces of material that used to line the seams of the wooden panels' joins now trailed uselessly in the water.

Day 13

More hippos — Three Rocks Camp

In the distance, surrounding a large rock in the middle of the river, there were four pairs of pinkish-grey ears twitching above the surface. We circled wide. Then further downstream, where we got stuck in shallow water, there were another two. While we were trying to dislodge the boat, the hippos silently bowed down. Just as we freed the boat and got back in to paddle, one hippo momentarily resurfaced just ahead of us. As we paddled hard to the other side of the river, the hippo reemerged twice and snorted loudly as we increased our distance. If only we could have paddled that fast since Faranah, we would have been in Bamako already.

After nearly two weeks, the long strenuous days with little rest were taking their toll. Lunch, by now, was nothing more substantial than the bland imported glucose biscuits. Instead, we took an extended break and put up the tent for an hour's rest where we would not be bothered by flies.

With places to camp becoming less frequent, we decided to stop that evening when we saw three flat rocks the size of our tents in the middle of the river. Lars took the left, I took the right, and the central one we used as a kitchen and built a small fire on it. We enjoyed another beautiful sunset perfectly reflected in the still water and retired to our separate tents. Lars was reading, and I just lay there, drifting slowly to sleep.

A thunderous splash and accompanying snort ripped me from my dreams and back to reality on the Niger River. *Bloody hell! That was loud!*

'Lars, tell me you heard that,' I said.

All he could bring himself to say was, 'Yes.'

It was, unmistakably, a hippopotamus, which aptly means 'water horse'. It sounded like a stallion flaring its nostrils and snorting wildly at the scent of a mare on heat and like a whale spurting a tall jet of water skywards.

Neither of us had the foolish courage to get out of our tents. Instead, we each lay in our separate cocoons perched on our rocks and listened as the hippo next to us snorted playfully and enjoyed bathing in the cool evening air.

Day 14

Fast rapids — Stuck — Decision to stop

It was a successful start to the day, with calm open water. Boosted by our early progress and steady rhythmic paddling, when we heard the distinctive white water ahead and then saw the rapids, we kept paddling. On our approach Lars called back, 'Should we stop and check it out?'

I dismissively replied, 'Nah, sod it, let's just go for it!' I was too tired to care much about the consequences. I only wanted to reach Kouroussa, so I could stop paddling.

We sped between the rocks, dodged one here and one there, and made one sharp turn and then another. A couple of times I thought we would hit a rock, but either the water was strong enough to carry us over unscathed or we took evasive action just in time. When the water slowed, we directed the boat into the bank and caught our breath.

Around the next bend the river divided into many channels. We picked one and persevered, scraping the boat over rocks. For an hour we slowly shifted it forward inch-by-inch. Once we freed the boat into deeper water, a man who had been watching us walked over and then explained we had taken the wrong route.

'Why didn't he tell us that *before* we got stuck?' Lars vented at me once we were alone, voicing what I had been thinking.

Late in the afternoon we pulled up onto the riverbank to camp. I checked the GPS. 'I think we'll be in Kouroussa the morning after next.'

'Ah, that's great!' Lars said. 'You know, I think we should finish in Kouroussa.'

'Yeah, me too. We're running out of time on our visas to get to the border, and I'd need a proper rest if we were going to paddle more,' I admitted.

'I think we've paddled the most interesting part anyway. These two weeks is enough adventure for me, for now. From here, there will just be more people and less wildlife.'

'And more shallow water to get stranded on. I wonder if Joliba would have made it to Bamako anyway? She's leaking more every day.'

We sat awhile in silence, then Lars said, 'I think we should start seeing villages tomorrow. We'll be close to town, so we should be able to buy more food. Shall we have a big dinner tonight and finish up the pasta? We can always manage one night without if we know that we have only got to paddle a bit the next morning.'

'Good idea.' I was hungry most of the time now. Powdered cereal and dry glucose biscuits and one proper meal in the evening were not enough to sustain us.

'So it's our last full day on the Niger River tomorrow. I'm a little sad,' Lars added.

'Yeah, but I'm looking forward to the prospect of a hotel room where I won't be ravaged by sandflies and know that I don't have to get up in the morning and paddle or push.'

'And there'll be beer.'

Day 15

Too much sand — Kouroussa — Sell boat — Beer!

We began enthusiastically, knowing it was the last full day. Unfortunately, the river had other plans for us – shallow water.

Now there were no rocks, just sand. The whole frustrating morning we spent more time out of the boat than in it, standing in ankle-deep water while we mustered up the strength to inch the boat forward. We gradually pushed the boat over the sands until the water was deep enough to paddle a few strokes.

We stopped regularly, but I was exhausted soon after each break. Then, after lunch, we came to a long, deep section and we burst forward energetically.

'What is that?' I asked Lars. I was staring at something unusual in the distance and trying to decipher it.

'It looks like a truck.'

'Really?' We paddled harder.

As we got closer we saw lots of people and pirogues on the river, and there was a dirt road leading down each bank.

'We've made it!' Lars exclaimed.

I didn't let myself believe it. 'It can't be Kouroussa; it's too soon.'

'No, but Kouroussa must be very close. We could just stop here instead, and cycle into town. We'd be in a hotel tonight drinking beer. We would only miss a couple of hours paddling.'

Lars knew I could be persuaded by beer.

The next two hours was a whirlwind of activity. We unloaded and reassembled the bikes, sold *Joliba II* for small change to a fisherman – enough to buy a few drinks that night – left the rest of the equipment on the bank for the boys to use or sell, and cycled off. Before we knew it, we had checked into a hotel and were cracking open a celebratory beer.

'Cheers,' we said and took a swig.

Part Two
West Africa

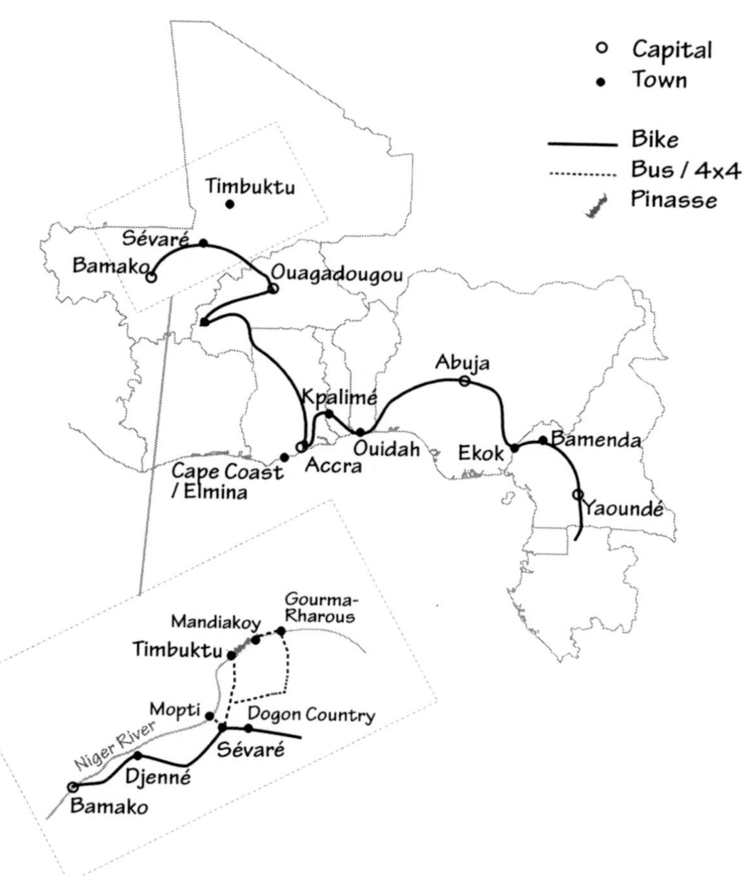

11

The Travel Blues

Mali

Mali is famous for its music, but I didn't hear much in my first week there. I had been singing my own sad song, the travel blues. After months of fun and challenging cycling along the lesser-known back roads of the Guineas and an adventurous time on the Niger River, the ride into Mali failed to inspire.

I was exhausted, and this manifested as a severely bloated stomach whenever I ate until I could barely cycle. Worse than the tired body though, boredom had set in. After eight months on the road, I was losing interest. Robbed of my natural curiosity, I was left with only apathy. I was going through the motions without interest, care or concern like an insomniac walking listlessly through life.

For hours I grappled with the thought that I could simply get a lift, but I knew there was nothing to be gained by this except an easy way out. There were bound to be rays of wonder shining through my cloudy outlook if I just persevered. My stubbornness and Lars kept me going.

'Why don't you carry on without me. I'll come on slowly and can meet you in Bamako,' I suggested as I lay on my back in the shade.

'I'm not going to do that now. We've come this far together; I'm not about to abandon you when you're not well.'

Part of me wished he would go, so I could curl up by the side of the road and go to sleep feeling sorry for myself. The other part was glad he stayed because troubles are halved when they are shared. He couldn't cure my stomach, but he was a shoulder to lean on for support (metaphorically speaking since our clothes were filthy and we stank, and body odour is not best shared). So I gritted my teeth and kept on pedalling.

We were entering the dry Sahel again as we headed north-east. The road followed the Niger River, and sometimes we caught a glimpse of it where the trees receded, beyond a field lattice strip of crops and irrigation channels. Villages appeared as green island shelters, and the great mango trees provided shade from the fierce sun, which failed to penetrate their thick coats of leaves.

We were in a land where there are only two seasons: hot and wet, or hotter and dry. It was scorching, and in those temperatures, food was merely sustenance and I took no joy in it. Except for the large ripe mangoes with juice that ran between my fingers as I cut into it and flesh that stuck in my teeth as I took a bite – the taste so tantalising and divine.

Water, however, was of the essence and became an obsession. In villages we filled our water bottles at the communal pump. It was always surrounded by women and children with a mass of jerry cans and metal bowls waiting to be filled.

Not a drop of water was ever wasted. The pump pipe was always too large for our bottles, so the water was pumped into a bowl first and then carefully decanted. Sometimes a large bucket was kept below the pump and any water that missed the bottles ran into it to be used for washing or cleaning. Then we would scoop a handful of water to wash our red faces, necks and dirty hands.

When our bottles were full we drank greedily the cool Elysian liquor that moistened our lips and quenched our thirst before a woman took the bottle from us, topped it up to the brim, and carefully screwed on the top without ever spilling a drop.

Only the water drunk immediately from the pump could be savoured. In a dry arid land my senses were elevated. I tasted the subtle sweetness from the earth on my tongue and felt the cool touch of the water as it flowed down my throat and coursed through me. Once the water had been in our bottles only fifteen minutes, it was warm. Warm water does not quench thirst or relieve a parched mouth. I would stop pedalling and guzzle the sometimes tepid, sometimes hot water. I could swallow a litre without taking a breath and still want more, my body and stomach saturated but never satiated.

* * *

I was not sad to be leaving Bamako. Our hotel was a depressing, dark sweat-box cell with mosquito inmates for company. I slept in my tent pitched on the bed of wooden slats with a foam mattress flattened by the bodies of old prisoners. The darkness never crushed the sounds of a city that didn't sleep. Restless noise troubled my torpid body and wrenched me from uneasy dreams. During the daytime the oppressive heat hammered me into submission. This was no place for recovery; I only lingered in limbo.

Lars was not suffering from the prolonged exertions of the last couple of months and when he could stand it no more, we packed our bags and departed for more pleasant pastures.

Bamako's roads were busy and filled with motorbikes. Scores of them screeched to a halt at traffic lights and swarmed off round the bend in a cloud of choking smoke. As we left the clogged arteries of the capital behind, I felt the freedom of life on the road begin to course through my veins.

I had become wary of Malian motorcyclists, having been scraped on the arm by one reckless youth passing too close during my first days in Mali. But over the river and out of town there was a bike lane – the first I saw in Africa – and I thought that I might just make it out of Bamako in one piece.

I should have known better. Motorbikes are bikes too, so while the cars had plenty of space to cruise along at top speed on the main highway, I had to try my luck with the hundreds of Malians on motorbikes dodging, weaving, braking and overtaking, and stopping and starting in the narrow bike lane. In Europe, their purpose is to improve the safety for cyclists. Here – who knows?

What I remember most, however, was the wind. At that time of year the harmattan wind blows from the Sahara towards the Gulf of Guinea. It carries sand and dust particles through the air, obscuring views. When particularly strong, it can carry sand and dust across the Atlantic to North America.

The harmattan, which had blown us along the coast road in the Western Sahara and hazed the distant horizon of the Fouta Djalon hills in Guinea, now worked against us. It blew northeasterly, directly into our faces.

The hardship of the battle against the harmattan was compensated for in many other ways. We were heading back towards similar latitudes as when we were in Senegal. Unlike the humid tropical forest of Sierra Leone where the atmosphere hung heavily over us and where there were always people when we wished for peace, the Malian Sahel was arid and sparsely populated. Now, when we were ready to camp, we simply pushed our bikes off the road and wound through the scrub until we found a clearing to pitch our tents. With so much tinder-dry dead wood, even lighting a fire to cook on was easy. Dust and sand covered all our belongings, but at least it was clean and dry.

Baobab trees stood solitary and tall, reminding me of easier, untroubled times. Through the black night when I lay back in my tent beneath twin baobabs that cradled the full moon as it rose between them, an owl hooted its wise words to the wind and I saw then my happiness written in the stars across the sky.

When we arrived in the predominantly Muslim town of San, Lars was quick to point out that it was Friday lunchtime. The shops were shut, restaurants weren't serving food, and the street stalls and market were eerily devoid of vendors.

We did have a knack of arriving in town on a Friday. When I finally arrived in a town on another day, it was a Sunday where Christianity was the major faith and still the shops were shut.

The truck-stop on the outskirts of town, however, was open. Even more unusual was the choice of food, not just the standard rice and sauce, but spaghetti and chicken, and other meat as well. Stupefied by the selection, I ordered rice and sauce. More surprising was when the waiter brought us a kettle and bowl for washing our hands. This ritual, together with eating with the right hand, which was common throughout Mali, I had not observed since Mauritania.

It was trivialities like this that highlighted our return to the Saharan desert enclave of Islamic belief and tradition.

Eventually, we arrived at the Djenné *carrefour*, the junction to the road that crossed the Bani River to Djenné. We bought a cold drink from one of the women with cool-boxes in a wooden shack and enquired about a lift along the dead end road.

'When will the bush-taxi leave?' I asked.

'Soon.' *Probably not soon enough.*

'How soon?'

'Maybe in one hour.'

When told that a taxi will leave in an hour, that means it might leave in two. First the taxi waits for the bus to arrive from Bamako, which is always late, and then the taxi must be filled. Only once it is brimming with people, arms and legs splayed in every direction, and every crevice jammed with belongings and the roof piled high with luggage will the taxi-driver consider leaving – we cycled into Djenné. We beat the bush-taxi by several hours; we beat my friend Catherine, who was coming out to visit, by a day.

Djenné is a sleepy place, except for market day when hundreds of people arrive in town, congregate and congest the streets. They usher in goats and sheep and set up shop on the street floor. They barter, bicker and trade anything from fresh and dried fruit, vegetables, spices, millet, rice and nuts to reels of cloth and second-hand clothes, shoes and sandals, football shirts, political campaign regalia, torches, batteries and bike parts, toothpaste, cuddly teddies, and sweets and cigarettes.

Locals know Djenné for the Monday market; tourists know Djenné for the Great Mosque, which is famous for being the largest mud-brick building in the world. The first mosque here was built around the thirteenth century. The mosque I saw was built in 1907 and is a replica of the original. Essentially, on the exterior, it is just a big mud-brick building and when I was there, a crumbling one. I do not know what it looks like inside – non-Muslims are not allowed to enter.

Each year the outer mud layer is eroded by the rains and then cracks and breaks in the ensuing hot day and colder night temperature fluctuations. To prevent eventual total collapse, the residents of Djenné repair the walls annually. Wooden scaffolding is erected and mud plaster mixed in large pits by the children, carried by the women, and plastered by the men, in an excellent example of the division of labour.

Lars was due to fly home soon, so we said goodbye. It was the end of a chapter, of the good and tough times we had shared together during the past five months. It was not a final farewell – our paths would cross again down the road somewhere in the future; we were sure of that.

Catherine was here now, and I was ready for a change. It was time to sacrifice the freedom of being able to go wherever or whenever I wanted with the bike for the inconveniences and aggravations of travel by public transport that most people have to put up with. Patience is a trait that must be learned; equally, it can be lost. I had forgotten how to sit quietly, passively waiting for the world to come to me rather than rushing headfirst with adrenalin pumping and pedals spinning.

However, when you pass through a country by independent means you miss out on many of the interactions of daily life. You can learn a lot about people by how they travel, and in Mali, most people travel by bus and bush taxi.

The minibus looked relatively new and roadworthy. My glass half-full of optimism emptied when I saw there were a lot of seats to fill – no vehicle left unless fully loaded. Then the empty minibus departed and was replaced by a smaller bashed-up tarpaulin-covered *bâché* for transporting people like cattle. *More likely to leave Djenné but less likely to arrive in Sévaré.*

Out of the blue, and the dust, people moved from idle bench-sitting to active baggage-handling and crammed into the back of the *bâché*. Once I would have said there was space for six people – now I know better – fourteen squeezed in. It was a slow journey. We stopped in every village; we even stopped between villages; eventually, we stopped in Sévaré.

There was little of interest at the crossroads in town although Catherine's fascination with everything was contagious. She was seeing for the first time what I no longer registered – goats and sheep wandering the dusty streets among donkeys pulling carts, and rusting cars with dented bumpers hanging off; women wore colourful *pagnes* wrapped around their waists and matching headscarves and carried babies who never cried on their backs, and when they reached for something on the floor they did so with knees straight and bulbous backsides mushrooming in the air; sisters wore different dress styles made from the same material covered in political party symbols and slogans; boys played endless games of rolling old bike tyres with a stick and pushing model cars they had fashioned from wood; and teenagers played table football outside in the daytime and put on long socks and jelly shoes in the evening to play football on a dusty patch of ground with goals made from sticks.

For me, it was now the same as walking down the high street in a typical English town where I know there will be the usual chains of clothes and phone stores displaying discounts, pharmacies, coffee shops and fast food stops, pay-and-display parking down side streets, and double yellow lines on the main street.

The biggest difference was that in Sévaré, as in most African towns, people talked to one another and smiled. I realised there was much to love about Africa and much to be reminded of from those who live there.

Our plans for travel in Mali were fluid, which was the only sort of plan likely to succeed. We both wanted to visit Dogon country and try to get to Timbuktu. Besides that, we would happily take whatever Mali offered like a dog given a bone. The crossroads of Sévaré led four ways. We had come from Bamako and Djenné in the south, Dogon country lay to the east and the road to Timbuktu led north.

First we went west to Mopti at the confluence of the Bani and Niger Rivers. It is the region's main commercial centre and is Mali's most important port. *Pinasses*, like large pirogues, but with a motor and a roof for cover ply the river from Segou downstream as far as Timbuktu and even Gao in Niger. They transport salt from the Sahara, people, food, and other goods as they have done for centuries.

We wandered among the eclectic ethnic mix of men united by trade as one nation under the banner of Mali. Fishermen threw nets into the murky water. Fulani traders and herders, distinguishable by their conical hats made of leather and fibre and decorated with cowrie shells, stood with their flocks of sheep. Tuareg 'blue men' in indigo robes and turbans talked. And Bambara, Bozo and Songhai in wide-sleeved, long-robed *boubous* and *kufi* caps mingled and made deals. There were only men on the riverbanks; the women were in the market.

Here, where the river was wide and the banks shallow, the muddy shoreline was paved with large flat stones. On these, stacks of the salt slabs, tied together with strips of cloth, were lined up until they would be cut into smaller sizes to be sold on. The sun glistened and glinted off the salt – Mali's mineral wealth – like jewels.

Another source of wealth is the tourist industry. Tourists like myself come to visit Dogon country because of the 'culture' and Timbuktu because of the name. The guidebook says to go to Djenné for the 'colourful market' and to Mopti to see the 'lively port' and 'beautiful mosque'. But every market is colourful and every port is lively, and I have never seen a mosque that is not beautiful. I have seen mosques in unattractive surroundings, but that only serves to make them more captivating.

12

To Timbuktu and Back

Mali

The road to Timbuktu was a long one. We travelled by bush taxi and bus until we needed a 4x4 to travel down the desert piste. We were told it would take about four hours from the road, but we reached Kourioume on the river in the middle of the night when there was no boat to take us to the other side. So Catherine slept on the back seat of the 4x4 and I on the ground outside, curled up in my sleeping bag. The other passengers took cover from the chill air beneath blankets. We had returned to the desert and while the earth was ablaze in the day, at night without the sun's warmth, the cool air made us shiver. At dawn, we huddled around a charcoal stove and drank coffee and waited for the boat to ferry us to the other side.

I can't remember the first time I heard the word 'Timbuktu'. It was a long time ago, before I knew it was an actual place, not some myth or legend. The dusty town sitting on the bend of the Niger River on the edge of the desert in northern Mali where 'camel meets canoe' was not as I had imagined.

Although originally inhabited during the Iron Age, it was only around the eleventh century that Tuareg Imashaghan of Berber origin founded Timbuktu as a market trading town. It soon became a celebrated cultural centre of learning and attracted scholars throughout the Islamic world. By the twelfth century there were three universities and 180 Koranic schools.

In 1324 the Emperor of Mali, *Mansa* Musa, made a pilgrimage to Mecca. He travelled from Timbuktu with a procession of 60,000 men, 12,000 slaves who all carried four-pound gold bars, and 80 camels carrying gold dust, which he gave to the poor en route. In Cairo he gave away countless gifts of gold that amazed the merchants and depressed the market for years. News of his wealth quickly spread through Europe, and so the legend of Timbuktu as an African El Dorado began.

Leo Africanus was a Moorish diplomat from Granada who visited Timbuktu in 1526. It is hard to believe the ensuing fervour that gripped Europe from his descriptions, of what was a typical city on one of the Saharan trade routes, awash with money. But it is a folly of human nature to believe what we want to believe, even when the truth is clearly otherwise, and especially when the facade is for fame or fortune. So many set out to 'discover' this fabled rich city, which they imagined to be glittering with roofs of pure gold.

Africanus talked also of the king honouring learning and he mentioned that many imported, hand-written books were sold for more profit than from all other merchandise, which in a land of salt, gold and slaves is fascinating and reason enough to seek the city, in my opinion. Coming from a background where education is seen primarily as a path to a better-paid job, I am not the only one who could learn something from a place where knowledge is valued more highly than wealth. Wealth and riches are only relative after all, and are dependent upon supply and demand, so that where there is less it is worth more. Knowledge on the other hand can continue to be acquired and like an antique it only appreciates in value.

Timbuktu's decline began when it was sacked by the Moroccan army in 1591. By 1828 when the first European, a Frenchman called René Caillié, reached and returned from Timbuktu, the city was a disappointment. His 'indescribable satisfaction' at arriving safely in Timbuktu was soon overshadowed when he looked around and found that the sight did not answer his expectations. He wrote, 'The city presented, at first view, nothing but a mass of ill-looking houses, built of earth. Nothing was to be seen in all directions but immense plains of quicksand of a yellowish white colour … all nature wore a dreary aspect and the most profound silence prevailed; not even the warbling of a bird was to be heard.' From that point on, Timbuktu's legend fell from fabled city to simply a far away place.

Caillié was not the first European to attempt to reach Timbuktu let alone set foot in the city. It is believed that Mungo Park reached the city on his expedition down the Niger River, but was killed before he had chance to report his findings. Gordon Laing, another Scotsman, arrived in Timbuktu two years before Caillié, but he was killed by locals who were fearful of European intervention.

When I travelled to Timbuktu, it was a relatively safe place to reach and leave, despite concerns of kidnappings by Islamic militants in the region. Unfortunately, the future of Timbuktu is uncertain. Tuareg separatists have been calling for independence since their first rebellion in 1916, claiming that they have been marginalised by the government, which allowed mining projects to damage important pastoral areas. Two years after I visited Mali, the rebels took control of Timbuktu. The Tuareg cause was hijacked by an Islamist group whose aim was to impose Sharia, Islamic law, throughout Mali. The mosques and ancient tombs were being methodically destroyed, and the fate of the libraries and thousands of ancient scrolls was equally uncertain.

It is still time-consuming to reach Timbuktu, unless you opt to fly, which would defeat the point of going since it is the difficulty of the journey there that is the main allure today. The town has not changed much since Caillié arrived. There is not much to do; there is not much trade anymore, or learning.

When we drew into the town the driver invited us to stay with his family. No encouragement was necessary, and soon we were speeding through the dusty outskirts. Only the main roads were tarmac, although in the north of town where the desert is encroaching they had to be swept regularly.

I asked for the driver's name, but all he said was, 'I am *le chauffeur*.' He lived with his family on the outskirts of town where a neatly laid out grid of wide sandy streets divides blocks of walled compounds. We entered through a small wooden door within the wall, and in the corner of the large yard was a small single-storey, mud-brick house, which had two rooms, one for le chauffeur and his wife and the other for his two sons. On our arrival, the boys were set to sweeping the yard and clearing their room for us. We all sat outside on the scattered, broken string chairs or upturned buckets and shared the pineapple and papaya we had brought with us.

The standpipe in the corner meant it was easy to get a bucketful for washing. The only novelty was the toilet. I have experienced my fair share of lavatories – porcelain flush, long drop squat with a bucket of water, and al fresco in the bush to name a few – but here was the rooftop pipeline long drop. First you walked up the ladder onto the upper open level of the building carrying your plastic kettle of water where there was a small concrete section sloping down towards the outer wall with a pipe sticking out. That was the toilet – aim and fire. Pity anyone walking the street below when they wonder why it is raining in the desert, or much worse.

Timbuktu was dusty streets, open sewers and telegraph wires strewn with cat-skins. It was common to see old pairs of shoes tied together by their laces, hanging from telegraph wires of towns on my travels, no doubt put there by miscreant boys. In Timbuktu this new tradition has taken an alternate form. Young boys hunt the town's cats and when they catch one they kill and skin it, leaving the skull attached. The meat is left to dry while the boys parade the houses singing and dancing, and the adults often give a handful of rice to appease the 'mighty' hunters, much like trick-or-treating at Halloween. The boys later return to cook the cat into a mean dish and sling the cat-skin to the wire. Before the telegraph lines were installed about two decades ago, the cat-skins were traditionally thrown into the trees. Boys will be boys, everywhere.

We wandered past the houses where the European explorers once resided. They are like all the houses, mud-brick with heavy wooden doors, except for a metal plaque with their names inscribed. There was little else to do except drink sickly sugar-sweetened green tea in shot glasses, as I had drunk in Morocco and Mauritania, while sitting on a carefully laid mat on the sandy floor of a shady recess.

I heard it could be hard to leave Timbuktu, so even before we arrived on the northern shore of the Niger River at Kourioume, I was already searching alternative ways to leave because we wanted to return by a different route. Word at the port was that a public *pinasse* would be leaving on Friday; at the tourist office in town we were told that it was too far into the dry season and that the river was too low to travel by *pinasse* at all. With the struggles of paddling the pirogue in Guinea still fresh in my mind, I could well believe that.

Shindouk, the knowledgeable Tuareg chief I had the privilege of meeting, ensured us that *pinasses* were plying the river, and he called the port to double-check. While there was no consensus on the Friday public pinasse, we were promised that they travel between here and Gao to trade, arriving in each village on their market day. By river to Gao could take anything from four days to four weeks and since Catherine had a flight to catch, we decided to market-hop halfway, to Gourma Rharous, where we could find a 4x4 to take us south along a piste back to the main road. This, Shindouk told us, would be the safest way. Although trucks travel down to Gao, many of the men are rough characters and would sell anything to make money, including two English girls to Islamist groups in the North. If we wanted to go by road he would put us in contact with reputable men, but we should not accept a ride with just anyone, he insisted. Pinasse it was then. My barrier for unacceptable risk may be higher than most, but I do still have one.

A pinasse would be leaving on Saturday to arrive in Gourma on Thursday. Saturday arrived, and we hitched a ride back to the river with Papa and his two friends. They enquired about the pinasse, but were told there was not one leaving Kourioume that day. Plans never go as expected in Africa.

Papa drove us downriver to Kabara and asked again with more success this time. We could go by public pinasse to Mandiakoy, which is halfway to Gourma Rharous. The cost was 2,000 CFA each until the pinasse owner saw that we were white and increased it to 5,000 CFA. We finally agreed on, and all felt hard done by, 4,000 CFA each.

When it was time to leave, we walked aboard along a slippery plank of wood with water and bread for the journey. Despite it being market day, there was only bread to be bought for our on-board dinner and breakfast and however many more meals on our pinasse ride of indeterminable length.

Like our pirogue, *Joliba II*, this pinasse also had a layer of filthy water settled in the bottom of the boat. The younger men and the driver, as regulars, had the best position sat on top of dry sacks and boxes. The women in the centre gossiped and laughed and cooked over a large stove that sent eye-stinging wood-smoke through the pinasse. The older Tuareg men sat silently, wrapped in blue with sheathed swords lying nearby. I was sat near one man who had a filthy habit of clearing his nostrils down the inner side of the pinasse, and sometimes the effluent was sent streaming on the wind.

The pinasse chugged down the smooth river. We were moving, and it required no effort on my part. Besides the driver who steered, and his mate who kept a good lookout for shallow water, the only other person working was the tireless old man who continually scooped out excess leak-water with a jerry can and poured it over the side. I balanced on a crossbeam and felt the breeze on my face as I leant over the side to watch the bow wave break and the river's ripples blur.

When the engine was cut and the boat drifted away from the setting sun obscured in the haze of the harmattan, everyone faced eastwards downstream and began evening prayers. Their mellifluous words resonated on the wind and round the wooden ribbed pinasse, which was our whole world right then. When prayers were said, the women got busy serving dinner. Then the engine started up again, and voices and laughter filled the insides. We glided through the water ever onwards for I don't know how long until a quietness reigned, and we all tried to find a comfy spot on which to rest because it was late.

The boat rocked gently, and I rolled in and out of sleep wedged between two logs, and when I could not bare the discomfort any longer, I opened my eyes and through the darkness saw the sky blanketed with stars, and there was silence as the boat slept. As I tried to sit by pushing up on my hands, I felt the cold water on my fingers below the branches I was lying on. The mat had slipped, and my bag was in the pool of water, so I moved it to a drier place and lay back down again as there was nowhere comfier. And so we drifted on through the night.

Morning came, the sun rose, bodies rose, people prayed, and the engine was restarted to take us further down the Niger River. We stopped to collect passengers in small villages where rice sacks piled high on the shore meant we were to stop there. At each village, the women on board left the boat, laid out goods on the sandy bank, and the bartering and trading of this mobile market began. Some villages were hidden beyond the bank, others were no more than nomads' canvas tents spread linearly along the shore with a light-skinned family stood outside watching and waiting. The women wore elegant, long flowing dresses while the young girls were beautiful in fine black headscarves with intricate flowers of golden thread. They resembled the Berber families of the Moroccan Atlas more than any of the other dark-skinned people in Mali. The boys wore cheap scruffy t-shirts and second-hand shorts from the market. Boys will be boys, everywhere.

We passed fertile green pastures with cattle grazing and horses resting, for the river is a lifeline through this otherwise barren region. We scooped water from the river to drink and ate the remainder of our bread. When the driver called to us, 'Mandiakoy,' we looked towards the sandy bank but there was nothing there; no village, no boats, no people. We looked imploringly at the driver. He assured us this was the stop for Mandiakoy and that the village was two kilometres away.

So we wobbled down the boardwalk that was a gateway from what we knew into the unknown, stepped into the shallows, and then onto dry land. It felt as though we had walked the plank and plunged into the fateful sea, stranded and abandoned. Except for those few words from the driver, no one had spoken with us since we boarded the pinasse. It was one of the few times that I truly felt an outsider, viewed as baggage or simply with suspicion.

When the pinasse pulled away, there were three of us on that sand bank: me, Catherine, and a young man carrying a briefcase, with kind eyes and an intelligent look. Dr Sidi was a medical student in Bamako returning to his home village since it was the holiday. We followed the doctor north across the dusty cracked earth, hard underfoot, between dried-up rice fields where cattle grazed. It was the end of March and the sun was fierce. The dust-filled air glowed white above us, and a wind blew hot and vengeful across the desolate expanse, and very quickly we could no longer see the river that was our lifeline and means of escape. There was no escaping the utterly oppressive heat, so we walked slowly in silence.

It was a relief when we came to a small river with a couple of boats and on the far side a grove of palm trees offering hopes of shade, if nothing else. A fisherman took us across, and we walked through the village. It appeared deserted apart from a couple of men sitting in the shade of a tree, and a few boys who ran past, absorbed in their games and oblivious to our presence. Sidi picked up the keys to his family compound from the school guardian, and we whiled away the hours inside the cool walls of earth, which had a blackboard on one side with the Arabic alphabet and numbers written on it.

When evening came, we strolled down the village's two sandy streets and bought some pasta at the under-stocked shop, and I wondered if it was always so or whether after market day tomorrow it would be resupplied. I doubted it. We offered to cook Sidi dinner that evening. He lit the charcoal stove then watched us chop and cook, but he quickly made his excuses to leave when it came to eating.

That night I slept deeply. Outside on the ground within Sidi's home compound was one of the most peaceful nights of the journey. It had been the same sleeping on the roofs of houses in Dogon villages. To sleep outside and feel entirely safe and need neither shelter for protection or a cover for warmth, with no need to listen out for wild animals or people and not be plagued by mosquitoes or ants and be able to open my eyes briefly as I rolled over, still half-asleep, and see where the moon had risen to and know what time it was by the position of the stars that shone brilliantly, unadulterated by artificial lamplight – that was my perfect night. It ended at first light, and not by the call of a rooster. Instead, I slowly came round to consciousness feeling well rested when the sun's rays reached me, and then I moved into the shade and wondered what the new day would bring.

It was market day, and it brought people. The village sleeps all week and then each Monday it comes to life. Down on the riverbank we watched as cartloads of families arrived at the shore. Boys rode loaded donkeys, and a turbaned Tuareg arrived on a camel with more following behind. Light-skinned Berber families came on foot, and Fulani men shepherded their goats to the pens. Stalls filled with the usual goods where yesterday the streets had lain empty.

When we had seen everything twice we returned to Sidi's home and spent our remaining time sat in the shade reading and occasionally talking. It was too hot to do much more. The hours slid by slowly until late afternoon when Sidi served up a sumptuous meal of rice. But before we had finished eating, Sidi's friend arrived saying it was time to leave right away. After endlessly whiling away the hours, time was now of the essence and we had to go immediately.

In a frenzy, we shovelled a few last mouthfuls of rice into our mouths, grabbed our bags, and leapt into the back of the 4x4, not wishing to miss this opportunity to leave because the next chance would be the following Monday.

Speeding over sand, alongside the river, was much faster than travelling by boat. We reached Gourma Rharous the same day. It was the height of modernity after days of simple living. There was electricity, street lights, and shops that didn't just sell the same essentials, but specialised in car repairs, electrical goods, and groceries.

We stopped in a side street, and the driver called a man over. This was where our ride ended; this was whom we had come to see. This was news to us. Rather than ask questions, we dutifully got out and waited to see what would happen.

Le chauffeur from Timbuktu has informed his friend in Gourma that we, *deux blanches*, would be arriving by 4x4 from Mandiakoy and since we were his friends, he was to help us. The most surprising part was that le chauffeur knew we had stopped in Mandiakoy. Mobile technology carries news faster than the wind, faster than camels, and faster than we could travel.

Even before the advent of mobile phones, news spread rapidly across the desert expanses. In 1880, Oskar Lenz the German geologist reached Timbuktu, the fourth European to do so. He commented on how everyone in town was well informed of all that happened in Europe through the constant connections with the Arabs of the Mediterranean countries. News spread with extreme rapidity that they knew of his plan to go to Timbuktu before he had even crossed the Atlas Mountains in Morocco.

Le chauffeur tasked his friend with feeding us, accommodating us, and finding onward transport for us. Like escaped convicts, under cover of darkness, a group of us assembled. One 4x4, distinguishable by its one broken headlight, had been cruising the streets of Gourma. When it stopped, we all piled in the back. I crouched against the back of the cabin, bolts bruising my back and shoulder blades, with my bags secure under my feet.

The full moon dimly lit up the desert. The wind was strong and cool. I wore a long top to keep warm, wrapped my kaftan round my head and put on my sunglasses in a vain attempt to keep dust from my eyes, but they still stung badly, so I rode most of the way with them closed. We arrived at the main road in the middle of the night. With nowhere to go, we slept behind a shack until daybreak. The return bus ride to Sévaré was quick and comfortable after that.

There I waved goodbye to Catherine. From now on, I would be alone. I was rested, revived and ready to see more of Africa by bike.

13

Storming a New Idea

Burkina Faso and Ghana

I fought the headwind and crawled slowly onward along the corrugated dirt road to the border. I stopped several times every hour to eat a mango and avoid another tornado. Columns of dust and debris marched across the desolate landscape, their path predetermined by the direction of the wind. One dust devil crept up on me unnoticed while I was sheltering in the shade of a tree and covered me with grit and sand. I hadn't the energy to move, only to hide my face in my shirt and shut my eyes and mouth until it went unhindered on its way.

It was now April, the hottest time of year. It was too hot to cycle for much of the day, like when I was in Central Spain in August. So I got up at four in the morning and was on the road with first light. The cool morning air brought only temporary relief. Pedalling hard, I tried to cover as much ground as possible before the oppressive heat tormented me and turned all my thoughts to one obsession: shade. By eleven o'clock I was assessing every tree and bush – there weren't many – as potential resting places. If there had been an air-conditioned bar, I would have stopped immediately. Anywhere I could buy a cold drink and sit without too much attention was great. But villages were few and far between, and as midday approached, any tree would do as desperation crept in. I used to lie on the ground with my tent as a rug, close my eyes and wait. Sometimes I read, occasionally sipping at my water and eating mangoes. Hours of inactivity passed until five o'clock when I could suffer an hour or two of the sun before it set.

As I gradually moved south through Burkina Faso and the weeks passed by, the hot dry season changed to the less hot, humid wet season. It took hours to cool down in an evening – any movement and I started sweating. Simply eating dinner, sweat dripped down my face. I used to lie in my tent in my underwear, sweating as the sun-soaked ground radiated heat upwards. By the time I fell asleep the temperature was bearable, but already the towel I lay on was drenched. I woke with a chill in the coolest hours of the morning when all heat from the day had finally dissipated and the sweat on my body had dried cold, so I put on shorts and a t-shirt, and drifted in and out of sleep knowing that there was only an hour or two left before I should get up if I was to cycle before the sun beat down without remorse.

One morning flew by on the road; the afternoon rolled on in a bar. In the cooler evening I cycled some more. Life was good; I was feeling strong and speeding along. The miles disappeared, and my speed kept going up. *How can it be so easy?*

I entered a large village and watched channels of dust and debris being whipped along the dirt road running parallel to the tarmac. Women ran to their houses, clutching skirts with one hand and headscarves in the other. Rubbish swirled around the compounds and was swept high into the air. *The wind must be really strong!* On the move, I had felt nothing as though inside a glass vacuum, protected from the elements. I was freewheeling effortlessly while the world around me was in disarray.

In this region, strong winds are harbingers of a storm. Looking back over my shoulder, I saw the ominous dark clouds chasing me. I pulled into a shack serving beer and chatted to the pre-teen tender. I planned to sit out the storm in this not-very-sturdy-but-at-least-has-a-roof shelter. I watched trucks stop for the drivers to cover the rooftop luggage with plastic sheets before continuing their journey. They too were preparing for the storm.

The air was electric. Alive. The wind continued unabated, but still there was no rain. People were uneasy, and I could not sit still. Having complained so bitterly about the harmattan headwinds, I was sat here, motionless, when the strongest tailwind I had experienced was blowing. *What's a little rain anyway?*

I got back on the bike and travelled fast until dusk, always just ahead of the storm. I pitched the tent, sheltered by some small trees on the edge of a small depression. Since I had stopped moving, the storm soon caught up with me. No sooner was I in the tent than all fury let loose. The wind howled, ripping the tent first one way and then the other. The rain lashed down relentlessly. Having secured the tent the best I could and made sure everything I wanted to would stay dry, I lay down and tried to sleep.

The centre of the storm passed overhead – flashes illuminated my two-man tent world, strobe lighting at a disco. Between flashes, the darkness returned, each time blacker than before. A thunderous crash came from everywhere at once. Explosive, striking right to my core and shaking my insides. It then rumbled and grumbled until my heart-rate slowed and the pounding in my chest subsided. Then another almighty flash, and crash and rip and roar, and rain drummed on the tent and pelted the ground, drowning all other sounds.

Late in the night I woke again; it was pitch black. The last drops of rain were falling in a pitter-patter of pity. Looking out of my sodden tent, I no longer saw a depression in the earth but a muddy-brown lake and I listened to the frogs croaking with the ferocity of the storm that had finally passed.

That was the first time I experienced the wrath and fury of the full force of a thunderstorm. It was immense, intense, electrifying – simply awesome. It was the beginning of the rainy season, and more deluges and electric blue skies were ahead. It was, after all, just a tropical storm, but I never knew it could rain so much in so little time.

I drifted in and out of sleep until I could discern the features of the inside of my tent, when it was light enough to get up. I emerged into the damp air and packed up. I was tired, the eyes-sore sleepy-tired-from-too-little-sleep kind, but I was feeling strong. The residue energy of the night's storm was now stored within me, coursing through my veins; my muscles twitched in anticipation, awaiting vigorous release. It was not often I felt that fired up.

The wind blew strong and helped me along, south to where the rains had transformed the land into dense, lush green tropical forest. Gone was the hot dusty Sahel and the barren beauty of the desert. Now rainbows reflected a kaleidoscope of colour, and rivers bled a rich earth-red. The rain had brought an abundance of nature that thrived on the excess – caterpillars crawled on leaves and sent beads of clear water running down to the green tips, and swirls of fluttering butterflies spiralled into the sky, and I was once again plagued by mosquitoes, ants, spiders, and everything else that creeped and crawled. And still the rain kept falling and more storms passed, but they were kittens' purrs to the last lion's roar.

* * *

The bike shook and rattled on the corrugated dirt road from the border, and I slowly rolled into my first Ghanaian town for a late lunch. Energy sapped, I stopped at a bar to ask where I could eat. It was strange hearing English after months of only French.

'We don't serve food here.'

'I know, but do you know where they do?' I asked politely.

'There are many places.'

'Can you recommend somewhere?'

'It depends what you want.'

'I don't care, anything.'

'But how can I recommend somewhere if I don't know what sort of food you like.' *Sigh.*

'Rice or spaghetti or …'.

'You can get rice opposite.' *That was harder than it needed to be.*

I had seen the rice stalls, but the loudspeakers next to them were blaring an indistinguishable racket. I wanted some peace as well as food, so I found another chop bar, which is what the Ghanaians call a cheap food joint, took a seat, and devoured rice balls and sauce. I sat and read while trying to recover some energy. Eventually, curiosity got the better of the other customers.

'Where do you come from?'

'Today, Burkina Faso.'

'Eéé! By bicycle?'

'Yes.'

'Where are you going to?'

'Wa.'

'Eéé! By bicycle?'

'Yes, by bicycle.'

'You can do that?'

'Yes.'

'Are you sure? It is a long way.'

'Yes. I know.'

'Where are you from?'

'England.'

'Ah, so you fly from England to Burkina Faso?'

'No, I travelled by land.'

'By this bicycle?' *Sigh.*

'Yes.'

'That is not possible.'

'Well I had to take a boat from Spain to Morocco …'.

'But the rest you travel by bike?'

'Like I said, yes.'

'Eéé! That is not possible!'

'Trust me, it is.'

'When did you leave?'

'Nearly 10 months ago.'

'Eéé! When do you go home again?'

'Well, I'm going to South Africa.'

'Eéé! For the World Cup?'

'No, I will be a year too late.'

'Eéé!'

And so the conversation continued.

The roads in town had been tarmac. I foolishly assumed that the poor dirt roads were behind me, but the orange dust returned and soon my energy levels were low. Need sugar. Must stop. Drink coke. Can't think.

A passer-by stopped.

'Where do you come from?'

'Lawra,' which was not so far away and an acceptable response.

'Where are you going?'

'Wa.'

'Eéé! By bicycle?' *Sigh. Here we go again.*

'Yes, by bicycle.'

'You can do that?'

'Yes, but not all today.'

'You stay here?' he asked.

'I don't know yet.'

'You stay here,' he insisted. 'There is a guesthouse.' *That's good to know.* The sugar rush from the coke had kicked in, and now I could form a comprehensive thought. The brewing storm was not conducive to camping and I was too tired to go further.

'So, where are you from?'

'England.'

'You always travel by bike?'

'Yes.'

'Eéé! You come from England by bike?'

'Yes.'

'Eéé! But it is a long way.' *Sigh.*

'Yes, I know.'

And so the conversation continued.

I found the guesthouse, showered, ate some biscuits for dinner and slept as the storm passed. It was over a month since I last slept in a bed. It should have been a quick start the next morning with no food for breakfast and no tent to take down. All I had to do was pay. I spoke with the only person around.

'I need to pay for the room.'

'Yes,' and then there was silence as the teenage boy stared up at me. *Maybe I should rephrase that as a question.*

'Who do I pay for the room?'

'In town.'

'What?'

'Yes, in town.'

'Is there no one here I can pay?'

'Not here,' and the boy scanned the courtyard. *I can see there is no one else here!*

'Is there not someone inside?'

'In town.'

'You're telling me I need to go into town to pay?'

'Yes.'

'Fine,' I sighed. 'Where do I go in town?' and there was silence as the boy stared up at me. I waited for an answer.

'I am sorry. I do not understand you.' *Now we're getting somewhere.*

I used the tried-and-tested method instead: I took money from my pocket, dangled the room key, pointed at the door, and then my bike, and said, 'I leave. Money for room. Who do I give?'

'Yes. Give me. I in charge.' *Finally!* I handed over the money, and he gave me the change.

I was exhausted and had not yet gone anywhere. At least now I could leave. I never had those problems when speaking pseudo-French.

* * *

It was a rush to reach Accra in time. I had booked a return flight home to get a new passport. The reason was that I'd had another idea. Like the idea to cycle to Cape Town and the idea to paddle the Niger River, it was a devil of an idea that sat on my left shoulder and whispered in my ear. It prodded and poked and played with my mind, and I couldn't ignore it, even when all the world on my right shoulder was shouting, *'Don't do it!'*

'Go on ... you know you want to,' said the devil on my shoulder.

'It's not safe.'

'The world's not safe but you've travelled and know it isn't all that bad. Besides, how do they know?'

'You could be robbed and raped, or worse. Murdered.'

'You're more likely to be struck by lightning. And what was that camping under those trees in a thunderstorm, you idiot? You could be run over by a bus tomorrow, but that doesn't stop you crossing the road.'

Thanks. I know I can be an idiot sometimes, but this idea isn't that stupid. Is it?

'It's not worth the risk.'

'Of course it's worth the risk.'

I know there are some potential dangers, which I would try to avoid, and the rewards surely outweigh the risks. You often find the friendliest people and most beautiful nature in the most unlikely of places.

'It's not like the rest of Africa.'

'It's not so long ago they were telling you Africa isn't safe.'

'But there is a war going on in that country.'

There is a war in part of that country, but it's a big country. That's like saying England was not safe during the Balkans War. Besides, I'm not that much of an ignorant idiot; I've done my research and have no intention of going into a war zone.

'But everyone there is corrupt and will try to steal from you.'

'Look at yourself – you're on a bicycle – you don't have much worth stealing.'

Thanks. I know I look like a tramp right now and need some new clothes, but I still have more stuff than most people here. The important point is that I don't care much for it. If it's stolen then so be it; I can either replace it or do without.

'You'll regret it if you go and something bad happens.'

'You'll regret it if you don't go.'

'You should listen to what everyone is saying.'

'Since when did you pay attention to what everyone else says?'

Shut up. I always listen to what other people say. I just don't always follow their advice. Surely it's more important to listen to myself.

'You can't keep taking unnecessary risks. You're not a cat with nine lives.'

'No, that is true. Maybe you have more.'

And so the conversation continued.

But I had made up my mind – to cross Central Africa through the Congo.

There is something mysterious about the word 'Congo'. Like 'Timbuktu', it is a word we all know but don't exactly know what it means. It is captivating and beguiling. You dare only to whisper the name for fear it may evaporate like a dream when you wake and that is because you know nothing about it.

They have stood strong against the tides of time. Even though Timbuktu may have passed its zenith of greatness, it is still alive and breathing languidly under the Saharan sun. But I think, perhaps, the Congo's time is rising like a sleeping monster that is beginning to stir. Whereas the Saharan desert was once a lush thriving expanse of plant and animal life, which has been swept away by the sand; the Congo's thick forests have stood tall since the beginning of mankind and its rivers will continue to flow for many millennia to come – its day is only just dawning.

I wanted to know more about this mysterious Congo and of Stanley, Brazzaville, King Leopold and Mobutu. Was it really the *Heart of Darkness* that Conrad wrote of? There are truths behind every tale of fiction, but a lot can change in a hundred years. So can nothing.

I had been bitten by the idea to cross Central Africa, and the more I read about the Congo the more I knew I had to see for myself. It was like a mosquito bite itching to be scratched, and the more I read the more intense the itch. I knew the only way to calm that feverish feeling was to go there – to see it would be the antihistamine.

I had mixed feelings – excitement, anticipation and a heavy dose of trepidation. The latter could be accounted for by having read the health section of the guidebook. It was similar to other African country guides, listing malaria, bilharzia, typhoid, cholera, schistosomiasis, and rabies among other illnesses and tropical diseases. Here though, there is also the occasional outbreak of ebola virus or plague. My doctor would have had an apoplectic attack if he had read this.

Desert Snow

If I was going to travel overland across Central Africa, rather than fly like my original plan, then I needed more passport pages for visas. Rather than waiting a month for a new passport in Ghana during the rainy season, I flew home to enjoy a month of the English summer. With it's unpredictable weather, there was always a risk it would be as wet as Ghana, but this way I could catch up with friends and family too. It turned out to be a gloriously sunny month. The change of scenery and rest were the perfect medicine. It was only once I returned to Ghana that I realised the effect on my body and mind of ten months continuous travelling.

14

Slaves to Religion

Ghana, Togo and Benin

One pannier now brimmed with sustenance for the mind. Besides a new passport, I returned from England with fifteen books and a large supply of chocolate, both commodities that were hard to obtain in Africa. The chocolate was rapidly consumed and the books I devoured soon after with equal relish. When I had read the books from cover-to-cover I gave them away to make space for food, which gave more energy for getting up the hills. I was then thrust into a literary black hole for months until I met another person with some to sell or swap.

Besides reading, I love pouring over maps. Reading the contours of mountain ranges and tracing my finger down winding rivers to the sea, following roads across continents with my eyes lingering on towns and villages, and wondering what it is like for the people who live there. The landscape of Africa, any continent actually, gradually changes as you move over it and pass through each geographical zone. The metamorphosis from desert to forest or mountain to savannah is like the transition of the seasons.

Maps of Africa have another distinct feature: a checkerboard of international boundaries. These are not like the borders of Europe and Asia that follow mountain ranges and rivers, which are real boundaries of hinderance to the traveller. Over half the borders are geometrically straight lines that disregard geography, which were drawn on maps in European boardrooms in the 1880s by people who had never been to Africa. They called the blank space of the interior they divided *Terra Incognita*, 'Unknown Land'.

It was David Livingstone, the Scottish missionary explorer, who initially claimed that European intervention was the only solution to drag Africa out of the dark age of slavery. The British had already outlawed the slave trade, yet while they were enforcing the law in West Africa, Arab traders were busy continuing it in the East. Livingstone was convinced that through commerce and Christianity, the continent could be civilised. This sparked the 'Scramble for Africa'. But the motives of the men in Europe were for conquest, not civilisation.

One British colony created during the Scramble was the 'Gold Coast', named because of the gold that was traded for salt and slaves. Then, in 1957 the country gained independence and was renamed Ghana after the ancient Ghana Empire, which rose to greatness around 900 AD and spread over southern Mauritania and western Mali.

It was the wealth of gold that initially attracted European nations and was what prompted them to build forts when they arrived to trade from. Scores of these forts are still standing as monuments to a murky past.

When the Portuguese first arrived here in 1471 they called the coast, *De Costa da el Mina de Ouro* – the Coast of Gold Mines. It is from this that the village Elmina and, later, the Gold Coast colony took their names. When the Portuguese were building their fort at Elmina, the British were just a few kilometres away at Cape Coast.

From Accra, I took a speeding *tro-tro* west to visit Cape Coast. The town, spread over the hills in a patchwork of colour, reminded me of Freetown. Painted houses with rusting corrugated iron roofs filled every space, clothes hung out to dry, and telegraph wires ran through the streets. Perched upon two hilltops were Forts Victoria and William, circular in construction and rotting around the edges; the original canons, now defunct, were still in place and used for drying laundry on.

The wind whipped up waves that crashed with a lion's fury and the rain lashed the shore. The wet grey day was fitting weather for visiting the depressing slave fort of Cape Coast Castle. I walked through the open yard, surrounded by stairways, arched walkways, and parapets – the walls are whitewashed, but that does not cleanse the past. Three graves lie in the centre, in memory of the governor, his wife and Philip Kwakwe who was the first Anglican priest of African descent.

But where are the graves of the many hundreds of others who died here? Lining the ramparts are canon sentries with their backs to the fort, turning a blind eye to the hundreds of cannonballs lying piled and discarded like the slaves who were hoarded and dumped in the dungeons below, where they were disregarded until of use, and then thrust into the sea – the sea is the slaves' grave.

I walked down a narrow corridor from the bright daylight into darkness. By the time my eyes had adjusted, I was in the dank dungeon surrounded by thick walls of stone and iron bars. If I had been a slave, the stench from the open sewage channel would have warned me in advance of my fate – not only stripped of freedom, but privacy, pride and prospect all ripped away when the shackles were bolted.

The underground prison was cold and unaired, and there was only one way out for the slaves: the Door of No Return. After waiting up to twelve weeks until a ship returned, the slaves were herded through that door and transported to the Caribbean. Most never saw land again; instead, they died on the gruesome voyage and were thrown overboard as fish fodder.

Inside the fort, if any slaves tried to escape or cause trouble, they were thrown into a small cell. The skull and cross-bones carved above the door foretold their fate. I stood in that cell, devoid of light or ventilation and tried to imagine how sixty slaves could even fit when the door was bolted and the world shut to them forever. In the darkness, those slaves were left to rot. The lucky ones died quickly. It was those whose fight for survival was the strongest that suffered the greatest, surrounded by death and decay as the bodies rotted around them. It is no wonder that those unfortunate souls tried desperately to claw their way out with their fingernails through the stone ground and thick door; the scratches they made are their lasting mark. The door was never opened until the last person was dead.

St. George's Fort in Elmina, built by the Dutch around a smaller Portuguese building, is smaller than Cape Coast Castle although the main features are the same. Here, the commander's quarters were above the female slave dungeons. From his balcony, he could look down and chose a slave whenever he desired, and they were sent through the trapdoor into his room.

The fort is situated on the shore, across a bridge from the main town, where colourful fishing boats lie side-by-side like sardines in a tin along the riverbank. Fishermen sat repairing nets as men have done since before the arrival of Europeans. Life, after all, goes on.

That evening, Ghana was playing the USA in the football World Cup. Anyone who owned a television had it turned on and tuned in. Most had brought them onto the streets, so as many as possibly could gather round and watch. Men, women, young, and old were all glued to the screens like iron filings to a magnet until the final whistle blew after extra time and signalled Ghana's win. The streets erupted. There was dancing and singing as a throng of united Ghanaians moved through the streets, blowing whistles, hooting vuvuzelas and excitedly waving flags. Children raced frantically up and down the roads while taxis and motorbikes beeped their horns and flashed their lights. This impromptu parade, a mass of red and yellow and green, moved in time to the official song for the FIFA World Cup, 'Give me freedom …'.

That, I thought, you have now.

To ease myself back into cycling I aimed for Aburi, a mere 40 kilometres from Accra. The peaceful botanical gardens in the town were less pristine than Kew, but here with the hot humid climate, the struggle was to hold back and tame nature rather than nurture it to fruition.

The idea of staying at the guesthouse within the grounds appealed. The dilapidated exterior failed to deter me. My legs, at least, were content to go no further. I walked to the reception desk that suggested it had once been a hotel of higher standing, simply because it had one.

'Hello. Do you have a single room?'

'No.'

'Do you have any room?'

'No.'

This was unexpected and perplexing. The hotel looked deserted besides one or two men wandering through, and I suspected they were gardeners, not guests. A wooden board on the wall, numbered with hooks and an array of keys suggested all but two rooms were unoccupied. I stood there sliding into despondency, debating the options.

Noticing either my dejected look or sweat-stained bike clothes and thinking I might not be a fussy customer, she broke the silence. 'Well, we have rooms of course, only there's no running water.'

I laughed. Running water was not a common feature of the hotels I had frequented in West Africa. Ghana, however, was used to foreigners with greater expectations.

'But you have water, yes?'

'Yes.'

'So I could have a bucket of water to shower with?'

'Of course,' and she looked at me as if to say *how do you think we wash here?*

'Can I have a room then?'

'Yes, of course. Would you like a single room, or double, a private shower, or a shared one. I can show you a few …'. Suddenly the options were infinite.

'I'll take the cheapest.'

The huge barrel full of water in the bathroom smelt stagnant when I lifted the lid, and I wondered how long this room had been empty while potential guests were told it was full.

The road further north to Atimpoku was a joy of gentle ups and breezy freewheeling downs with expansive views of the rolling green Akwapim hills over my left shoulder. Small townships brightened the hillsides with their pink, cream, and terracotta painted houses and dusty rusting corrugated roofs. In these sleepy towns the shops were painted brightly in red, yellow, or green – the primary colours of Ghana's national flag. They are also the colours of the three major telecommunications companies – red for Vodafone, yellow for MTN, and green for Zain.

The mobile phone industry, besides single-handedly keeping Ghana's paint manufacturers in business, has revolutionised communications in Africa. Rather than laying thousands of kilometres of telephone wires, they have skipped generations of technology and rapidly erected radio masts that were now a defining feature of the African landscape. Even in the remotest of villages, the locals carried mobile phones.

As with second-hand clothes, there was no shortage of cheap second-hand mobile phones. As necessity breeds ingenuity, the issue of powering these millions of mobiles has been readily solved. In towns, there were small manned kiosks covered in electrical sockets, all connected to one of the few working power supplies in town, usually a privately-owned generator – simply plug in your phone, pay a small fee, and return to collect later once fully charged.

Still unfit from the lazy days in England, I resorted to hauling the bike along on foot as I climbed further into the hills. Sweat dripped down my face, neck, back and arms. Thankfully, the following day as I cycled into Togo, my legs finally remembered the art of cycling.

There was more uphill after the border. I just had to keep the pedals turning – low gear – slowly, slowly. When I reached the top, I stopped a few moments to catch my breath, got back in the saddle, and off I went round the bend, changing up through the gears – faster, faster. I felt the wind against my rosy cheeks, and the sweat-drenched shirt stuck to my body and felt cold to the touch, and I savoured every shiver because it was so rare those days to feel cold. When I reached the highest gear and could not go any faster, I stopped pedalling and looked out across the endless green blanket of the tropics spread through the valley. I forgot about the hard work it took to get to the top and that in minutes I would be right back down again, and I thought of what a beautiful day it was and if I hadn't made that one decision to cycle to Cape Town, so long ago now, I would never have seen this sight and …

Bump.

I hit a pothole. The rest of the descent was spent watching the road surface, until I reached Kpalimé where I checked into a cheap hotel, had a real shower, and spent the rest of the afternoon sipping cold beer in the courtyard.

As with most nights in a hotel, it was a restless one. The mosquitoes were noticeable by their absence. Instead, the rain thundered down on the metal roof. No sooner than it had battered me into unconsciousness and I was rudely awoken by a cat-strangling wail. *Someone's in pain. Should I go and help*? Then I made out words – Hallelujah and Praise the Lord! – that bellowed from the depths of the darkness. I prayed only for silence.

Eventually, my body gave in. I drifted in and out of sleep until the predawn chorus of bright, cheerful gospel music, which is what church singing should sound like, erupted. It would have been the perfect start to the day if only morning had broken a couple of hours later. By six o'clock I was wandering through the cool, misty streets of Kpalimé. The town was already awake and dressed in Sunday best; men, women and children were all walking to church. I was dressed in my best (only) bike clothes and searching for a kick-start coffee.

With legs of steel forged out of lactic acid and long hills, the ride to the capital on the coast was a breeze. I passed small villages united in belief on this good Lord's day. Families sat on benches under thatched shelters with no doors or walls and only a simple wooden pulpit at one end. An enthusiastic teenager clanged the bell strung between two poles outside, which reminded me of the dinner bell at school.

Christianity in this region, from Ghana to Nigeria, is followed with the same fervour as Islam in the desert and Sahel. Whereas once I had been woken up regularly by the *muezzin's* call to prayer, I was now repeatedly roused from my dreams by gospel choirs and preachers' sermons.

Although most Christians are Protestant or Roman Catholic, there are an overwhelming number of smaller denomination churches. Every town, in Ghana especially, has scores of boards advertising them. Signs for Presbyterian Methodist, Seventh Day Adventist, The Twelve Apostles Church, African Faith Tabernacle, Ebernezer Healing Church, Bethesday Church Mission, Jehovah Nissi Church, The Church of Light, The Healing Hand of God Mission, and Lighthouse Chapel International. And so the list continues.

The 'Eternal Sacred Order of Cherubim and Seraphim of Mount Zion' and the 'Practical Church of John 14:6, 15 and Acts 1:8 and Matt 5:16,44 and Rom. 12:20' both needed oversized boards for their full names. But I liked the sound of the Happy Go Lucky Church of God Almighty In Jesus Name Amen, the Jesus Never Fuck Up, and the Run For Your Life Ministries.

It's not necessary to go to church to hear the Word, but merely turn on the TV to be confronted by a selection of religious-based channels and be affronted by a smart-suited evangelical preacher with a microphone in hand, who looks less like a humble servant of God than someone who does big business. The Reverend of the Apostle General of the Royal House Chapel in Accra holds three services every Sunday, each with a congregation of 10,000 worshippers. The Ebenezer Miracle Worship Center in Kumasi is the largest church building in the Ashanti region of Ghana and holds a congregation of 18,000. In England, crowds that big gather for the football or cricket, not Christ.

Togo is a narrow slither of a country next to a fatter Benin, both of which are sandwiched between English-speaking Ghana and giant Nigeria. In four days, I passed through Togo and into Benin.

It was market day in Aneho, the town before the Benin border. Women sat in brightly wrapped *pagnes,* surrounded by second-hand clothes with flip-flops and shoes piled high, although finding a pair was a near impossibility. There were bowls of rice and nuts, piles of manioc and onions, and handful-size stacks of peppers and chillies. Neatly lined-up bottles of hairspray and mosquito killer (don't get them confused) were a backdrop to aluminium pots and pans.

I walked to the far end of the market looking at the floor to make sure I didn't step on the fresh fish, dried fish, shrimp, crabs, leg-tied chickens sitting dejectedly in the sun as though their pea-sized brains knew what fate awaited, or dried skins of... *What is that?*

Is that a crocodile skin? I stopped to pay closer attention to the first thing I had not seen in all the other African markets I had walked through. There were dried skins of crocodiles and antelopes; shrivelled, sun-dried bodies of chameleons that had no colour to change and withered birds with no feathers to fly; rows of monkey skulls, big and small, and many unidentifiable more; and talisman armies of hand-sized ebony wood statues decorated with cowrie shells and wearing grass skirts and bright feathers lined the floor. *So this is where you buy your Vodun fetishes.*

Vodun is the predominant animist religion here. Its roots go back 6,000 years and the name derives from the god of the Yoruba people who lived in this region of West Africa.

It was the slaves who introduced Vodun beliefs to Brazil and the Caribbean. Animist religion was forbidden amongst the slaves, so they outwardly practised the Catholic religion of the missionaries and secretly looked to the Vodun spirits for guidance. Where clay figurines of the Virgin Mary and Jesus sat on tabletops, out of sight below were the Vodun fetishes. It was this syncretism of Vodun and Catholicism that led to the formation of what is known as Voodoo in Haiti and Cadomblé in Brazil.

When the slave trade was abolished, some freed slaves returned to West Africa and settled on the coast near Ouidah in Benin. They brought this syncretised religion back with them, and it is their descendants making up the majority of the Beninese population who practise it today.

I cycled into Ouidah and came to Place Chacha, the square that is overlooked by the former residence of Brazilian Governor Don Francisco de Souza. It was in this square beneath the large tree that the slave auctions were once held. The slaves were traded for merchandise from Europe, and bought and sold like cattle. Those in their prime and in peak physical condition bought the highest price. Once sold, they were held in the Portuguese Fort, which is now a museum, to await shipment to Brazil and the Caribbean. When the time came, the slaves were walked through town, back past the square where they had been sold, and trudged down the dusty track to the coast.

The day I cycled the four-kilometre route from the fort to the sea, which is known as the Route of Slaves, it had been raining. The dirt clogged my bike wheels as I navigated around the orange puddles. I passed a few guesthouses, restaurants, and symbolic Vodun statues such as the three-headed man, a panther, and a serpent devouring its tail. There are no slaves shackled by the neck and ankles walking in line to their fate now, only a steady stream of men on motorbikes throwing up mud. On the beach, at the end of the road, an imposing columned gateway marks the Door of No Return, guarded by metallic statues representing Egun-Egun, the spirit of the slaves.

15

Home of Hospitality

Nigeria and Cameroon

'Nigeria is dangerous, unsafe, corrupt. Expect trouble on the roads,' people said. When you are told something often enough, you begin to believe it. I had been conjuring up scenarios of kidnap and robbery.

Then I crossed the Nigerian border and my fears and suspicions diminished by the minute. Everyone waved as I passed and wished me well. The sun shone, the sky was a clear blue, and it seemed as though everything was right with the world, so I smiled and waved back. Downhill the pace quickened – faster, faster. Then ahead, I saw what I had been dreading: a roadblock.

Overlanders often cast aspersions on the military and police and condemn them as corrupt. Whereas cyclists have a hard job mustering the energy to get from one place to another, so those in motorised vehicles have their own difficulties in the way of paperwork and vehicle registration, and because they travel much faster, they spend a disproportionate amount of time dealing with bureaucracy. There are, however, more overlanders than cyclists travelling through Africa, and it was their view that predominated my thoughts. When I was back in England, I did meet one man who had already cycled through Africa.

'So Dan, what about the roadblocks in Nigeria?' I asked.

'Oh, they're not that bad.'

'Well, it's alright for you to say that now. But like, how did you deal with the police?'

'Oh, it's fine. Just don't stop. Just cycle straight through and don't stop.' I had not considered that. I looked at him sceptically, wondering if he were having me on. *Maybe it's worth a try.*

There I was, rapidly approaching the roadblock of wooden planks, with long nails protruding upwards, laid across the road to stop vehicles in their tracks. There was a gap between the board and verge, enough space for a bike. *Shall I do it?* I scanned the canvas tent erected and saw several plain-clothed men sitting in the shade. I saw no uniforms, no guns, or motorbikes. *Go on, just do it. They can't shoot you without a gun or catch you on foot.*

I flew past at 50 kilometres per hour with my head down, ignoring their shouts to stop. The bottom of the hill came sooner than I would have liked, and I was pedalling furiously to get up the other side when two cars overtook and pulled me over, angry men shouting with arms waving frantically out of the windows. They were furious with me. *Little, innocent me? What have I done?* Already, I was conjuring up the lies that would diffuse the situation the quickest.

'Why didn't you stop? Why did you ignore us?' the red-faced driver roared at me. 'We are security and here for your safety …'. And so the tirade went on.

I saw his mouth moving and watched his face going redder and redder until I wondered if it were possible for a face to explode like an overripe tomato. I heard only noise, not words. *How the hell did I not see the cars? And how much money are they going to extort from me for this?* I tuned back in.

'… would you?' He was silent now, staring at me. He leant in close trying to intimidate me. His bloodshot eyes locked on me like a wolf that sees its dinner and knows it is just a leap and lethal bite away. My only thought was that his breath smelled bad.

'Sorry, what?'

'You wouldn't behave like that in your home country, would you?'

'We don't have roadblocks in England.'

'You have police though, don't you? And you wouldn't behave like that, ignoring the police, in England.'

'Our police wear uniforms. How do I know you are police?'

He waved a filthy card, dirty from overuse or misuse with the laminated edges peeling apart. His tirade resumed. He still wanted to know why I didn't stop.

'I didn't know I was supposed to,' I lied. But he didn't hear me because he was shouting again. 'Look. It is done. What are we going to do now?' I raised my voice in retaliation. Not used to having someone answer back, he was silenced.

'Show me your passport.' Reluctantly, I showed it, and he grabbed it off me. 'You must go back to the roadblock,' he said. Now I was furious with this man I did not trust, and I refused to go anywhere until I had my passport back. Without it, I was powerless and at his mercy.

With a promise to go with them, he handed me my passport. But since my chances of escape were low, I pedalled back to the tent with one car ahead and one crawling behind.

The angry man gradually calmed down as he meticulously recorded my details onto a notepad of pink headed paper advertising a hotel. I calmed down too and suggested we start again. He ignored me.

The immigration official also needed to see my yellow fever vaccination card. His tight pink t-shirt, far from accentuating his muscular physique made him look like a big cuddly teddy. After scrutinising it, he informed me that I was fully vaccinated, that the vaccinations had not expired, that the signature was in the correct place, and the stamp there too. I tried to look enlightened, glad there was no excuse for a bribe.

Next the transport official wanted to speak with me.

'What is the registration of your vehicle?'

'I'm on a bicycle.'

'But what is the registration number?' he insisted seriously.

'It doesn't have one.' *Are you stupid?*

'I need a number.' I debated making one up, but decided not to.

'The make is Thorn,' I offered. 'Will that do?'

'No.' *Is this going to be the excuse for a bribe?*

'Can't you see it's a bicycle? Bicycles do not have registration numbers. Have you ever seen a bicycle with a registration number? No, of course not. It is black and has two wheels. So if you need a number, will the number two do?' I paused and held my breath. *Perhaps I should have just made up a number.* I used to be submissive in the face of authority – that was hard to believe now.

It was a relief when the other men started laughing. *And breathe.* The transport officer was silent with embarrassment.

'You are free to go, but next time you must stop. We are here for your safety,' the red-eyed officer reminded me.

In the 160 kilometres during my first full day in Nigeria, there were 21 checkpoints. Customs men wore grey uniform, the police were in black from beret to boots with an automatic rifle slung across the shoulder, and immigration had tank tops like your grandfather would wear with 'Immigration' knitted across the midriff. No one wanted to see my passport and some stopped me only to ask questions. *Where are you going? Where have you come from? When did you leave England? What is your mission? Will you marry me?* Some just wanted to shake my hand. *I love you! Be my wife! What's up? Can I have your number?*

The first city was the crazy, chaotic Abeokuta. The roads were a traffic-jammed maze weaving round the hills and crisscrossing at random. Police in bright orange bibs stood at junctions, supposedly directing traffic. Some drivers followed the hand signals while others decided for themselves. Mind alert, strong arms, steady balance, I held the bike upright and slowly negotiated the taxis and motorbikes jostling for position, putting a hand on the car bonnet to steady myself if I wobbled – determination to proceed was the key.

I didn't know which road to take and everybody I asked pointed me in different directions. Eventually, I despaired and employed the guidance of a taxi driver. Gradually, peace returned, and I rode through a sea of hills, over a peak and down to a trough, across the huge green swell of Nigeria.

Nigeria is seven times the size of England. With a population of 170 million, it means that one in every six Africans is Nigerian. According to projections, by 2050 its population will be the fourth largest in the world, ahead of the USA. Of the 100 largest African cities, 18 are in Nigeria and nine of these have a population exceeding one million. I passed through three of them. There are a lot of Nigerians.

And it does not go unnoticed when travelling through the country. I met Yoruba, Hausa, Igbo, and Fulani. I met policemen, customs officers and many other government officials, students, professional engineers, teachers, preachers, international businessmen, labourers working for the ministry of transport and many other ministries besides, truck drivers, families running restaurants, and countless people trading all things on the streets.

Despite its size, I spent only two weeks in the country, but covered 1,400 kilometres. Had it been another time of year, I would happily have stayed longer. But it was the wet season, and I was racing to overtake the rain. Instead of ambling along lesser-trodden tracks and camping in the wild, I sped along tarmac roads and checked into cheap hotels at night. Without food to cook in the evening or a tent to take down in the morning, I spent more time cycling and speaking with the people I met.

At a guesthouse in Ibadan's rundown suburb, I met Tayo. He introduced himself when I sat down in the hotel restaurant. 'Would you mind if I speak with you?' he asked.

'No, of course not.' If I had wanted peace and quiet, I would not have sat alone at a table – it invited company. For time to myself, I had to stay in my hotel room and even then I was often disturbed. The desire to be alone comes from our western lifestyles and was not understood by most Africans.

The lady returned with a plate of rice and beef that I had ordered. The other option was rice and chicken.

'Oh, I see you are going to eat. Please, have your dinner. I will come back when you have finished.' When people sat down to eat here, they ate. They didn't talk. There was always enough time for talking afterwards.

'No, it's fine,' I said, but Tayo went anyway and came back later.

'Every two weeks I travel between Abuja, my home, and Ibadan for government work. I always stay at this guesthouse. It is cheap and clean,' he explained. That was why I chose to stay there too.

'My family lives in Abuja. I have a wife and two boys, eight and ten years' old. It is my eldest son's birthday next week.'

'Oh, that's great. They grow up quick, yes?'

'It's true, too quick.' He let out a sigh and went on talking, 'I don't know what to do. He keeps telling me that he wants a bike for his birthday. I think he's too young. I'm scared he will have an accident. Drivers are bad in Nigeria.'

Eleven did seem a young age to be driving a motorbike. *I wonder what the age limit is, not that anyone pays much attention to it, I suppose.*

'The drivers aren't so bad,' I countered, 'It's the vehicles that aren't roadworthy. I saw a lorry crashed today. The cabin had separated from the tanker and careered into the bush while the tanker just lay on its side in the road. The driver and his mate were sat on the top, mobile phones in hand, waiting to be picked up. I couldn't believe they weren't hurt.'

'How are you travelling?'

'I'm cycling.'

'But aren't the roads too dangerous?'

'You know, it's not that bad,' I lied. I had been run off the road by an overtaking lorry that morning. With two lorries storming side-by-side towards you and a long deep air-horn blast of pending doom, it is surprising how quickly you can scramble up a steep bank with 50 kilograms of loaded bike. 'If you take the smaller roads, there's not so much traffic. It's a great way to see the country.'

I went on to tell him about my journey, not because he had asked, but from habit.

'My son would love to hear these stories. All he talks about is getting a bicycle. His friends at school have them you see.'

'Oh, I thought you meant he wanted a motorbike.'

Tayo let out a laugh that burst from deep inside, as though he did not often find something to laugh about, and then he said seriously, 'No. I will never allow him one of those.'

We sat there quietly for a few minutes. I finished my coke, sipping it from the glass bottle with a straw, and we watched the TV. There was always a TV in Nigeria's hotels. It was the sign of a modern establishment; Wi-Fi was another world away.

'I hope you don't mind, I think I need to go and sleep. It was a long day today,' I said.

'Of course. It is getting late. I should go to bed too. Thank you for speaking with me.'

'A pleasure.'

'You know, I think I will get my son a bicycle,' he said after a pause. 'There is a shop near our home. I could buy it when I return next week.'

'You changed your mind quickly,' I smiled.

'I think if you can cycle all the way from England, he will be OK on our street.'

'I think so too.'

'I will let him cycle, on the pavement, to the end of the road and back. No further,' he added adamantly.

'Oh I doubt you'll be able to stop him,' and I laughed a little.

Tayo looked serious and vacant and then sighed, 'My wife's going to kill me when she finds out.' That is a common phrase the world over.

After Ibadan the highway runs north. It is the main route between Lagos, Nigeria's largest city on the coast, and the North. Old oil tankers and trucks were a steady stream of rumbling, choking, thundering trade. The lorries hurtled past me on the good sections of road, churning black diesel fumes into the air. Slowed by the potholes that spanned the width of the road, the trucks slowed, backed-up, and tried to overtake regardless of oncoming traffic, and often they broke down causing yet more chaos. The roadside was littered with burned-out wrecks; rusted skeletons were all that remained of many.

Here, two wheels won – I dodged around the potholes, found the flat line, and continued unabated overtaking the backlog. When the smooth tarmac returned, the lorries caught up again and overtook, with the driver's mate waving to me out of the window.

I was going to Abuja to collect visas and once they were stamped in my passport, there was no reason to stay. The city sprawl faded into the distance and was replaced by vast expanses of fields interspersed with rural settlements of round thatch huts.

Daylight was fading fast, and I could barely see the illegible scrawl in my journal as I wrote, sitting on a wooden bench in the courtyard of a cheap hotel. The indecipherable code was unimportant; the simple act of writing tattooed the memories in the mind as permanent blueprints of my past for future recall.

I was waiting for the electricity to come on, although I am not sure why because the low wattage bulb hanging by an exposed wire from the ceiling would only show me that my room was not worth the few dollars I spent on it. It would highlight the peeling paint on the walls and a spider's web in the corner, the wooden-frame bed with a thin foam mattress permanently depressed from a hundred other tired bodies, and a cockroach scurrying to the drain in the bathroom where there was no shower, only a bucket of water and a plastic scoop.

None of this mattered because when I had used one bucket of water someone would refill it for me and if I gave some money they would return a few minutes later with a cold beer and my change.

I turned on my head-torch and continued writing. It had been raining again and in the interlude insects had returned as winged menaces of the damp air. Attracted to the head-torch light, the bugs fluttered around my face, and the mosquitoes found exposed flesh to feast on. I went into the room, shut the door, and lay on the bed in the darkness with my eyes closed. The only benefit of the rain was that it was cooler, so I no longer lay with sweat seeping into the foam mattress.

At some point I opened my eyes and noticed that the light had come on. I must have fallen asleep; it often happened after a long day cycling. This time I turned it off and went back to sleep. Other times, when I didn't feel so tired, I lay in bed reading and eating regardless of the time of night. With no alarm clock set, I slept only when I was tired and woke when my body was rested, unless there was a mosque or church nearby, which was often.

* * *

The guidebook says it is beautiful. Even my map showed the roads as 'scenic' – a web of green winding lines scrawled throughout the region. Experience had shown that often there was little difference between the 'scenic' roads and those deemed not worthy. Experience had shown that 'scenic' on the flat fold-out map translated to 'hilly' in three-dimensional reality, and since I was looking at the Cameroon highlands, this theory seemed valid. All I needed to do was cycle from the Nigerian border, lying at little above sea-level, to these highlands, which by definition were at considerable altitude – incomparable to the Himalayas or Andes, but substantial relative to the Sahel.

It was getting late when I reached the bridge crossing the river that separates Nigeria and Cameroon. I put a smile on my face and patiently answered the unofficial questions of the border officials, questions that African men ask young white females.

'Are you married?'

'Yes.' I usually told the truth, but I hoped that this answer would speed up the subsequent interrogation. It didn't.

'Where is your husband?'

'In England.'

'And he let you leave?'

'Yes.'

'He let you travel by yourself through Africa?'

'Yes,'

'If I was your husband, I would never let you leave me.' *That is one of many reasons why we would never be married.* 'Why didn't he come with you?'

'He's working.'

'What does he do?' I told the border officials about my fictional husband's fabricated job. What I was doing or where I was going were of no interest. Who would they be more interested in if I were a man with my wife at home? The concept of a woman travelling alone is unusual here, but that a husband would allow it is stranger than fiction.

My groaning stomach forced me to cut short the officer and ask if I could leave. It was a relief that the conversation ended before it came back round to sex.

Sat in a bar earlier that day, I had been talking with three men, drinking beer. We were all sheltering from the rain falling in streams from the sky and had time, if not much money, to spend. It was the same conversation.

'Do you have a boyfriend?' the biggest of the three asked. He was a charismatic, larger-than-life guy who talked loudly and laughed a lot, smiling all the while with a big wide grin that showed his full set of teeth.

'No, I'm married.'

'That may be. But do you have a boyfriend while travelling?'

'No.'

'But, what do you do when … you know … "need things"?'

'What do you mean?' I asked innocently, not entirely comfortable with this angle of questioning from a stranger.

'Sex. You must need sex.' *Sigh.* It didn't matter if I were married or not. I was still an eligible target simply because I am female. It is much easier to say you are single, take their mobile number or exchange email addresses, and be done with it.

I stared outside, up at the grey uniform strip of sky between the corrugated roof of the bar and the shops on the other side of the road. There was no sign of the rain easing.

'You don't need sex; you only need some self-control.'

'Of course you need sex,' and he stared at me, unable to decide if I were lying or an anomaly of nature. 'Me, I have several girlfriends. I need sex every few days. I can't go a week without it. See, I *need* lots of girlfriends. But I satisfy all of them, of course. They are all happy.' He was a guy who guiltlessly indulged in all life's pleasures. If food and sex in excess can make you eternally happy, then he had life all figured out better than I did.

'Sounds like you've got your hands full. You won't be needing a girlfriend from England then,' I said in jest.

'Well, I've got enough girlfriends you know. But if I can make another girl happy then I would.' His mates, who had been sat quietly, now looked at him and laughed. They had seen his game before.

Across the bridge separating Nigeria and Cameroon, I divorced my hypothetical husband since I was as uncomfortable lying as I was breaking free from my English prudishness. This sped up the questioning on the other side. Christian was in charge of the immigration office. He walked with me up the hill to get my passport stamped. He showed me to the best guesthouse and introduced me to the bona fide money changer in town. Christian was uninterested in whether I was married or not, thankfully. He knew that ten minutes of his time, saved me thirty. My tired legs followed his footsteps like a dog at heel to the man who feeds it.

I went to the little wooden house at the end of the road for dinner. The young woman my age, was breast-feeding her baby girl when I sat down on the wooden bench by the plastic-covered table. She pulled the baby from her breast and with one hand pushed her swollen breast back in her shirt while simultaneously handing me the baby. I asked if I could exchange the baby for food – fried noodles with eggs, onion and the ubiquitous fiery red pepper.

A young boy of twelve came out of the house and shyly said good evening before wiping the plastic table dry of spilt water. He had outgrown his trousers, which now ended halfway down his shins. They were the same colour as his t-shirt – the greyish brown of ingrained dirt that is the colour of every workman's clothes here.

Back at Tina's Inn, I sat outside in the dark talking to two truck drivers. Their truck was stranded on the Kumba Road, so now they were stranded in Ekok with nothing to do except wait and drink beer and ask me questions. *Are you married? Where are you going? Where have you come from?*

'You have come all this way on a bicycle?'

'Yes.'

'But you are a girl.'

'Yes.' I lost count of the number of times in Nigeria I was told I was a girl. It's better than being called 'Sir' or 'Brother' or '*Grand-père*', which happened later in the Congo. A girl riding a bicycle alone in Africa is like snow in the desert – a rare occurrence that must be seen to be believed and when you do, it causes you to step back and double take, or if you have a phone, which most people do now, to take a photo for proof and posterity.

Then it came back round to sex again.

'Will you sleep with me tonight?'

'No.'

'OK, but if you change your mind, I am in room number two.'

The next morning I went for coffee at the same house. I seated myself at the same bench. 'Good morning,' I said to the same woman.

'Same?', she asked.

'Same,' I replied.

Satiated on noodles, I sat back, opened my book and sipped the sweet, milky coffee. The same young boy of twelve came out wearing the same grey-brown short trousers and said good morning as if I were an old friend. After he had cleared away my plate, he hovered beside me, curious about the book I was reading.

Barely above a whisper, he said, 'Excuse me, can I have your book?'

'Oh, sorry, I haven't finished it yet,' I replied. The boy's head lowered, and he began to apologise. It was a sorry of shame for having asked, even though he had been building up the courage ever since he saw me with it. 'But I will finish later today, and of course you can have it,' I added.

The biggest smile I have ever seen spread across his face. He looked at his mother, and then he looked back and said, 'Thank you, thank you,' and shook my hand with a little bow. 'Thank you.'

I had a guilt-free lazy day at Tina's Inn, reading in my room or watching TV in the lounge with the same truck drivers. The rain went on, pounding on the roof and rebounding off the ground.

That evening, I wandered back to the same house. It was busy now; the two tables were full. A young man smiled to me and said, 'Your friend will be home soon.' I presumed he meant the young woman, his wife. I sat quietly with my journal as he served coffee and bread and noodles to those who wanted it. When he had finished, he brought me a coffee and then a dish with plantain and plums that an old lady had been grilling by the roadside.

Slowly the other customers departed. I stayed and wrote my journal in the dim light until there were just three of us left. When the young boy appeared from the house, I gave him the book. His face filled with the broad grin, and he shook my hand again and made a little bow. He cleared the empty plates urgently and then sat with his friend to look at the book. Their English was not good, but they could both read the words slowly. I don't know how much of it they understood, but that didn't matter.

Much later the young woman returned and gave me a kiss on each cheek before saying something to her husband and disappearing into the house. When I next looked up, a hot dish had been placed beside me. The fish and plantain stew smelt delicious, and it was only then that I realised how hungry I was.

16

Up to the Highlands

Cameroon

The dirt road from Ekok wound its way round and up and down through the thick, overgrown forest where trees competed to grow the tallest, reaching out above the canopy to feel the sunlight on their leaves. Hillsides vanished into a mass of green, where fast-flowing waters loudly rushed out-of-sight and cut steep ravines. The wall of trees, liana vines, and grasses towering up on either side of the track obscured the view.

I felt small and insignificant and alone, afloat on a forest sea of green that rolled on, wave after wave, until it poured into the Indian Ocean. My bike made tracks in the wet earth and when it was steep uphill, my worn shoes made footprints too. But when the next rains came, and they would come as surely as the sun rises in the morning even if I do not see it through the clouds, those tracks would disappear and no one would know that I had ever been there.

It is never silent in the rainforest – the stillness that pervades the heavy humid air only amplifies every sound and disturbance. Each bird has its own unique call and they 'kaw-kaw' and 'ko-ko', but rarely come into view. The lizards rustle through the undergrowth and the cicadas rhythmically call. To see things in the rainforest you don't look with your eyes but listen with your ears.

I heard an unusual noise, faint in the distance. The noise became louder and when it was clear enough to recognise, I realised it was neither animal nor bird, but a chain-saw. The large pile of logs stacked by the road finally shattered the illusion: I was not alone. Now the curtain was pulled back, I saw spaces devoid of trees and the orange-red earth revealed where man had made his mark and staked his territorial claim.

Then out of this stage-set, a small village appeared by the road. Women sat outside talking with other women and men sat quietly beside other men. The first young child to see me, who had been playing in the dirt road with a stick, pointed at me and shouted, 'White!'

The child next to him looked across and he too called out, 'White!' and several other children heard. They appeared from behind houses and stood up from the shade where they played.

'White!' each of them called. 'White! White! White!'

Soon all the children were looking and pointing and shouting, 'White!' They shouted all together, but never at the same time, and when one started to run after me with arms flailing and flapping wildly in the air, the others gave chase too.

'White!'

All the while this flock of little boys (they were always boys) like *Finding Nemo*'s gulls squawked, 'White! White! White!' It was the same through every village that morning – the call, the chase, the escape.

My mind was telling me to persevere with the poor roads and climb the hills to Bamenda. My legs said to sod that and head for the coast. Still undecided when I arrived at a junction, I stopped for the day.

A lad in a blue and black striped football shirt came over to meet me at the unmarked guesthouse, 'Hi, I'm Denis. I'm very sorry, but do you mind waiting? I've got football practise to go to now. I train every day and never miss it, but my brother will be here very soon.'

When Bless arrived, he showed me to a room that was clean except for the cobwebs lining the corners of the walls. It looked as though the room had not been used for months. With the floral bedspread and matching curtains, it looked like it had not been redecorated for decades. Importantly though, there was water, electricity, and a comfy bed. Everything else was immaterial.

During the last hours of the afternoon, I sat on the porch with Bless, and we read. It was unusual to see locals reading anything, except sometimes a newspaper in town. Bless was a qualified lawyer, although he had never practised, and I wondered what he was doing running this small guesthouse.

Denis returned and when a young boy came over with a shoe bag slung over his shoulder, Denis said something to him. The boy took out a pair of football boots and showed them to Denis, who checked them over with motherly attention, saw they were clean, and gave them back.

The three of us sat on the veranda that evening, looking out into the darkness and watching the frenzied flying insects swarm around the porch light and the thousands of small winged bugs crawling in confused disarray over the floor. As the bugs encroached on the veranda in a writhing mass, we inched our chairs back towards the wall.

'How was football training?' I asked without taking my eyes off the bugs.

'It was OK, but I couldn't concentrate. I keep thinking about my exams. I get my A-level results in two days. They're really important.'

'So, you've finished school now. What do you want to do?'

'If I pass, I'm going to study geography at Buea University.'

I looked up at Denis now, intrigued. 'So you don't want to be a footballer then?' I joked.

'Of course, but I play for fun and to keep fit. It's not a job.' Denis was clearly under no illusion that he would make a living using his head, not his feet.

Bless, who had been quiet and passive, became animated when we started talking about British politics. He avidly read the BBC News and seemed better informed than most of the British public. Like every Cameroonian man I met, he would like to work in England one day.

'You know we study the same syllabus as you do in England? We do GCSEs and A-levels.'

'Really? I didn't know that.'

'Cameroon used to be part of the German Empire, but it was divided into French and British-administered territories after Germany lost the Second World War. So, here in the West of Cameroon, we lived under the British. That's why we speak English here, but when you go to Yaoundé, you will need to speak French. Then, in 1972, there was a referendum to dissolve the two territories in favour of a United Republic of Cameroon. Fortunately, they decided to keep the British style of education and now it's taught nationwide. It's the only good thing they kept, and now they are talking about changing it.'

It was a common sentiment in Anglophone Cameroon that they got a poor deal with the 1972 referendum, and that they are under-represented by government and largely ignored. If I mentioned the poor state of the roads, they replied that the rest of the country's roads were good; if I mentioned the lack of a constant water supply in villages, they replied that it was different in the rest of the country.

The conversation tailed off, and I was left wondering why Bless, who was clearly intelligent, was here and not in the city being a lawyer or working abroad. When Bless quietly disappeared into the guesthouse, Denis pulled up his chair next to me, too close for comfort. I was thinking that here was an impressionable eighteen-year-old with hormones running high and that he was going to say something embarrassing and awkward that I would not know how to respond to.

In a soft, low voice, barely audible above the night-time noise of the cicadas, Denis spoke as though whispering a secret even though there was no one else to hear. I leant closer and noticed a tiny white light fly across the darkness behind him – just a firefly. Focussing back on Denis, he told me that he lived in the small, simple house next door with Bless and their younger brother and two younger sisters.

'I've got two older sisters as well who have finished university and are now working in the city. Four years ago our mother died and then last year our father passed away also.' I listened quietly. He didn't say how they died, and I didn't ask. He would tell me if he wanted. 'So me and Bless run this guesthouse that our dad built, so we can look after our little brothers and sisters because we want them to go to school, not work yet ...'.

Denis continued talking without stopping. Like a burst water pipe, the words flowed forth until Bless returned armed with a broom. Denis immediately fell silent, and in the brief instant they made eye-contact, I saw a hundred words of silent animosity exchange between them.

Denis pushed his chair back, realising that his chance to confide was over, and we both watched with amusement as Bless swept away the thousands of bugs crawling on the floor only for more to take their place in this unstoppable insect inundation. *What was the point?* We all laughed at the futility of it. Eventually, Bless put the broom down, and we watched the insect tide inch closer.

* * *

My head won the battle of mind over muscle, and my legs bore the brunt of the decision. The Cameroon highlands were, after all, where I wanted to go. My muscles will always recover from exertion, but my mind may never get over the regret of the things I don't do. To be forever wondering *what if* is infinitely worse.

The road cut through the wall of thick grass, tall trees and hanging, twisting, entwining vines, before I crossed a bridge over a river of still water, an ink-black pool that might swallow anything that touched it.

On the other side, the tarmac was replaced by a 'road under construction'. The government may care little about the state of the roads in the Anglophone West, but the Chinese care little for politics. If there was a job that needed to be done and money to be made, they would do it. It was only business.

The road was roughly laid with rocks. I weaved slowly from left to right and back, focussing intently on picking the least potholed path. When the road levelled out, I picked up speed until a village emerged and from somewhere out of view, I heard a child's voice shout out, 'Nĭ hăo!'

Yes, the Chinese have definitely been here.

'Nĭ hăo,' I called back. 'Hello!'

Where the corrugated earth road was blocked by heaps of dirt and a broken-down digger, I took a smaller path instead. The shuddering of an abused two-stroke engine shattered the silence. Around the bend, a motorcycle careered uncontrollably down the bumpy hill. We diverged from the collision path, and then I returned to the original worn trail that wound steeper uphill, so that I had to walk, push, and drag the bike until the track rejoined the wide earth road.

Around another bend were trucks and diggers, Chinese men in clean shirts and safety helmets, and lots of local workers in dirty trousers and once-white vests.

Some waved, but more often they gave a thumbs up and shouted, 'Hey Baby, what's up?' or 'My Sister!' The Chinese either looked at me with a bemused expression or did not see me at all as they stared intently into their paperwork.

Diverted down another overgrown track, where the forest was re-staking its claim, I rode downwards past a steady stream of water rushing off the steep hillside. Thick, slick, slippery mud covered the wheels and brakes, and I slid into the edges of the deeply carved tracks. My front pannier jammed against the verge and was forced off the bike to lie abandoned in the quagmire until I could slip-slide like a cat on ice to retrieve it.

I sweated and pedalled hard going uphill and let gravity do the work going down – faster, faster. I was overconfident (some may say reckless), and I misjudged the ruts.

Thud.

The front wheel plunged down, the handlebar bag vibrated wildly and then the back wheel hit the hidden rock.

Crunch.

I looked sharply over my shoulder to see a pannier somersaulting down the track behind me. *Shit. Slow down. This isn't a race.*

But I was going slowly, so I didn't have many breaks because I didn't think I deserved them, and I got more and more tired until I reached the top of the hill, and when I saw a bar I just had to stop. The workmen were on their break too. They were mostly students working the roads part-time during their summer holidays. I stopped for only one drink because I had a long way to go if I was to reach Bamenda that day.

The track swept round into the next valley and opened out. I could see for miles to the next town lying in the midst of the hills. The collection of houses scattered on the slopes sparkled like diamonds when they reflected the brilliant sun. There was no sign of construction or improvement to the road after the village. The track zig-zagged upwards, always up, looping wide onto the next hill and then switch-backing to greater heights. It was mostly too rough to cycle, so I pushed slowly.

By now it was clear I would not reach Bamenda, so I aimed for Bali, 20 kilometres earlier, instead. A truck stopped alongside me, 'Do you want a lift?'

'No, thanks.'

'I can give you a lift just until the tarmac and then it will be easier for you.'

'Thanks, but I'm fine,' I said, although my legs were screaming otherwise.

'We understand – you are doing this for the challenge and to see the places you are passing. Is that it?'

'That's exactly it,' I smiled. *Finally, somebody understands.*

Several bends later, the top was still nowhere in sight, and I wished I had listened to my legs and answered differently. *Just keep pushing.*

It was with relief when I reached the top and looked out at the ridges of hills disappearing into the misty distance. Soon everywhere was enshrouded in a wet mist and by the time I reached the tarmac it was raining lightly. *Not far now.*

I was exhausted. It might have been a tarmac road, but it was a roller-coaster ride. I should have stopped in the town where I saw a sign for a hotel. I should have stopped in the next village, and although it was too small for a guesthouse, I could have camped. But I didn't. With dogged determination I persevered to Bali, foolish with tiredness.

Eventually, I came to a long downhill. *Only two kilometres to go. Perhaps Bali is at the bottom. I sure as hell hope so.* It wasn't. On the brink of complete exhaustion, I got off the bike and started pushing again.

Around the corner, I saw houses and people walking on the road, and when I stopped to ask where Bali was, they said it wasn't far, and I was filled with relief to hear that until I looked upwards to where they pointed. It was too steep and seemed far away, and I wasn't sure if I could make it. I just stood there, looking up at this insurmountable wall, my legs fixed like cement. *Take a deep breath and take it slow. You can do this.*

I took three steps and stopped, three steps and wheezed, three more steps and stopped again. My heart hammered hard and my head pounded with the exertion, and I could feel my chest tightening. I looked around despairingly and my eyes pleaded with anyone to help me, but no one saw my pain through the darkness. Tears welled up and when I wiped my eyes the sweat made them sting. *Don't Cry. No point thinking it's too steep and you can't make it. You have to make it. You're on your own.*

There in the darkness, I thought that last hill would never end. But it did. It ended at the market crossroads with men calling to me, 'Hello!'

I collapsed over the handlebars and tried to calm my breathing until I could talk.

'Where is there a guesthouse?'

'Down that hill,' one shadow pointed, 'and up the next. Then take a left, and go down and up …'. I looked into the darkness and felt my throat constrict. I fought against the tears that I didn't want and my body could not control.

'Is there another one?' I whispered hoarsely.

'Yes, near the hospital.'

'Is it closer?'

'Yes.' *Thank God.*

'But I need food first.'

Someone led me to a bench in front of a house.

'What food do you have?'

'Fufu.' My heavy heart sank into the pit of my empty stomach.

'Nothing else?' I asked hopefully. I hated fufu. The lady shook her head.

'OK, fufu and coke, please.'

'No coke.' My body rebelled at this response, and again I was on the verge of tears of exhaustion. *Need sugar.*

The lady dished me out the heavy mash and cold cassava leaves and went in search of a drink for me. Beyond exhaustion lay a complete lack of appetite and it made that fufu look like consolidated wallpaper paste. I ate a few mouthfuls, but could manage no more. When the lady brought a bottle of coke, I downed it so fast it overflowed down my cheeks and I almost choked. Several months later, when my hunger levels were restored to their all-time high, I was actively searching for fufu to fill me. How needs must!

I paid and went in search of the guesthouse. No one I asked knew of it, so I followed the sign for the hospital down a dark path. I never felt so lonely – a stranger walking blindly down the pitch-black side streets. I stumbled on until I saw a light and slowly wheeled the bike towards it – the hospital. I could see no guesthouse. If I had not been in a town, I would have pushed my bike off the road and camped. Yet, although I could see nothing, I knew there were houses and people all around.

'Can you tell me where the guesthouse is?' I asked

'This is not a guesthouse, this is a hospital.' *Now I may be exhausted and a foreigner, but I can see that.*

'Where is the nearest guesthouse?'

'We don't know,' the lady at reception replied, having looked first to the nurse for help. 'You should go to the market on the main road and ask.' My shoulders slumped and the last drop of energy drained out of me. I managed to collapse onto the bench before the tears started rolling. I couldn't help it. I didn't want to cry, and I tried to laugh at myself, but crying was the final thing my body seemed capable of doing then.

'Oh, don't cry,' the nurse consoled as she put a comforting hand on my shoulder. 'We will find you a guesthouse,' she said, as if she had the power to fabricate one from the thick forest air in this empty hospital waiting room.

The nurses conferred, and I wiped away my tears. 'We'll show you to a guesthouse,' one said. Led out of reception, I walked along the corridor bumping into the side wall because my legs were so weak they would not go in a straight line. I collected the bike and was shown to a private room. There was a metal bed, a cot, a tray covered with a thick layer of dust and a bench in the room with flaking mint-green painted walls.

'You need to leave early tomorrow though. This is part of the hospital,' the nurse said. 'It's not really a guesthouse,' she whispered to me in confidence. *I may be exhausted, but I can see that.*

'OK, what time do I need to leave?'

'Six.' *That is early!* I nearly collapsed again.

When she had left, I washed and crawled onto the bed and watched two cockroaches scurry into the shadows. *At least I'm not seriously ill.*

Before I drifted into a restless sleep, there was a knock on the door. *Maybe they'll go away.* I didn't have the energy to move. The knocking resumed. I forced myself off the bed and stumbled to the door. It was the doctor. He was concerned about me and said I could go to his house if I preferred, where his wife would look after me. I looked back at the bed a few feet away and even that looked too far. Leaving the room now was definitely out of the question.

* * *

The streets of Bamenda were a hive of activity with men in business suits walking through the bustling sidewalks that were lined with stalls selling mobile phones and CD's with Bob Marley and Whitney Houston competing for prominence. Young men in trendy jeans and bright t-shirts talked and lingered in small groups. On street corners corn was grilled and trays of fruit and nuts waited to be bought.

The backdrop of houses lining the cliff-top was hazy in the morning cool. By afternoon, if the sun shone, the rocks reflected brightly and every ridge and crevice was in sharp relief. When it rained, the white water cascading down its face turned to muddy orange, and that was when the power supply for the town was cut. Then the roads emptied of motorbikes, and people sheltered in doorways or tightly up against buildings and watched the wall of water as the roads turned to rivers. If they had to go anywhere, they ran with an umbrella to the nearest taxi and got their feet wet. Only a forlorn stray dog skulked by with wet coat stuck to its thin body, and a couple of boys having searched through the market rubbish wandered off with their finds of some netting, rope, and a tyre.

My rest days were spent reading and writing and drinking beer. One morning I washed my bike and cleaned my clothes in a bucket of water, as I always did. The Omo washing powder didn't clean the dirt off the clothes, but rather disintegrated the outer layer of fabric and fingertips.

It would have been worth my time to pay someone else to do the hard work, but African women clean clothes by scrubbing them with vengeful vigour before beating them to death on rocks, so that after a couple of cycles there is little left but rags even if they are cleaner than I could ever get them. This would then necessitate an earlier-than-planned excursion to the market in search of more clothes. The explorer Henry Morton Stanley insightfully said, 'I foresaw a brilliant future of Africa, if by any miracle of good-fortune I could persuade the dark millions of the interior to cast off their fabrics of grass clothing and don … second-hand costumes … See what a ready market lies here for old clothes!'

Whether from his idea or by coincidence, the second-hand market is integral to the African town and the best place to shop for replacement clothes while travelling. If you love hunting for a bargain among the sale items of your favourite department store, this is heaven. For someone like me who detests shopping, it is a veritable nightmare. Having to sort through pile upon jumbled pile in search of shorts or a top that is respectable and suitable, and then among that heap find ones that will actually fit without the aid of a dressing room to try them for size could only be worsened if I had a fear of crowds too. That was why I washed my own clothes and fooled myself that it was only to save money, which I then spent on another beer instead.

I cycled out of Bamenda, refreshed after the rest. The road swept around the green hillsides, and I looked down the valleys into the distance that reminded me of England on a crisp clear summer's morning before the sun warms the air. Except that when I looked closer, I saw palm trees and women selling bananas outside their corrugated-roof homes. Besides, the grass never grows that tall in England, and people use lawnmowers to cut it, not machetes.

During break-time, children in school uniform carried machetes to the playing field and cut the grass. They were student caretakers paying for their education with labour. Men lined the roads and cut back the embankments with long low sweeps, back and forth, back and forth, and they worked up a sweat as they shredded the grass.

I stopped at the first bar I came to when the black clouds released their deluge of water. The local men were handing round a bottle of milky palm wine. They consumed three bottles between them while I was there, and I suspected they had drunk at least three before I arrived. The jovial word-slur was impossible to understand, and I could not even tell which language they were mumbling.

People in Cameroon love their alcohol, especially beer. If beer is unaffordable, the locally-made palm wine is an acceptable substitute. It was not unusual to see several people sat in a bar at nine in the morning eating breakfast with a bottle of Castel or 33 Export or any of the other beers served in Cameroon, where the choice was wider than in most British Pubs.

They said it was downhill all the way to Foumban. I had been dreaming of freewheeling along endless miles of quiet earth roads, winding through the hills and admiring the views. What a shock I got! When you build your hopes upon other people's words you are destined for disappointment, especially if they mention the words 'downhill' or 'tailwind'. It was better to set my expectations low or not at all – then I was guaranteed to be pleasantly surprised at the least and sometimes exuberantly elated.

Desert Snow

The green line on my map was an accurate interpretation of the road – it was both scenic and hilly. Whether the obvious visual attractions compensated for the physical exertion was disputable. I have to believe it was worth the effort. Given the same choice, I would push for the wet highlands again. I think.

17

An Ailing Bike and Long Night in Yaoundé

Cameroon

In many ways, I was disillusioned about this journey. The cycling was meant simply to be a way of getting around – a side activity that would let me see Africa slowly and up close. It didn't turn out like that. The cycling became the all-consuming constituent that not only made the journey possible, but was the journey.

At some point I stopped waking up in the morning and thinking, *What a great day to go cycling, so where shall I go today? The whole world is laid out in front of me like an unopened book and I can turn to any page I wish.* Instead, I woke up and did not think at all. I simply got on my bike and pedalled down the road, just as I used to get in the car and drive to the office. It was my regular job. Don't get me wrong, I would not have exchanged one day of my unpaid pain-in-the-arse (yes, I had a very sore backside some days) job for anything else.

When I had returned to Ghana with my books and chocolate, I also brought back a bike tyre. It seemed a sensible thing to do. I had been carrying a spare with me, so with a second one, I could have a new set of tyres on my bike that should get me to Cape Town.

I'd had a series of flat tyres in Guinea, but that was only because the rim tape wasn't substantial enough, and the adhesive patches I had to repair the punctures caused by the spokes didn't stick in the humid atmosphere. I discovered too late that the holes in the wheel rims were too small for the Schrader car-tyre type valves, so I was forced to reuse my punctured ones over and over. A solution had to be found.

An avid cyclist-mechanic in Freetown promised he could fix it all for me. My eagerness to hand over the two bike wheels to a virtual stranger, who I knew only as Eddie and nothing more, was concerning. That busy corner of Wilkinson Street could easily have been the last time I saw him or the bike wheels and that would have been a substantial setback in the endeavour to cycle to Cape Town. I would have forgiven him – the wheels, especially the back one with the Rohloff hub, cost more than he would earn in a year. Outrageous, I know, but that's the unequal world we live in.

Eddie was good to his word, as most people are. He taped up the rims, drilled out bigger holes, and procured several inner tubes with Schrader valves, which were hard to find, by going to a bike shop on the other side of town, which was a timely undertaking in that chaotic city.

Some people have a strong attachment to their bikes and even give them names like their pet dog, or after some fictional character that epitomises their journey. 'Rocinante, my trusty, noble steed of steel that was always with me on my worldly misadventures,' they say. Dogs and trusty steeds, however, will move of their own accord without the need for energetic input on my behalf.

There was no love affair between me and the bike I was riding. If it worked and helped get me from one place to another quicker than I could walk, then great. But that is what bikes are built for. I am easily pleased and was content as long as it got me there, even on the days that we went slower than walking pace. If it didn't, then like some old marriage, it really started to piss me off.

The animosity, acrimony, and at times, outright anger that arose in me towards that inanimate object of steel and rubber can only be explained if I did love it just a little. Like it or not, I needed that bike. Technically, any bike would do, but the one I had, I was well aware, was much better than any of the other heavy, single-speed Chinese imports I saw in Africa.

I bought that bike because it was the bike that would require minimal maintenance. I was happy to clean the chain with a toothbrush, even several times a day on the really dusty roads, to wash it in the shower or with a bucket and cloth when I got a day off, and to oil the squeaks and creaks in appeasement. Despite all that, after I returned to Ghana, there were growing signs of discontent and that the bike needed more attention if it wasn't going to either break up on me or die.

Use something enough and eventually it will wear out; it doesn't matter how much care or attention you give it. Stay in Africa long enough and eventually you will get malaria (my doctor did try to warn me); taking a prophylaxis pill daily only delays it. Some things in life are inevitable.

It started with the chain slipping shortly after I left Ghana. That was temporarily treated by removing a link and tensioning it. The only cure was to replace the chain entirely. If I was going to do that, then I needed to replace the sprocket too, which by then had worn itself down into a lethally sharp ninja throwing-weapon. I ordered new parts and the tools to replace them from England and had them sent on to Yaoundé in Cameroon.

There was one constant murmuring though that grumbled on unhappily. It was so small at first, I don't know when it started, but gradually the rear wheel wobbled more and more. My worry was that it would crescendo to a dramatic, cymbal-clash climax with fatal consequences for the bike and possibly, of more concern, for me. Since these sorts of things usually happen at the most inconvenient times, it was bound to happen where I was going. I figured I might as well get everything fixed up at once.

The consensus via the Internet, from people who knew more about bikes than I did, was that the bearings in the hub were worn. Naively, like the locals I talked to about it, I thought it was simply a case of taking the hub apart, replacing the bearings and putting it back together.

I collected the bike parts package from the embassy where they had been sent and asked, without much hope, if they knew of a bike shop in town. They didn't. They suggested trying the Chinese Auto Garage. Off I went clutching a hand-drawn map. The garage was no use, but the gentle-natured man back at The Foyer, where I was staying, tried to help. We failed to remove the sprocket, but he was convinced that the mechanic on the street outside would be able to help with the aid of a vice and wrench. He couldn't. Instead, the mechanic directed me to the hardware store where I was told to go to The Briqueterie.

'The What?' I asked.

'*Le Briqueterie*'

'Like I said, what?'

Realising I was a hopeless case they went straight to the final answer, 'Just get a taxi and ask for *Le Briqueterie*.' I hailed a taxi and was amazed the driver knew of it.

It was the road where all the motorbike mechanics had their street-side workshops and where there was also one that specialised in the pedal bike variety. I was optimistic – there were even padded cycle shorts for sale, although they were clearly second-hand and well worn.

The two young guys set to work with the sprocket removal tool and chain whip. They broke the chain whip, got out their own one and broke that too. I was beginning to despair when the owner, a huge tough guy, came back. He looked at the wheel carefully, tried with the now-broken chain whip, failed, put it down and picked up a big hammer and blunt-ended chisel. *I'm not sure this is a good idea*. He was going to bludgeon the expensive hub to scrap metal. Since I was running out of options, I just watched him work. With three solid bashes the sprocket was loose; the internal mechanism was dented in the process, but he tapped it back into roughly the right shape.

I showed him how the wheel wobbled, and he too said it must be the bearings and although he'd never seen a hub before, he set about unscrewing everything to take a closer look. He was the kind of guy that if he had ever gone to school would have worked out an equation from first principles if he couldn't remember it. It soon became apparent that we couldn't fix it, so we put it back together and off I went.

With an email to the manufacturers, it was clear that the only solution for the wobbling wheel was a replacement hub. Assured that I wouldn't do more damage if I continued riding, I opted to stick with the wobble and maybe replace it later in Kinshasa. It would take three weeks to get a new hub sent out, and I didn't have time on my Cameroon visa.

That should have been the end of the bike maintenance proceedings in Yaoundé. But with the new sprocket and chain attached, I discovered that the gear shifter would no longer turn. In the few days of inaction, it had completely seized up. Nothing would induce it to move. Ten months of dirt, sweat, and rain had cemented the shifter solid and welded it onto the handlebars. Three days of soaking in WD-40, which was easy to get hold of because I now knew where the hardware store was, and with a hammer and chisel I got the shifter off the bars. The street mechanic worked from basics to get the shifter apart with a strategically placed nail, gave it a good clean and reassembled it.

Now that the gear shifter twisted, it would only change through 12 of the 14 gears. By now, I was considering exchanging the bike for a cheap single-speed Chinese import. I could guarantee it wouldn't have the same problem. The only solution was to go to the bar opposite that served a mean rotisserie chicken and fried plantain, which was my favourite meal then, and wash it down with a beer or two, which was always my favourite drink. I ate there every evening for a week. Yes, it took over a week to fix the bike. None of this mattered though because I was waiting for a visa from the Gabonese embassy.

It was Gabon's Independence Day when I handed my passport over to the security guard. 'I'm sorry, but all the government officials are celebrating with a week-long holiday. If I see someone, I will ask if they can get your visa done quicker.'

'Thanks.' I wasn't hopeful.

When I returned a week later, the security guard told me the embassy was still shut. I returned the next day, but not deemed smart enough to step inside the embassy building despite wearing my smartest (only) trousers and shirt, the guard went to ask for my passport on my behalf. He returned empty-handed and said to come back tomorrow, which I did.

Wearing the same clothes, a day dirtier, I was this time allowed into the offices. Beckoned to a large desk by a member of staff,

I asked for my passport. Two piles were lifted from a cardboard box lying abandoned on the floor and searched. It was clear that my British, maroon-coloured passport was not among the green and black ones.

I was always very careful about keeping my passport in a safe place. It had never crossed my mind that it would be lost at an embassy. Yet another thing to go wrong in Yaoundé. I was told it was being processed and to come back tomorrow. I sat there in outward disbelief while I raged inside. There would be a fight tomorrow, that was certain. I calmly walked out and vented my frustration on the guard, who had probably heard it all before but listened anyway.

He called to his colleague and told him about my missing passport, who then leant over and opened the draw in the guardroom – miraculously, there it was.

Now I had my passport back, I was free to leave Yaoundé, as soon as I got the last two gears working on the bike. This I was determined to fix myself. I sat down one afternoon and methodically took apart everything that had been touched in the previous days, which now it was all clean and degreased was easy to do, and found that the internal mechanism had been reassembled incorrectly. *If a local who's never seen a hub before can figure it out how it works, then there's no reason why an engineer with a degree cannot.* So I figured how it worked, realigned it and put everything back together, and it really wasn't that hard.

I was confident that any problem with the bike I would now be able to fix myself, except the wobbling wheel. I later replaced the front chain-ring quickly in Kinshasa and when the gear cable later frayed between towns, I calmly sat down and fixed that and then replaced the internal mechanism with little difficulty. A broken axle in Namibia, I had not counted on. But Namibia and broken axles could not have been further from my mind that last night in Yaoundé.

It was a long night.

The Foyer had a curfew. There was a long list of rules, and one of them was that you had to be back before a certain time. My relationship with the family who ran the hostel got off to a bad start when I was late back the first night. Generally, I dislike rules but will stick to them, at least until I know which ones can be broken without too great a consequence.

Dutifully, I returned five minutes before eleven o'clock on my first night. Unfortunately, lockdown was at ten o'clock. I knocked and apologised, and they reluctantly let me in.

The mosquitoes in the room forced me to put up my tent on the bed – the tent pole broke. That was the first thing that stopped working in Yaoundé (the next was my bike computer, and then my bike). The second night I went out, I made sure I was back before ten and although the door was unlocked, they had wedged a chair under the handle. The third time the door was locked even before their lock-down time. And it happened yet again, but the security guard woke the woman up. She let me in and I got a telling off even though I had stuck to their rules. It was infuriating.

Then came the last night. It would have been great to stay out late, to have a few beers before hitting the road and to celebrate having fixed my bike, but I returned before ten. I should have expected it – the door was locked, again. This time the security guard would not wake up the woman.

'You can sleep outside.' *No chance.*

'Look, you can have my blanket.'

'No, you need your blanket, and I want to sleep in the bed I have paid for.'

I knocked loudly on the door: no response. I walked around and knocked on their window: no response. I called out. Eventually, the woman opened the door.

'What are you doing?' she screamed at me.

'I'm trying to go to bed, but you locked the door.'

'It's after ten. You know we lock the door at ten.'

'I was here before ten. I've been trying to get in for twenty minutes. Why would you lock the door before ten? You have these rules you expect everyone to obey and then do your own thing anyway.' I was angry and that helped my fluency in French.

'We lock the door because this is not a safe area. We lock the door for your safety.'

'You locked me out! You were content for me to spend the night outside,' and I realised the battle could not be won because logic and reason were more a foreign language to her than French was for me. 'Don't pretend you care. You lock the door for your *own* safety.'

'This is a dangerous place.'

'Fine. I shall make it easy for you. Give me five minutes to get my bags, and I shall leave. Then you can lock the door and go back to bed and sleep safe and sound.'

I marched upstairs, grabbed my belongings, and exited the building. *That was rather a rash decision. Where am I going to go now?*

'We won't be responsible for your safety,' she called out as I left.

'That's fine, you never were.'

Now I needed a plan. I went back to the bar across the road, parked my bike in the front and bought a beer. By the time my glass was half-empty I realised it was also half-full – now I could go out for the night as I had originally wanted to do. It wasn't ideal to have all my stuff with me, but I would manage. So I polished off the beer and ordered another, and told Christiane the barmaid my plans.

'But we close at eleven.'

'Seriously? Oh well, maybe I'll go to the *Le Cabaret* then.'

'That closes soon too.'

'Seriously?' My night-long bar crawl idea wasn't looking so feasible.

'What are you going to do?' she asked as she sat down beside me on the sofa.

'I suppose I'll go back to The Foyer and camp in the garden.'

'You can't camp. It's not safe there.'

'I promise it'll be fine. Plenty of people camp there.'

'No, you come and stay with me. You'll have to wait until I lock up and my boyfriend arrives though.'

'OK,' I gave in. Sometimes it is good to accept help, and this way, I could avoid any further confrontations.

At eleven she told the last people to leave. I collected the bottles, of which there were many, and she washed the glasses, of which there were few. The ratio of beers drank to people present was always high. Then, when John arrived I locked up my bike, and she locked the bar.

Stood in the dark street waiting for a taxi made me uncomfortable. I never wandered the city streets late at night with more than a few notes of the local currency. Now I had all my valuables on me, and John was carrying the pannier with my laptop in.

'John always comes to pick me up after work when he's on leave from the army. It's a dangerous area and I don't feel safe by myself.' This was the first place on this trip that anyone had said was really dangerous, and now I was hearing it a lot. Beyond the pink lipstick, Christiane struck me as a tough lady who could look after herself, but I had to admit that having John by our side made me feel more secure.

As we were on our way to Christiane's neighbourhood, a man hailed our taxi and the driver pulled over as there was space for one more. The man opened the back door, leant over me, and thrust his arm at Christiane's chest. She let out a loud yelp and then slumped over her knees. *Oh, shit!*

I watched, hardly believing what was happening and looked at the man's arm, waiting to grab the knife if he tried anything else. In that instant, which lasted a lifetime, I wondered how badly she was hurt and whether I knew enough first aid to help and if the hospital was far away. *What just happened?*

Thankfully, there was no knife. The man was trying to grab the handbag from Christiane's vice-like grip. I sat there helplessly, wondering why he hadn't tried to grab mine instead.

The fight for the bag went on until Christiane, using the only weapon she had, bit down hard into the man's forearm. He retreated rapidly once she let go. John shouted at the driver to move, and we swerved away from the curb into the middle of the empty road. I reached to close the door and then looked at Christiane, who still had her bag but was shaken.

'Are you OK? Are you hurt?' I asked her because she was feeling her lip and teeth and then looking at her finger for signs of blood.

'No, I'm OK,' she said. 'My life is in this bag. My purse, my phone, the keys to my house …'.

It was the same for me and my handlebar bag – it also had my camera and passport with the Gabonese visa that had taken over a week to obtain. But these things were not worth our lives.

When we got to the neighbourhood where Christiane lived, we went to her local bar and had a beer while John called his friends in the police about what had happened.

'Don't worry, we're in my neighbourhood now. It is safe here,' Christiane said as we picked our way along the guttered, unpaved path. And when we reached the front door, she added, as though trying to allay my expectations, 'It's not a big house, but it's my home.' That summed it up perfectly.

The living room had a wicker sofa, hanging pictures, a TV, and a plant in the corner, and the small kitchen was out the back. Her clothes hung out of drawers in the bedroom, and there were trinkets on the shelf and a cuddly cow toy on the bed that mooed and said something ridiculous when she pressed the belly.

And that was the end of a long last night in Yaoundé.

The next morning, I said goodbye to Christiane and John, and when the bar reopened, I collected my bike and left the city I was ready to leave – into the unknown.

Part Three
Central Africa

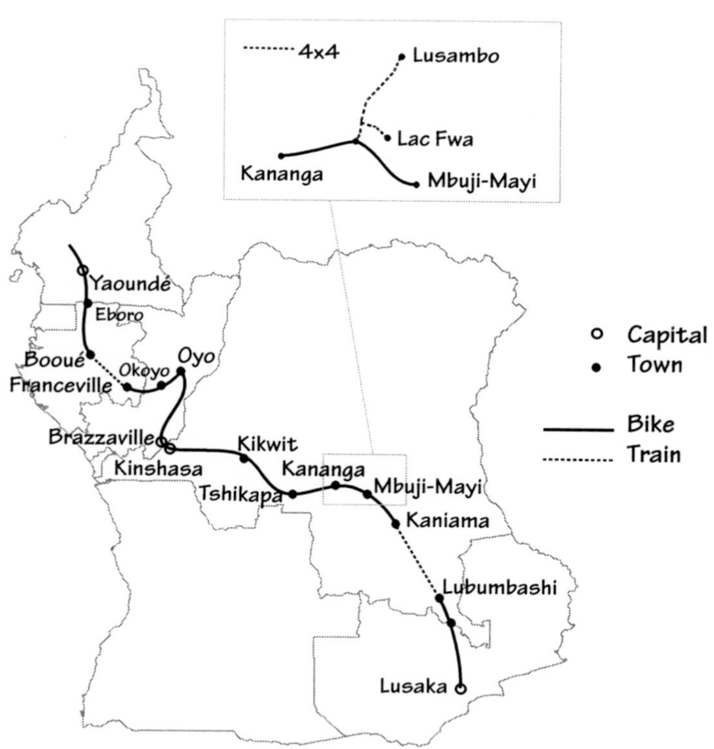

18

Into the Wild in Central Africa

Cameroon and Gabon

Yaoundé was the doorway to something that had been hidden from view. The similarities throughout the West African countries were rapidly fading into the past.

Whereas people had carried goods from the market in plastic or calabash bowls on their heads, in the Cameroon hills they carried wood from the forest in rucksacks fashioned from baskets woven with liana vines. Leather-skinned men with sinewy arms, worn by weather and hard work, marched head down with short quick strides up the winding paths carrying large piles of wood strapped securely to their backs.

People still waved as I cycled past, but now they sometimes waved a dead animal too. Did I want to buy bush meat? I could have the small antelope strung up by its neck. *Is that an armadillo shaking its claws at me?* On a slow day there were chickens for sale, hanging unceremoniously upside-down.

There were cane rats, which looked like giant guinea pigs, although on menu boards they were listed as grasscutters – it sounds more appetising, I suppose. Hunted and caught in the wild, they are the one animal classified as bush meat that is not endangered by the trade. It's another matter for the antelope and our closer primate relatives.

Central Africa was carnivorously crazy. West Africa had been fruit and nuts and, where there were rivers, an abundance of dried fish in varying sizes of crispy, flat brass-coloured flakes. Rather than servings of rice, the meat was now dished up with glutinous translucent lumps of manioc or heavy balls of fufu, which I ate out of necessity rather than for the taste, texture, or nutritional content.

The meat, whatever it was and it was often hard to tell because it was served generically as *viande*, I ravenously devoured and washed down with beer. *Singe* I avoided until I checked the French translation and then continued to avoid it because I would prefer to see monkeys swinging in the trees than served on a plate.

It became harder to camp, not because there were always people to see me, but because the forests were largely impenetrable. The desert had been open, dry and clean – sterile, as though nothing could live on the face of it – and only an occasional shrub or dead-looking wood lay waiting for the rain. Underground was where life simmered gently, plant roots reaching for deep water reservoirs and creatures hiding in the sand, all biding their time for the moment when they would spring forth and flourish, if only for a moment.

In the thick equatorial forests, the air and trees bubbled and overflowed with life – buzzing, flying, flapping, howling, creeping, crawling, croaking, singing their joys and groaning their sorrows. Yet the earth on which this abundance of creation balanced was layer upon layer of rot and decay. Between the tropic of Capricorn and the equator, nature had flipped itself like a coin and life and death now lay inverted.

I pitched my tent on moist, moss-covered wood that crumpled like day old crisps and watched from inside as moths, mosquitoes, stick insects, spiders, and a score of unidentifiable species drew in and reoccupied the ground I had stolen from them. Throughout the night, dew fell from the canopy above in solid drops onto the sea of leaves. With so much water in the air, I thought it was rain. Leaves came crashing to earth with such force that I shuddered to think of the noise if a tree were to fall and I was the only one to hear it.

Once, the hardest part of cooking dinner was collecting enough wood for a small fire. Now wood was plentiful but saturated with moisture, and I couldn't light it. Besides, there was rarely a clearing large enough and, irrationally, I feared burning the forest down, although I could barely keep a kindling bundle alight.

In the next big town, I visited a supermarket run by Lebanese businessmen, as they always were in Gabon and neighbouring countries, and bought a cheap Chinese imported gas stove. Next door in the hardware store, run by the Lebanese businessman's brother or best friend (I couldn't tell which) I bought a blue gas canister, and then I stocked up on lighters from a market stall. Everything still had its place – not always logical, but consistent nonetheless – that never changed.

In towns, hotels were now advertised with room rates by the hour and discounts for 24 hour stays. Otherwise they were unchanged. They ranged from respectable, clean en-suite rooms to dark-and-dingy mosquito-filled ones with a muddy walk to a latrine by torchlight. When I was soaked through and exhausted from a day cycling in the rain, I was willing to overlook the obvious deficiencies as long as there was a bucket of water and a bed.

People still sat around doing nothing, not because it was too hot, but because there was nothing better to do. They always talked and drank. Usually I listened and drank. Beer was an important part of any hour of the day in Cameroon and the Congo and that was fine with me.

Music proclaimed a similar importance and was boomed through loudspeakers that lined the roadside stalls. Decibels were deemed more important than melody so that only crackling noise with ear-splitting drumbeats reverberated down the road.

People were still surprised that I was cycling, and they still wanted a way to keep in touch. On passing a broken down bus, the driver asked where I was coming from and going to.

'From Yaoundé to the border at Eboro,' I replied.

'*Merde!*' was his ultimate proclamation, whereby several lingering passengers nodded in agreement.

'Can I have a lift?' one called out.

'Sure, I'm faster than your bus,' I replied in jest. 'I can take three of you on here.' I turned round and patted the back rack of the bike.

'No, no, just take me. Don't worry about the others,' he replied in all seriousness. And the last thing that reached my ears as I cycled into the distance was, '…1 38 26. Call me!'

People no longer asked if I was married, but what my mission was. They looked at me uncomprehendingly when I said I was just a tourist. They thought I must be a spy. Did you ever see James Bond on a pushbike? But they didn't know who he was.

They were under the impression that I must work for the government, which would pay me grandly to come to such a far-flung corner of the continent. There could be no other reason for my presence there. When I explained that I was cycling to South Africa, they asked whether the government was sponsoring the expedition, seemingly oblivious that times had changed since the first European explorers ventured inland. To say I was paying for it myself, they replied that I must be rich. I tried to explain that it did not cost much money to travel as I did. Could they not see that their bike had a motor and their trousers did not have holes in them? Still, we all agreed that it was a chance privilege that I had been born where I was, which allowed me a British passport and the opportunity to see the world, although if they were in my position, they would not have chosen this particular corner.

One teenage girl told me she was studying hard at school and hoping to go to college, 'I don't want to be grilling maize for the rest of my life. Tell me, what do I need to study to become a tourist like you?'

Fewer people saw me as a passport to England. It was always difficult to explain that my home may not be the promised land they imagined. It was a relief to not have to explain that I didn't have a friend or family member in the Foreign Office to whom I could go and ask a favour, to get my new friend from Ghana or Cameroon or wherever a visa. What was a man who looked after goats or grew manioc to do in London? These men looked at me like a naive child if I suggested that it might be better to be a farmer in Africa than without a job in England. As far as I could tell, you can get by with little money here. But my government would have to give them jobs and a home and take care of them if they got ill, they said.

When you are coming from two completely different backgrounds and points of view, it is impossible to find a common understanding.

It was not our languages that were incomprehensible to each other, but our lives.

You would be mistaken to think these were the only conversations I had with people I met. We also talked of sport and the weather, of food and drink, of politics, partying, and what we had done that day, or more commonly, what we should have done that would wait until tomorrow – sometimes interesting, at other times inane, and usually inconsequential – just chat.

One afternoon I talked with Yasmine who was only 22-years-old. With a fit lean body in tight black jeans I could not tell she had two sons, the eldest already eight. She showed me faded photos of them dressed up at school plays and parties. We sat behind the wooden bar under a corrugated iron roof when the plastic seats by the road filled with young men drinking beer and laughing loudly. We chatted as she fanned the stove with a piece of card to heat the coals. She spent her days grilling fish for anyone who wanted it and that was how she provided for her boys.

'I'm not married you know. I had my boys early, too early. I didn't know what I was doing, but I do love them. I love them so much. I'm so happy I've got them.' That was when she got out the photo album, and it seemed to me that they were her *raison d'être*. 'I would like to get married though, but this is a small place and it's hard to find a good man, especially because I'm so busy looking after my boys.'

'I know what you mean,' I said. 'Even in a big world it's hard to find a good man that isn't already taken,' and we both smiled a confiding conspiring sisterly smile.

She leant over towards me and whispered, 'Do you know anyone who might want to marry me? Perhaps when you return to England, you can ask any single male friends of yours if they would be interested. I can give you a photo to show them.' She flicked through her album. I started making a mental list of all the single men I knew and was surprised I had never done it before.

'I'll see what I can do,' I lied. I didn't have it in me to bring up the practical improbabilities; instead, I let the romantic idea roll on.

'Don't think I'm asking you because I want to live in England. Cameroon is my home, but I would leave if it meant I could find a good husband. I just don't want to live forever in this village.' I could understand that – I had grown up in a small village too.

* * *

A Land Rover drove past, stopped, and reversed. The window was wound down, and two white faces peered out. 'Are you Helen?' *Not again.*

'Yes,' I admitted hesitantly; for a short word, it took a long time to say.

'We were just talking about you.' *That's disconcerting.* I didn't say anything.

It transpired that they had just met another English cyclist. All the way from South Africa they had not met any, and now there were two of us, like buses, only slower.

I knew Wayne was ahead of me. He had heard about me at roadblocks in Nigeria and one of the police had passed on my email address. The day I left Yaoundé, I received a message from him and realised he was only half a day ahead, going the same way. Reports on the way had suggested I was catching him up. White cyclists do not go unnoticed here.

I caught him up later in the afternoon. We stayed at the Catholic Mission in town and spent the evening drinking beer as English cyclists in Gabon like to do. The nuns at the mission were not avid alcohol enthusiasts, but there were no attempts at conversion by either side, so we got along amicably.

My aching legs needed a rest day. Wayne needed to continue because of an expiring visa. That was what we told each other. In truth, we were both content cycling alone, which was fine because we owed each other nothing. That was the last time I expected to see Wayne as we had different routes planned from there on. You never can tell though.

It was a pleasant, peaceful morning following the bamboo-lined River Lara downstream, with few villages and little traffic. When I reached a sharp bend in the road I stopped by a rickety stall and bought food, parcel-wrapped in a large leaf and tied with vine. It was fresh, boiled fish in soup and tasted divine. But my body was craving carbohydrates, and for once there was nothing of the sort. I dug into my precious bread reserves while I debated which road to take.

The shortcut to Booué appealed. Firstly, it was shorter, although that did not mean it would take less time. Secondly, I was ready for an off-road adventure. Still, I was hesitant. When I had ventured into the unknown before, I'd had a good map and company. Now I was alone and could determine little from the inch-long line that joined my present location to the next place on the map. My GPS was useless – it gave my precise location, pinpointing me to the middle of empty space. It was hard to know if I had enough food. On top of that, a significant number of red blotches had appeared on my arms and legs, and they concerned me too as they didn't itch like bites. Heading further from 'civilisation' didn't seem wise. It is easy to find excuses when you want.

I looked down the laterite road and let logic and reason overcome my anxieties and tried to trust in my abilities and instincts. I made a mental check of my physical state: no fever or headache and my heart rate was normal; and a check of my questionable mental state: still normal. I could always turn back.

The dirt stuck to the hairs of my arms, flattened against my skin by the sweat that seeped from my pores with nowhere to go. Like a chameleon, I turned a bright orange of the earth as each logging truck thundered past and cloaked me in a cloud of dust. I stopped and squeezed my eyes shut and covered my mouth, and still I choked as the convoys rolled past. Then, once the dust settled and the silence overtook me, I continued.

Trees were being torn from Gabon's heart and carried down arterial tracks as loaded lumber. It was clear that logging was still a major source of income for Gabon, even if the economy is now sustained primarily from oil revenues.

Oil has made it relatively rich in this region and that was clear too. Houses were larger and made of more permanent materials, with fenced-in gardens, and goats grazing or laying on large ceramic-tiled memorials. The houses either had their own water pumps or were connected to a pipeline that ran through the front gardens. Grass verges were kept clean and cut short using a strimmer, not machetes. Restaurants had menus and more than one food to offer, and there were *salons du thé* and cafes serving real coffee and even one with a flat-screen TV. Most people spoke fluently in French as well as their native language. They dressed smarter too. I saw fewer children, and those I did were in school uniform. It was a long list of little things.

Once the last logging trucks passed by in mid-afternoon, there was nothing left except the forest and the flies. Sometimes there were sidetracks, and I took a couple in search of a place to camp. Even though the tracks were wide, they were carved deep from the earth, and either the verges were too steep to climb or the wall of nature too thick to pass. On the one occasion I saw an opening, there were deterring signs of several empty shotgun cartridges and the thick trail of a large snake.

As it was getting dark and I was coming round to the idea that I would have to forge my own trail into the forest, a gap appeared. An area the size of a tennis court had been cleared of trees. It was bumpy and uneven from the lorries that had churned up the earth, but it would suffice. I pitched the tent and started up my new stove to boil water. I had used it for coffee in the mornings, but this was to be the maiden meal.

I dismissed an uneasy feeling as an overactive imagination. In the pervading silence of the moonlit evening, I felt the forest watching me – the intruder. I scanned the trees with my head-torch, but it was weak and showed nothing except the moths and crickets that fluttered and jumped towards it. There was nothing but shadows. It was easy to understand why people used to believe in spirits, and still do.

Then, from the corner of my eye, I noticed a light near my tent. I spun round and saw a flame spouting from the stove. I ran and tried to turn it off, but the adjuster burnt to touch. I moved the stove further into the open and managed to save the half-cooked pasta. Wild flames engulfed the stove; they peeled round the bottom of the plastic casing, and I could do nothing but watch the ball of fire. The plastic blistered and bubbled, turned black, and melted. As the seal burnt through, the stove fell away from the base, and where the gas canister was pierced, a flame jet spewed several feet into the air burning blue and bright white. I watched, mesmerised.

In the end, I left it to collect some wood to make a controlled fire to cook on, and by the time my pasta was al dente, the jet had finally died down to a feeble outflow as the last gas particles burned. Once the prolonged firework display had finished, I was convinced that I was the only person in the vicinity – any people would have been drawn to the spectacular and any creatures would have been frightened away. I lay in my tent listening to the leaves that fell, and then I heard the crunching and cracking of someone, or something, trampling their way through the jungle. *It's probably a deer.*

Then, in the middle of the night, a vehicle stopped on the road. Separated by only a few bushes, I heard car doors open and three men talking. *What are they doing?* I heard the footsteps of one man come into the clearing. *He must have seen the tent.* The voices continued, muffled by the trees, but when a woman called from inside the car and the men laughed, I knew there was nothing sinister. The presence of a woman and laughter changed that. *But why, in this vast forest and long jungle road did they choose exactly this spot, beside my tent, to stop?* Some nights you get no peace.

Daylight brought with it bees under the fly sheet and an incessant hum, which was worse than an alarm clock that cannot be stopped.

The road narrowed into deep, pristine jungle – wilder, older, taller. With no people to make their mark, it had taken on its own character, an amalgam of all the animals that lived within it. Although I couldn't see them, it was as though they spoke to me through the breeze on the leaves of the tall-standing ancient trees and the call of the birds.

There was a loud, slow *whoop* of air being forced aside by the strong wings of a large bird, and then at the very top of the tallest trees, way up on the hillside, I heard a rustling of leaves and saw several sandy bodies, with long limbs and dextrous tails, leaping between branches and disappearing deeper into the forest. Then nothing – as though the monkeys had alerted all of nature to my presence.

Chance encounters with wildlife in the wild like that were a humbling privilege, made all the more special because only I was there to experience it. While I may regale friends and strangers with tales of mishap and madness from this journey, it was those moments that were the most magical and what I remember most clearly. Those were the moments that made me stop in my tracks because I realised – and I took a slow deep breath and savoured the sweetness of the air – *Wow, I am the luckiest girl alive.* And it made me want to jump and shout and tell the world about it.

It was midday and even the cicadas were silent; it was too hot to stay still for long. Besides, the profusion of flies that descended on me when I stopped was unbearable. It was better to cycle and feel a breeze. If I pedalled fast enough I could outpace the flies, but the slightest incline or corrugations and they launched another attack. They buzzed around my ears and eyes and nose, and landed on my arms. To swat them by cycling one-handed over the rough ground risked a swift exit from the bike. It was the ones hitching on my handlebar bag that infuriated me the most. I hated their ugly, fat, raisin-like bodies and blood-red eyes, and I flicked them away in disgust. But they always came back.

As I entered the next village, the flies dispersed; there were always fewer flies in village clearings. I filled my empty water bottles at the pump and guzzled a litre immediately because I had run out a while back and was mouth-dry parched where my tongue stuck to the roof of my palate and I struggled to swallow.

Soon after that, I felt weak and nauseous. I ate the last half of a squashed banana and pushed my bike up the hill. Still queasy, stomach-uneasy when I reached the top, I celebrated by hurling half the contents of my bloated belly into the ditch. An old man pushing his bike came over the hill, saw me, and stopped. He stared at me draped limply over my bike. I looked up at him and then dropped my head again and spat. We were both motionless twin peaks on the hilltop. Then I vomited the other half of my stomach contents. When I looked up, wiping my mouth on my shirt, wishing I had something to drink that wouldn't make me puke, the man broke his frozen stance, nodded to me because he realised I wasn't spitting at him and continued past without a word. I stayed rooted to the spot until I could muster the energy to move.

Those last kilometres into Booué were a struggle. I announced my arrival in the town square by throwing up against the telegraph pole. Now everyone in the shops and dusty street stopped what they were doing and stared as my body convulsively drained every last drop from me. When there was nothing left, and I was retching like a cat with a fur-ball stuck down its throat, a hand touched my shoulder and a voice said, 'Ça va bien?' *Well, of course I'm not OK.* I didn't say that though, not because I never say what I mean, but because I was trying to detach myself from the drool that was hanging from my mouth and reaching for the floor. I used my shirt sleeve again.

'Ça va bien, madame?'

'I'll be fine,' I said with a sore throat and bilious taste in my mouth. 'I think I just need some water.' The man shouted to someone, and soon I had a cold bottle of mineral water in my hand. I took a cautious sip followed by long swigs and instantly regretted it. The water ricocheted off my stomach and onto the telegraph pole again. I doubled over from acute embarrassment. Such are the hazards and diversions of travel in Africa.

19

Sandy Tracks and the President's Driveway

Gabon and the Congo

After a tortuous, torpid, bedridden day in the tropics, I forced myself to look around the town. It reminded me of Kouroussa in Guinea, with its tumbledown colonial buildings among the overgrown and recently burnt grass.

Booué lies on the wide Ogooué River, which spans the country from the Republic of Congo to the Atlantic Sea. The brilliant blue water is lined by golden sandbanks and palms, and the flow is broken by glistening black rocks poking above the surface to the horizon and beyond where cataracts churn the water white.

Two Europeans of note travelled to Gabon at the end of the nineteenth century and explored this river. One was an English lady, Mary Kingsley. With little more than unsuitable Victorian dresses, a keen eye and sharp wit, she ventured into the interior employing the aid of the local Fan people with the aim of studying the fish, botany, and other biology besides. She did it neither for fame nor fortune nor going where other Europeans had never gone before; although, she sometimes went where the locals feared to follow. She did it for science and curiosity's sake. A typical woman, maybe, except made of steelier stuff than her time deemed tolerable.

Heedless of danger, she jumped into things with little thought for the consequences. If the risks were pointed out by more cautious souls, she merely brushed them aside and commented on the upside. There is always an upside.

Mary Kingsley only travelled as far upstream as Ndjole, which is downstream of Booué where I met the river. In between, the forest has been named Lopé National Park, the allure of which was overpowered by my lack of energy. I heard from others later who drove through there that it was a severe disappointment. Tracts of

Gabon's forests have been named a National Park for the reserve of wildlife only now that all the mineral wealth has been extracted, the land fully exploited, and its assets expended.

The first European to explore the river, twenty years before Kingsley, was Pierre Savorgnan de Brazza. Born in Italy with the name Pietro, which he later changed, he was always fascinated with exploration. With strong connections in France, he joined the French navy and travelled to Gabon on the boat *Venus*. With the help of influential friends, he obtained French government approval to explore the Ogooué River to its source. He hoped to find out what lay beyond.

Brazza travelled with three fellow white companions, ten Senegalese sailors, and a number of Gabonese guides, interpreters, and boatmen in nine canoes. Most of the cost was funded from his own pocket, and he carried few trade goods beyond a few trinkets and some fireworks for entertainment.

Looking down to the Ogooué River, I saw the rail line linking Libreville on the coast to Franceville, which was founded by Brazza in 1880 for resettling former slaves. That was where I was going next. The rail line gave me an alternative to recuperating in a hotel I could not afford in a town with no distractions. Cycling at this stage was not a realistic option.

The train stopped at three in the morning, which gave me ample time to make two more tours of the town. I walked past the concrete statue of a train, commemorating the day that Booué was connected with the rest of the country, and past an Independence Day memorial, commemorating the day in 1960 that Gabon elected their first president, Léon M'ba.

M'ba's campaign had been heavily funded by French logging interests and there was widespread discontent. As was commonly the case, an army coup followed four years later. It was quashed when French paratroopers, in a blatant act of self-interest, flew in to restore M'ba to power. It was only when M'ba died that his vice-president, Omar Bongo Ondimba, took over.

Ondimba ruled Gabon as his own private estate, happily transferring money from state coffers into his personal bank accounts for 42 years. His presidency ended in 2009 when he, too, died. Bongo's son was elected the successor. Democracy is a wonderful ideal.

Besides the two statues, there was little else except some dogs asleep in the dusty road and a handful of taxis that passed on their circuit between the town and the train station. There was no other traffic – it is hard to get a vehicle here. I could see no reason for the train station being a few kilometres from the town centre. Town planning appeared entirely focussed on making the most of the available space, of which there was a lot, spread out simply because it could be.

Once I had exhausted myself exhausting the sights, I cycled to the station and discovered the reason for the town's lack of life. Everything was there. Goods arrive by train to be sold, so the market is naturally near the station, and where there is a market, there are people. Where there are people travelling and trading, there will be a supply of cheap lugubrious accommodation. When I discovered this I had already bought my ticket. The appeal of Franceville, being one of the larger cities in Gabon, was too great.

Like the rail line in Mauritania, the trans-Gabon railway's primary function is for transporting ore from the inland mines to the coast. There used to be a Cableway for this, but it went via the Republic of Congo, so the railway was built to keep the manganese in the country, under Bongo's tight control.

The train is also used for passengers. Considering the state of the roads, it is understandable why the carriages were full when I squeezed onto the compartment bench. It is the easiest, quickest way to travel for the majority who cannot afford to fly. Compared to cycling, it felt like flying as the train glided through the night smoothly towards dawn. Swiftly and steadily, it steamrolled on, from the forest wilderness with clearings only for a village or pile of lumber to the deforested hills that reminded me of a bleak and beautiful Wales. It only slowed down to halt at a station where people lined the tracks surrounded by bags, ready to meet and greet or clamber aboard.

I sat and watched and drifted to sleep, and woke when my head banged the window or someone near me moved. If you don't mind being squeezed into a tight spot for eight hours, it was a pleasant enough way to travel through the country, and more so than the Mauritanian dust trap.

The hotels in Franceville were above my meagre price range, so I went to the smartest one, as they were usually run by an expat European, and asked if I could camp discreetly on a patch of grass or the corner of the car-park. The owner was happy to oblige. For his generosity, I spent the money I saved twice over in the bar. This was common practise.

After a few days of rest, I was straining at the bit to test my resolve on what was a notoriously tough track across the border. There was no hesitation or doubt in my mind this time.

The 'tough track' to the border began with inexplicably smooth tarmac. By this stage I had learnt not to question and simply accept things the way they were. Reasons usually became clear if I was patient; if they didn't, it was reasonable to assume there wasn't one.

The tarmac passed through the village of Lewai, although it was no longer called this and was more of a town. Lewai was the birthplace of the president, Omar Bongo. With extreme hubristic tendencies, he renamed it Bongoville and channelled state funds into several glorifying public works that distributed the oil money into the hands of his Bateke tribe's elite. Bongoville is now home to an Olympic-size soccer stadium. This explained the tarmac road. There is also a Bongo airport, Bongo University, Bongo Gymnasium, and some Bongo hospitals throughout the country to his name.

It is said that one time Omar Bongo vouched to make a multi-million dollar donation to charity, and when a diplomat asked whether it would come from public or private funds, he was truly bewildered that there was a difference between them.

The tarmac road ended abruptly at a large signpost indicating a right turn to the Republic of Congo. *This is where the fun begins.* There was nothing except a deep sandy track running like a scar across the green grassland savannah until it disappeared over the horizon. The equatorial forest was behind me, for now. Beyond the horizon, fourteen kilometres later, I would find immigration.

I turned the bike around and pedalled furiously for the sand pit. In sand, speed is your friend. Low gear, legs spinning. The wheels hit the sand, slipped and slid, and I fought to steer straight and keep the speed up. The back wheel spun, and we sank and stopped. *Sigh. All that effort for a measly ten metres.*

I pushed the bike onto level sand for attempt number two: a non-starter. Number three: failure. It was futile. There was only one solution: push. *This is not going to be fun after all.*

I dragged and pushed and sweated and strained, then stopped to catch my breath. *Calm down. Try again.* I dragged and pushed with sand filling my shoes and sweat streaming down my neck under the illusion that by pushing as hard as possible I would reach the immigration post quicker, so I could put this sandy episode behind me sooner. How naive. There was only one speed – painfully slow. The sand continued.

While eating biscuits I considered whether to give in gracefully and hitch a ride. *No, don't be such a wuss. You finally got what you're looking for, and now it doesn't look so good – tough.* I resolved to slog it out. There was no one to hitch a ride with anyway.

After a few more hours, I finally reached immigration and was absolutely shattered. In the bamboo frame shack, the officer sat behind a wooden desk studying my passport and reading every stamp. I sat down on a wicker chair, emptied my shoes and removed what was left of my socks. Realising this grave error as a pungent odour arose, I rushed outside, washed my feet, buried the socks, and studied the blisters and raw rotting skin. I retrieved plasters and the last pair of socks from my panniers, bandaged up my festering feet, and returned to the shack. The officer was busy copying all the details from my passport, or writing a poem for the time and concentration it was taking.

I leant back in the wicker chair and closed my eyes. Somewhere in trying to calculate times and distances and average speeds and how many days it would take to reach the main road if I kept up this pathetic pace and where I might be able to buy surely needed extra food, I fell asleep.

'Excuse me, madam. Madam?' The officer was leaning over his desk with an outstretched arm, 'Your passport.'

I opened my eyes and was sorely disappointed to see that nothing had changed. I was still in the arse-end of nowhere. I feigned a smile, said thank you, took my passport, and sat back. Noticing my reticence to leave, the officer invited me to stay and rest in his quarters. I made assumptions of misguided intentions and declined. He offered me a drink instead.

'But I can only offer you water, I'm afraid. It's all there is left.'

His quarters stood adjacent to the identical rustic 'office' and served as bedroom, kitchen and lounge. This was his home. Once every couple of weeks, he or his co-worker took the motorbike to Mbie for more supplies, and once every two or three months they went further afield. It surprised me that he was content passing his time in solitude where there was little to do except collect water every couple of days.

'I like it here. It is peaceful, and I have everything I need,' he said. He did have a point.

After another hour on the road, it became possible to cycle short sections and, eventually, the road descended down and down until I came to the village of Mbie. It was a short-lived elation, when the policeman said there was no shop and no food to buy. He suggested the best thing to do would be to camp within the compound and continue the next morning. The tipping point was when he mentioned I could have a shower. He meant a bucket shower, but it was still a chance to wash. I leapt at the chance of anything that would calm the itching of the sandfly bites that covered my body.

Once clean, I rested in my tent and read, involuntarily scratching in my upturned-beetle legs-in-the-air position. When evening came I talked with the policeman over a beer. Dmitri had grown up in Pointe

Noire, a modern city on the coast. He was a long way from home and despondently bored with the monotony of the three months' backwater posting. It was not what he had in mind when he joined the police, but he followed orders and went where sent.

The officer at the border had been a man in his late fifties who had experienced what he wanted to in life and was now happy to while away any extra hours he was granted in relative peace. It was different for Dmitri, a young officer with high hopes and dreams. He would not realise them here.

'There is nothing to do, besides drink,' he said. We were on our third bottle by then. 'I do my job, but that doesn't take much time because there is never trouble here. At the end of the day I come here and eat dinner and drink beer, and there's no TV, so I just go to bed, in there.' He pointed through the doorway of his rustic hut that was dimly lit by a kerosene lamp with fumes that burned the back of my throat. 'So tonight is just like every night except you are here. And we are talking, and when we have finished drinking, I will go to my bed in my room and you will go to your bed outside in your tent. It's a shame for us both to sleep alone when we could easily sleep together. It's always better to have company, don't you think?'

I tried to decide if I had misjudged Dmitri as harmless and whether camping where there was only this armed man was a sensible thing to do. I instinctively scanned the room for exits and other weapons. I wondered how I would cope if I did have to put up a fight. I liked to think, as all girls do, that I would put up a good fight, just as all men think they are good drivers. Most likely, I would fight like a girl with no fingernails and only flailing arms and pathetic palm slaps.

'Sometimes it is good to be alone,' I pondered.

'Yes, but I am alone a lot, and tonight I don't have to be if you don't want either.'

'Well, thanks anyway, but I'm going to sleep in my tent tonight,' I replied as if I had simply turned down an offer of coffee. And that was that. We finished the beer and went to our own beds, alone.

The tarmac road ran down from the police compound to a bridge, across the river, and up the other side where it ended. From then on it was sand and dust. I cycled when I could, and if my pannier came off as it jammed against the dirt, I stopped and picked it up, and when I couldn't cycle, I pushed or dragged or carried the bike. When the sandflies became too much, I changed out of my shorts and put on my trousers despite the heat and humidity, and I realised I should have changed much earlier because my cycle shorts were not made for walking in and had rubbed me raw. I didn't consider giving up, but just accepted it calmly as the way it was to be. I wouldn't have accepted a lift then even if a truck had come by, which it didn't. The only truck was stranded, dug into the middle of the road, sand up to the undercarriage and cabin tipped forward, in a poor state for repair. It had been stuck for three days. A road that you can walk faster than you can drive deserves a different name.

As the light faded and I reached Okoyo, I asked a lady sat by the roadside to direct me to a hotel if there were one or to the *gendarmerie*. 'Come,' she beckoned and I followed her down to a concrete compound with high walls and wire running along the top like a prison. 'Follow me,' she said when I halted outside the gate.

Inside, there were two blocks of buildings facing each other. She walked to one of the doors and knocked. I heard voices, and then Michel, a Frenchman, called me inside. He showed me the spare bedroom and gave me towels for a bath and told me to make myself at home. He had to go out, but would be back later, and if I needed anything to just ask Roger the cook or Aurelle the cleaner. Then, like a whirlwind, he was gone, leaving me dazed and confused.

It was an air-conditioned, beautifully furnished apartment with a blend of Moroccan and oriental styles, a flush toilet and actual bath in the bathroom, a large sofa and huge TV in the lounge, and a big double bed in my own room, to sleep in, alone. I couldn't believe my luck. *Who is this guy?*

'Roger!' someone squawked. 'Koh-koh-koh.' That's what people say when they come to your house. It hails from the days when houses didn't have solid doors, so people imitated a knocking sound to announce their arrival. 'Koh-koh-koh, Roger!'

Roger didn't appear, so I went to the front door and opened it. No one was there – strange.

'Roger!' I jumped and spun round and there, in the corner, was an African grey parrot watching me with his beady eye, 'Roger!' *Idiot.*

The following day that parrot had me looking in the microwave to see what was cooking. 'Beep-Beep. Beeeep, Roger!' Roger was a wanted man – no wonder he kept himself scarce.

Michel worked for a German engineering firm and was overseeing construction of the Oyo-Boundji-Okoyo road by the Chinese. It was the first stage for a fully paved trans-equatorial road linking the Congo with Gabon. He said he had been working there too long. He looked tired and jaded and came back each lunchtime to sleep. In the evenings, he regaled me with stories of how it was impossible to get work done in the country and to get it done well was another thing entirely.

Michel promised me that the hard part was over. It had taken only two days from Gabon. I had expected worse – I was a little disappointed. Hardships are quickly forgotten when surrounded by the luxuries of modern living.

It was hard to imagine that in 1878 Brazza had been forced to turn back near here. Once Brazza had gone as far up the Ogooué River as possible, he had continued over land and reached the Alima River in the Bateke tribe's territory. He was told that the clear water came from a big river that flowed north and then east, on which sailed many pirogues from far off places to trade with the locals. Brazza wondered if this water were indeed the Congo River, which was what he was searching for. Despite the warnings, Brazza left the safety of the Bateke's land and continued his search. However, he was forced to retreat by the fearsome Apfourou tribe with their cannibalistic war-cries when he ran low on ammunition. He had been only 100 miles away from the Congo River when he had to turn back.

At the same time Brazza was exploring the Ogooué, an Englishman was making his way west from the East African Lakes along the Congo River, which he called 'The Livingstone'. Henry Morton Stanley was being financed by *The Daily Telegraph* to solve the last great mystery on the African continent, by tracing the Congo River from source to sea. Stanley reached the sea after 999 days, exhausted and half-starved.

Whereas Brazza had travelled by river, I continued along the sandy road across open savannah that was split by shrubs and sporadic copses. When I passed through villages, I saw women carrying oriental parasols to shelter from the sun – a sign that the Chinese influence had extended beyond construction.

When I reached Boundji, as Michel had promised, the tarmac started. Then it was a smooth ride to Oyo where there were vast administrative offices, hotels, a massive sports complex, wide avenues and obligatory statues, as well as a large airport, devoid of planes, on the outskirts. The home village of the Republic of Congo's president, Sassou-Nguesso, lies just north of here. Like Bongoville in Gabon, the money has flooded in.

Along the Alima River, which flows on the south side of town, luxury powerboats glistened in the sun, and I thought of Henley-on-Thames gone tropical. The opulence of Oyo did not extend far along the 'President's Driveway' to Brazzaville. In the next town the market was eerily devoid of produce. It was a far cry from the 'colourful and lively' markets of West Africa. The villages were little more than a few rectangular huts with large barrels at their corners to collect rain water – the only accessible drinking water.

There was little traffic on the road too. Several locals were on bicycles, and occasionally a truck passed, overloaded with goods. People sat precariously on top, bleating goats were tied to the sides in three lines like bunting with legs and bodies bound, and a bundle of empty jerry cans sprouted from the back like a bunch of balloons.

Eventually, there were no more villages, and I wound through green, rolling hills that gradually became more rugged with rocky outcrops. Then the road rose steeply to a plateau. It was a bleak, washed out day – I could have been in Wales. The clouds hung low, clinging to the cliff top that rose formidably up ahead, and the air was full of moisture.

By the time I reached the first village on the plateau, the wind had picked up. It was the prelude to a deluge I had no desire to be caught in. So I sat in an open-sided shed with two other guys, and we watched the trees thrashing in the wind and the dirt whipping up and swirling in the air. People rushed to their houses, frantically finishing whatever they had been doing. Everyone knew the rain was coming and no one wanted to get wet. Then the wind died down, and for a short while there was calm. That was always the way.

Then it started – there was no gradual build up. Instantly, torrents of water streamed down, shattering the silence as it pounded the ground with a forceful rebound. We shouted to be heard, but soon gave up and watched the water fall in streams. Only trucks driven by the Chinese thundered past in a cloud of spray.

When the rain stopped it was late afternoon and people began to grill food by the roadside. Smells of marinated meat drifted on the cool breeze, tempting me to stop. I did, and I devoured half a chicken and drank a bottle of beer.

The road descended from the plateau, but before I reached the city centre, there was Poto-Poto – a chaotic mess of traffic and people – to negotiate. It was as though the whole population of the Republic of Congo was crammed into this one suburb.

Poto-Poto was originally demarcated by French colonisers in 1909 as a residential neighbourhood for African and migrant workers. The centre of Brazzaville was reserved exclusively for white residents only. I could see the Nabemba tower, the city's sole skyscraper reaching out of the sprawl like a beacon. It looked impressive, as it should do. It cost six million dollars to reconstruct in 1997 after it was damaged during the civil war. Its maintenance costs alone are supposedly three million dollars each year, which is money the government could surely put to better use.

Brazzaville centre is a modern city with a distinct French flavour. I spent several days wandering down the wide, tree-lined avenues running through the exclusive embassy district and down the high street filled with suited men walking on the pavements, and reading a newspaper and drinking coffee in the cafes. There was an abundance of excellent restaurants, mainly Lebanese owned, where I ate cheap shawarma and chips, or pizza and ice cream. There was no shortage of bars either, or beer. I had nothing that needed to be done; it was pure indulgence that I stayed a few days.

From here my plan was to take the ferry to Kinshasa. I had no idea what to expect there or in the whole Democratic Republic of Congo, often referred to simply as the DRC or Congo. The only thing I did know was that it would be very different to this taste of Europe.

First, I had to get there, across the Congo River.

20

The Congo River and Kinshasa

DRC

Getting in to the DRC was surprisingly easy. There was never a time when I thought I would not be able to enter (leaving was another story). The only uncertainty was how much it would cost. If I had come straight from home and landed on *The Beach*, the name given to Brazzaville's port, I would have been overwhelmed by the chaos. Now, it was just another game. Navigating *The Beach*'s bonkers bureaucracy was like a treasure hunt in a lunatic asylum.

First, I paid to enter. I gave the man stopping the taxis a few notes and was handed a receipt in return, as if that piece of paper made it official. I then flew straight into the cuckoo's nest on my bike and quickly stopped. There were no signs or indications of which way to go, and it was impossible to tell the difference between those in charge, un-officials and other passengers.

I tried to buy a ticket from the disinterested figure behind one counter. When he could no longer ignore my incessant demands for attention, he told me this was not the ticket office. He indicated I should leave by pointing at the door. The ticket office was a small plain room with two desks stacked high with paperwork and three men sat talking. I couldn't buy a ticket because they needed my immigration form. They said I could get that from the office I had just come from.

Back to being ignored in the immigration office, the disinterested figure pointed at the form to be filled in. He checked my passport, stamped the form, and then demanded money. No one else was paying, so I refused. I waited; he ignored me. I got angry; he ignored me. He, apparently, needed to write my ticket number on the form before handing it over. You get a ticket number for the immigration form by buying a ticket, but you can't get a ticket until you have a completed immigration form. *Sigh.*

Bemused and bewildered by this Catch-22, I explained the quandary. He reluctantly gave me the form, but retained my passport. I returned to the ticket office to buy a ticket, but now they needed to see both the immigration form *and* my passport. *Enough of this ludicrous nonsense.*

I marched right back into the immigration office, leant over the counter, picked up my passport while the man had his back turned, and walked straight out with the was-disinterested figure now very much noticing my actions and shouting that I owed money and must be stopped. His demands fell on deaf ears.

Back at the ticket office, I handed over the form and passport and money and asked for a ticket for me and the bike. But, they said this ticket office was for passengers only they. As I had baggage I must buy my ticket elsewhere. So I wheeled my bike further into the port where police and touts and people with piles of bags and sacks lingered.

There was one desk to buy tickets for passengers who had luggage, another one to buy tickets for the luggage, and then a third to pay for a baggage handler, who was required to handle the luggage, regardless of whether you could carry it or not. Wheeling the bike on board myself was not an option. So I walked across the ramp with my handful of tickets, followed by a teenage boy in a bright bib wheeling my bike. The tickets I had bought were checked by other officials, one for each ticket, and then, finally, I was allowed on the boat.

It was only twenty minutes late leaving. Sometimes it is good to wait. I spent five minutes speculating how the officials, touts and hawkers at the Kinshasa port were going to extort money from me and the other fifteen talking to officials and other locals sprawled atop sackfuls of merchandise. I soon had a small army of Congolese willing to escort me through the port and border formalities on the other side. Of course, I suspected they were only helping because they wanted money, but I played the game and left that fight for later.

The polio-afflicted and other physically disabled, whether paraplegic or an amputee through a traffic accident or the recent civil war, were carried to the front and sat upon a jerry can or, if they had one, a wheelchair. There was a surprisingly large number of them compared to other passengers. There was little room for sympathy, and no one was asking for it. On the contrary, the disabled women were confident and commanding, issuing orders to the *bagagistes*.

Thanks to a law passed by the ex-president Mobutu in the seventies, disabled passengers are exempt from paying taxes on their transported goods. They also receive a discounted ferry ticket on Mondays, Wednesdays and Fridays. Whereas their disabilities may have once left these traders stigmatised and with no source of income other than through begging, they can now use this tax-free status to their financial benefit. Since the average cost of return travel between the two cities is 40 dollars, which is what most people earn in a month here, ferry travel for trade is largely inaccessible to the able-bodied, who also struggle to earn a living here.

It was a grey, cloud-covered day, the water was choppy and the wind chilly. Slowly, Kinshasa's skyline grew larger and emerged from the haze. The industrial port outline of cranes and crates hid the city's true identity, whose spirit of ten million souls sprawled far beyond.

Barely two steps off the boat at the Kinshasa port, my passport was demanded by the first uniformed official to see me. The dilemma was whether to stay with my bike or follow the official with my passport. I followed the official. He said my bike would be safe with the *bagagiste,* and he was not someone you disobey, white tourist or Congolese porter. Taken into a small office, I shook hands with the boss who had two young men employed under him. It took both men the best part of an hour to record my passport details onto a piece of paper.

If your passport is nearly full, it is worth getting a new one before coming to the DRC. Congolese immigration officials love passports and paperwork. Every official wanted to make a copy of every detail.

It doesn't matter that you might have travelled through Guatemala ten years ago, the information will be recorded. Thankfully, my passport was only four months old. No doubt, if I had shown an expired house insurance or Tesco's shopping receipt from three months ago, by the end of the day a hand-written copy would have been made and at least twenty friendly but curious Congolese would have scrutinised it, asked an array of irrelevant questions, and known more about me than some of my best friends.

It was a relief to find the *bagagiste* and my bike exactly where I had left them. He looked anxious and apologised greatly because he now had to catch the return ferry. I didn't even get a chance to tip him before he rushed off. From there, I simply walked out through the port gates.

Welcome to Kinshasa.

* * *

Chris was a South African living and working in the city. He had a small modern flat and offered me the sofa to sleep on while I waited for a package of bike parts to arrive and worked out how to cross the country.

My first idea was to take a barge up the Congo River, following Stanley's route to Kisangani, called Stanleyville during colonial times, and then continue overland on my bike to Rwanda. If that was not going to work, for logistical or safety reasons, I could go by boat to Ilebo on the Kasai River and continue east from there. Besides flying, river transport is the main mode of long distance travel; for that reason, a journey by boat appealed. Alternatively, I could cycle the main road, and then continue east to the Tanzanian border. If that was not possible for some unforeseen reason, I could take the road all the way to Lubumbashi in the south-east and continue into Zambia. As a back-up, I made several trips to numerous cashpoints in Kinshasa until I had enough dollars to last me three months and to pay my way out by any means, if I absolutely had to.

I walked down to the river station from where boats for upriver left. The gate was padlocked shut, but an adolescent barefooted boy in ragged shorts told me there was another way in. I followed Danny over a semi-collapsed stone wall, across wasteland, and into the port where several large barges in various states of rusting decay were chained. The man I spoke to owned one that would be leaving for Ilebo in a few weeks' time. The no-frills boat looked river-worthy to my untrained eye: it was floating. The barge from Kisangani was expected any day, which meant it might arrive tomorrow or in two week's time and then who knew when it would leave.

Meanwhile I visited the tourist office, out of curiosity rather than expecting useful information. It was a series of rooms in an office block, with the most important person on the top floor where the air was fresher and there was more light from the window. We laid out maps and discussed possible routes and places to avoid. No one foresaw any problems although the boss gave me his phone number in case of an emergency. I failed to mention that I didn't have a phone, and he forgot to mention that he could not have done anything anyway.

My guidebook said that describing what 'to do' in Kinshasa was difficult; it is a city 'low on sights, but high on atmosphere'. But that is true of many African capital cities.

Kinshasa's main street is named after Independence Day, *Boulevard de 30 Juin*. The road had been resurfaced to celebrate fifty years of independence since 1960. Now there was an eight-lane highway complete with pedestrian crossings. Generally, African drivers are bad drivers, and the Congolese were no exception. They drove fast down the centre of the road regardless of oncoming traffic, possibly because on most roads there was no oncoming traffic. Confronted with black and white stripes on the boulevard, the cars all stopped, probably because the drivers didn't know the rules or what else to do. This order among chaos meant that this road was one of the safest in Africa to cross. However, if you were simply walking along the roadside that had no pavement, the chance of being hit by one of the speeding blue and yellow minibuses was high. I also had to watch out for the *pousse-pousseurs*, boys pushing registered carts – Congo's capital courier service – who had goods to deliver and paid scant attention to the idle ambler.

Kinshasa has a massive expat community. I saw them through tinted windows of shining Land Cruisers and in the supermarkets full of imported goods. The rest of their time was spent hidden behind crumbling walls that on the inside have air-conditioned rooms, swimming pools, and fully stocked bars at European prices. Walking along the streets, I would never have known these elite enclaves existed. It is not how the majority of Kinshasa's residents live, most of whom survive on less than a dollar a day. In some households the boys eat one day and the girls the next, and when they don't eat, they will be trying to earn money any way they can.

The main thing to do in Kinshasa is to drink beer. Most African countries have one brewery that brews one beer, like Castel, Flag, or Star. The DRC has several breweries and several different beers and countless bars in the capital at which to drink them.

In the seventies, as part of Mobutu's *Zairanisation* programme, he nationalised the entire industrial sector. Run on a political basis rather than with good business practises, many companies were bled dry financially. The breweries are one of the few industries that survived and, now privatised, they are thriving. In Kinshasa, Primus was the prime choice of beer, but I also drank Doppel, Turbo King and Mutzig. Ngok has a crocodile on the label and is imported from across the river. The beer doesn't travel well though, so as I moved across the country I became familiar with Skol and then Simba (meaning Lion) and Tembo (meaning Elephant), which are produced at the Katanga Brewery in the south-east.

I quenched my thirst at street-side bars where I shared a plate of goat meat and watched the world walk on by. There was not much else to do. The rich aroma of meat juices and fat dripping from the grill wafted by, and the smoke hung low in the sultry air.

With each day, more clouds appeared in the afternoon sky. The rains were on their way and it was only a matter of time until the air could no longer hold it back. It was still early in the season, but like most things here, it runs on its own schedule and cannot be predicted from one year to the next. I only hoped that I would be well on my way before the rains came.

The replacement bike parts arrived at the embassy. Inside the high-walled secure compound was everything a diplomat needed. A colonial era throwback, they lived in modern, furnished apartments, and had someone to clean and cook, so they could go to the bar for an evening drink after a swim, and hob-nob with colleagues and partners over dinner or some after-work club, all without leaving the safety of the embassy grounds or talking with a local *Kinois*. It was not really my style. I turned down an invitation to a garden party in favour of an evening with Chris and his friends drinking beer in Kinshasa's bars and clubs.

The barge from Kisangani had still not arrived over a week later. I decided then to cross the DRC by bike. I could be halfway across the country before the next barge even left. I had already made a two-day excursion to visit some of the sights around Kinshasa and the Bas-Congo province. The 200-kilometre tour and two weeks I spent in Kinshasa showed me enough to realise that there was nothing to fear about setting off across the country. So it was that I left Kinshasa on my bike, no longer with trepidation but with excitement.

21

Cycling Across the Congo

DRC

It was a pleasant surprise to discover that the first 500 kilometres through the country to Kikwit were smooth tarmac across a plateau that lay like a flamenco dancer's dress with pleats of rich green grassland falling gracefully into valleys, fed by the fresh waters of the Congo River Basin.

In the fifty years since the Belgians left, almost nothing has been done to improve, let alone maintain, the infrastructure. Now the Chinese, who are good at building roads, are here. However, there are still few vehicles to be driven and fewer reasons to drive. There are other ways to get around – rivers do not require maintenance.

Of the few decrepit trucks that make a journey, fewer reach their destination. I saw more abandoned skeletons of lorries and trucks in mid-repair than moving vehicles. People who made the journey spent most of the time waiting for repairs or walking up the hills, both because the engines were knackered. The advantage for me was that on every steep hill there were willing volunteers to help me push the bike.

Despite the huge natural resources in the country, nothing is manufactured except beer and cheap cigarettes. It is as though they are the only industries untouched by war, when everything else has been destroyed, because everyone, regardless of which side they support, knows that when peace comes and there is nothing left, life still goes on and you can survive without these things as long as there are beer and cigarettes to give some small pleasures.

Everything else is imported. Central Africa is largely forest and you need only one tree to make a thousand matches (so the song goes), yet still the DRC imports them from South Africa (with a lion on the box) and India (with a tiger on the box). It was no surprise to see that all the vehicles were imported too. There were new 4x4s driven up from South Africa as well as used vehicles that have surpassed their useful life where they originated, like the bright red 'bristolbusandcoach.co.uk Every 20mins!' bus I saw in the middle of Bandundu province, which probably passes every 20 days. There is always another use for things here.

There were several small villages between Kinshasa and Kikwit. I could see them from a long way off by the cluster of trees on the otherwise sparsely covered horizon. Each village was a small collection of simple palm-thatched huts lining the roadside. The bigger villages also had a couple of kiosks that were run independently, open all hours, and sold the same cheap supplies. Unfortunately, they lacked in diversity as well as quality. If powdered milk, glucose biscuits, cigarettes, sugar, tinned tomato puree, or Maggi stock cubes were on the shopping list, you could get them there. For everything else, they were out of stock.

There was no difficulty finding fresh fruit and vegetables: mangoes, bananas, pineapples, and peanuts. They were all readily available to buy at source, although surprisingly lacking in the nearest town market. When I craved mangoes, I simply looked for a mango tree; there was one in every village. In one village, I asked the elderly lady with the toothless smile if I could buy some mangoes from her. Her smile widened, but that did not mean yes. She did not understand what I had said because I was speaking French and she knew only the local languages, Lingala and Kikongo. She was smiling because I was a white foreigner and had stopped to speak with her. I took out some dirty Congolese francs and pointed to the mango tree. Instantly, the toothless lady had a team of small boys scrambling with long sticks and soon it was raining mangoes.

When I entered a village, the children, and often the women too, called out, '*Mondelé!*' which is Lingala for 'white'. At least it made a change from *le blanc*, *branco*, *toubab, oporto,* or *obroni*. They shouted and waved and ran down to the roadside to watch me with big smiles.

When I stopped, I was surrounded and bombarded with youngsters wanting to practise their French. '*Bonjour, maman. Comment ça va? Comment t'appeles tu?'* If I replied to one, the rest asked the same question and each wanted an answer. It was tedious saying that I was fine over and over, especially when I really was not fine because I was tired and hungry and just wanted some peace and quiet.

The best thing was not to stop in a village. The problem was that many villages were at the bottom of a hill, being closer to water. Therefore, leaving was an uphill slog at a pace that the entire village could keep up. There was no escape; I could not outrun the masses.

When tired, my frustration grew as the children's screams pierced my ears, and their hands on the back of the bike made it wobble, and I fought to stop it falling over. When I shouted back, the children momentarily stopped in their tracks, stunned like rabbits in the headlights, and then resumed the pursuit with renewed determination. I was the reluctant pied piper of the Congo, luring hundreds of eager children away from their homes. When I did get back on the bike at the top of the hill there was always a loud cheer and several hands tried to give me a push-start.

The first time I ever truck-surfed was on that road to Kikwit. The tiredness and children had got to me. They surrounded me as I walked and ignored me when I told them to go, and when I pleaded with them to leave me alone, they mimicked my words. Finally, I vented my anger. I stopped suddenly, turned around and shouted at them all, 'Piss off!'

My words were returned with a rock thrown by one of the older girls, and that was when the first tear trickled down my face. At that moment, we all heard the long low repeated blasts of a truck's horn. As if it were Moses, the children parted to let the vehicle pass and then surged back until the road was drowned in the patter of tiny feet and tormenting screams.

The driver's mate leant out of the window and signalled to me to catch up. Mustering my last reserves of energy, I got on the bike and caught up the truck, which had slowed to a crawl. I grabbed the back and held tight as it accelerated away. We stopped after a few kilometres and the truck driver apologised for the behaviour of *les sauvages* and hoped that I wouldn't let them ruin my impression of the country.

Getting through the larger villages without stopping was also hard. Immigration officials insisted I stop, so they could check my documentation and ask an array of irrelevant questions. The informalities were always the same. I played the game and used the breaks to rest. I got out bananas and nuts for my lunch, which I could now eat in the shade away from the prying, hungry eyes of children.

Once the immigration officers had copied every detail of my passport, they handed it back and asked for a beer or coke. When I refused them, they simply replied, 'OK, no problem. We understand – you are a tourist.'

But the problem was that I did not understand.

* * *

I was always happy to arrive in a town – good food, cold drinks, a bed and a bucket shower. Usually, I was happier to be leaving town – peace and quiet, less hassle, good views and fresh air. Kikwit was no exception.

The Kwilu Hotel, once a luxury establishment, was not even a shadow of its former glory – fallen into decay and falling down. In the last fifty years only the prices have gone up.

The shops were equally disappointing. Considering their quantity and size, I expected a plethora of imported goods. They merely stocked what the kiosks in the little villages had; only they sold it in bulk, which was not helpful for a lone cyclist. It was made worse by the infuriatingly slow process to purchase anything.

First, I had to give a list of what I wanted to the man behind the counter when I reached the front of the queue. It is not easy when you don't know what the shop has because all the goods are behind a glass screen, stacked in a warehouse facing away from you. Flummoxed, I listed the only things I could see, which were biscuits and mayonnaise. Then I waited while a second person got the items on the list and put them in a bag. The bag and the list were taken to a third person who checked that all the items on the list, and nothing more, were there. He passed it on to a fourth person who added up the cost of all the items. Then I had to pay a fifth person and wait while he wrote a receipt. *All this bother for a jar of mayonnaise!* With the receipt in hand, I was allowed to collect my bag. Finally, I could leave. As I walked out of the shop door, a security guard stopped me to search my bags and check the receipt. *Sigh.*

It is the old colonial administrations that are to blame. The system ensures maximum employment for the locals, gives each person minimal responsibility while ensuring that only one person, the clerk, who would have been white in the past, remains in control of the finances. After that, I limited myself to bread, onions, Maggi stock cubes, and glucose biscuits bought from the village kiosks.

I returned to my hotel room, collapsed on the bed, and whiled away the evening in a mosquito-killing spree between sips of beer. They were the only things in abundance here. I vowed to leave the next day.

The Kwilu River runs wide and slowly through Kikwit with its surface softly broken by whorls and swirls, subtle signals of a powerful fluid force in the depths below the dark surface. The road crossed the river, rose out of the water's reach, and wound round the hillside through speckled shadows of the midday sun squinting through the forest leaves. Cycling was a joy again. Not everything, everyday, had to be a struggle or challenge.

I was joined by Jean and Joel who were on a bike too. Joel hitched a ride on the back when we went downhill and ran alongside when we climbed. The company was something I would soon have to get used to, like it or not. They stopped in their village at the top, and I continued alone to the shouts of, 'Stop, you must pay *vélo tax*.'

I turned around and called back, 'No, I don't. I'm a white tourist.' They laughed. I could play their game.

As I entered the next village, I hoped to pass the police sleeping in the shade of the roadside tree, but one spotted me and took me to his office at the front half of a small thatched hut. The back half, partially hidden behind a faded curtain, was his bed. The 'office' had a low wooden table covered in papers and a Bible, which was being used as a paperweight.

Not a day went by now without an encounter with immigration. I thought I had it mastered and knew all the cons, but there was always another one. It started the same as always – he checked my passport and told me that my visa had expired because he was looking at the Republic of Congo visa, which had expired, but was not the right country. I showed him the DRC visa, and he told me that too had expired because he was reading the date I got the visa and not the date I entered.

'What is that?' he barked like a chained Rottweiler.

'That is not important.'

'Show it to me.' I handed it over and after several minutes he told me, 'It is a visa for Ghana.'

'Yes, I told you it was not important.'

'What is that?' *Sigh.*

'My vaccination card,' I said as I handed that over too. *I must remember to hide this paperwork.*

'It is out-of-date.' *Sigh.*

'They are the dates I had the vaccinations,' I explained slowly as though talking to a retarded monkey. 'Here it says how long they are valid for.'

'You have come from Kikwit?'

'Yes.'

'You went to the immigration there?' He was sat calmly now with his eyes fixed on my passport, slowly turning it over and over in his hands.

'Yes, when I arrived, the police took my details, called another office and the boss said I was free to travel.' He stopped playing with my passport and looked up at me with ears pricked.

'Ah! So you didn't go to the office and pay the fee.' *Sigh.*

His expression was unchanged, but I thought I saw a glimmer in his red eyes. It may just have been the conjunctivitis, which was almost as common in men here as the bloated stomachs of children suffering from kwashiorkor, malnourished on a protein-deficient diet. Either way, he thought he was about to catch this prey.

'What fee?'

'You haven't paid your resident's tax.'

'What? I am not a resident.'

'Of course you are a resident of the Congo. When you arrive in a new country, you become a resident of that country. You have been to …' he flicked through my passport again, 'Cameroon. Yes, when you were in Cameroon, you were a resident there. Then when you went to … where did you go after Cameroon?'

'Gabon.'

'So when you arrived in Gabon, you became a resident of Gabon. Now you are a resident of the Congo and must pay the resident's tax.'

I slowly and meticulously explained that I was a tourist and he slowly and meticulously explained that I was a resident. Back and forth. Ping. Pong. It was match point, and neither wanted to lose this game. We both had time on our side, so we sat in silence staring at each other.

He was fat, with pockmarked skin and yellow-stained teeth from years of smoking the local unfiltered cigarettes, and his weeping red eyes did not make him pretty. He also has vitiligo, a condition that causes depigmentation of the skin, so that his hands and around his mouth were whiter than I was. He had been dealt a duff hand in the beauty stakes, but it was his attitude I found distasteful.

So many people here have something wrong with them. We all do, I suppose. But here, they don't try to cover up what many would call imperfections, be it a missing eye or amputated arm, scars or crooked teeth. They are not flaws – they are tattoos of a life story and should not need to be hidden from view. They are a part of us and there is no shame in that. Besides, it is our actions that define us. We are so used to being bombarded with images of perfect-skinned models and straight, white-teeth smiles of Hollywood actors that we forget this.

I was still in silent stand-off with the red-eyed Rottweiler. This game could not end in a stalemate, so I made a move.

'How much is the resident's tax?' I asked.

'450 dollars.'

I burst out laughing and then with a straight face said seriously, 'I am on a bicycle. What makes you think I have that much money to give?'

'150 dollars.'

'I'm not paying. I'm not a resident and I'm not paying a resident's tax.' I paused and then said, 'So what are we going to do?' This was the question I was always asked, along with, 'How can you help me?' What we really meant was, 'I understand this is a two-way exchange and you have done something for me; now, what do you want in return?' It did not matter that this was part of his job. What mattered was that he did not get paid enough to feed his family to the end of the month and must use other ways at his disposal. The uniform gave him an opportunity.

'Give me 20 dollars,' he demanded. There was no talk of taxes now. It was a simple exchange between me and him – passport for cash. I waited silently.

Unexpectedly, he placed the passport on the table equidistant between him and me. His fingers lingered over it while he considered this manoeuvre. He was testing me. Fatal move – the winning shot was mine. I picked up the passport. I could walk out whenever I wanted, and he knew it.

Now that the 'formalities' were over, we were like best friends. We chatted and smiled and laughed, and we shared my bag of nuts before I got back on the bike, and he wished me a safe journey.

Dark grey clouds had gathered to my left and right, and lightning flashed and struck the distant horizon of the flat green savannah. Curtains of rain connected the clouds with the ground. I pedalled quickly, in the hope I would pass before the storms converged on the road ahead. I got drenched.

In the next village a woman called out from a hut, 'Come, come!' Soon, I was safely installed in the room with my bike and Anne, Kendai her husband, the five children, two rickety wooden beds, and a small fire smouldering in the corner for cooking and warmth. There was barely room to move. Anne stripped me of my dripping clothes and dried me with a cloth as the rain pelted down outside, turning the cleanly swept yard to mud. Three of the children shared *fufu* from a common bowl while Anne breast-fed the youngest, and I was offered what little food they had.

After a couple of hours the rain eased, so I collected my wet belongings and headed out the door. 'Thank you, thank you,' Kendai said as he shook my hand for giving them a bag of pasta. 'Can we have your water bottles?'

I hesitated. I could not give away everything I owned to anyone who asked for it, or I would have long ago given away my last belongings. Plastic water bottles were always in high demand. The ones I collected regularly disappeared whenever I stayed in a hotel. I had just managed to get hold of a third one – it would make life on the road easier by having to refill less often.

'It is for my wife,' he said. 'It will make it easier to collect water from the river.' I handed over one. Three were a short-lived luxury of excess, and excess and greed had no place here.

At the other side of the village, the road ended. The deep rutted sand started. I got off the bike and began pushing and dragging across the sodden landscape. At the next village, I filled my water bottles and pushed on. Some men watched me struggling, and then one shouted, 'Come back. There is a good path through the village.'

I backtracked. 'But where does it go?' I asked. I had no doubt what they said was true, but it did not mean the path went anywhere other than round the houses.

'You can follow it to the next village. A motorbike took the path earlier today, so you can just follow the tracks.' The paths were not on my map, but I decided it must be better than following the main sandy route that the trucks had gouged out and destroyed.

On the narrow path, it was possible to cycle. I followed it through the village, weaving between the huts and neat yards with pretty flowers lining the edges and wooden fencing marking one household from another. The motorcycle track faded on the hard earth and disappeared. I followed the only path, out onto the open plain and down to a stream, which I crossed at a small earthen bridge. The water flowed underneath, fresh and cool and clear. I refilled my bottles and drank, savouring the sweetness of the pure water, and then washed my face and felt the water trickle down my neck.

The sun had come out now and was burning hot. I sat under the shade of a tree and ate a mango. It was turning out to be a great day, and I looked out over the lush green countryside for I don't know how long. I had never thought I could be so happy.

The path continued alongside the small stream that flowed into a larger river where I crossed the deeply rutted main road again. I continued on the path straight between giant pylons that scarred the landscape, and when the sun faded behind me, I pulled off the track to camp and watched the women returning from their day of work in the forest and the fields to where they would begin their evening work in their homes. The women's work was never finished.

The Luange River marked the border between Bandundu and Kasai Occidental provinces. A new bridge, completed by Chinese contractors a year earlier, meant I could cycle across rather than having to rely on a boat. There is a Chinese saying, 'to end poverty, first build a road'; before that though, you must build bridges across the rivers. There was still a long way to go here.

Back on the main road the going was slow. I followed other bikes through the sand. They were local bikes, fully loaded with eight yellow jerry cans of water on handmade wooden racks along the bike's sides. Each bike was pushed by two or three men. Those at the front had the hardest job picking a route. The rest of us positioned our wheels in the rut that had been carved out by the one in front, so they would not slide sideways. With heads down, we strained and sweated, and heaved and pushed the bikes slowly, slowly, up the hill.

At the village, I stopped in the shade to rest and eat. Several more bikes were parked there, all loaded with the yellow jerry cans, either waiting to be unloaded or taken for the return journey to the river. These men had tough jobs. Sometimes their bodies can't take the strain any more, and when they lie down to rest by the side of the road, they never wake up. Their hearts … stop. Just like that.

Here, a path wide enough for bikes had been cut through the forest. It was fun weaving between the trees and braking suddenly when I heard a bell ring, which meant there was someone cycling towards me and they were not going to stop because they had no brakes. Along these paths there was always a manned barrier of rope or a wooden plank blocking the route where a *vélo tax* had to be paid. Those without money waited until another person came and handed over enough notes to let others through too. We were willing to pay to travel on a good toll track than have to push through the horrific main road of sand and dirt. It was another example of where the government had failed to provide basic services, local enterprise was thriving. The Congolese always survive.

Towards the end of the day, clouds gathered, and when the wind picked up, I knew it would rain soon. It was one endless village after another with nowhere to camp. So I stopped and spoke to the *chef du village*. He was an elderly man who moved slowly, hunched over a walking stick. He did not speak French and I did not speak Kikongo or Lingala, but a stick-thin lady, all skin-and-bones and broad smile, translated – I was welcome to stay for the night.

That was the first of many nights I spent camping in a village in the Congo. A hundred eyes stared at me with intense curiosity as I put up my tent next to the chief's hut, where he had swept the ground clean. They watched with amusement as I lit my stove and cooked dinner. The women occasionally looked to each other and whispered something with nods of approval as though watching a bargain shopping channel and they had just seen something useful for the kitchen. Once my pasta was cooked, I said good-night and turned towards my tent. Out of the corner of my eye a young woman ran forward and swept up the empty tin of tomato puree I had left on the ground. There is no rubbish where everything can be reused. Then I entered my tent and zipped up the door. I could not eat dinner under the scrutiny of so many.

Soon after, the rain thundered down, and I knew that everyone would have gone back to the shelter of their homes. I was preoccupied with moving my bags out of the water that was rapidly filling the end of my tent.

It was a wet, windy, thunderous night, and I slept fitfully until morning when I packed up my gear and hit the waterlogged road in the damp drizzle. The villagers returned to watch me leave, and for two hours I was followed by the children. Like a relay, they ran to the next village, passed the baton with their screams, and I continued with a new crowd until the next changeover. On and on we went. It was an endless chase with no escape.

At midday I arrived in Tshikapa town. What a relief! I checked into a hotel room, and for the first time that day, I was alone. *Peace.* I ate food without being watched and drank beer without having to share it. It was my selfish indulgence behind closed doors.

Tshikapa was a busy town with dusty streets. Small market stalls run by locals sold local produce – fruit and vegetables. Then there were the large buildings in clean compounds and glass-fronted shops run by foreigners who also bought local produce – diamonds. The Congo is mineral rich, and people here live for diamonds. Between the fruit and veg and the Lebanese businesses were small shops selling anything and everything of use in this trade, mostly wetsuits and compressors. Locals were employed to dive in the rivers to gather alluvial deposits and pan for diamonds. They use a hose pipe connected to the compressor as an unregulated regulator, which supplies the oxygen with a little leaking fuel mixed in.

By mid-afternoon I was following paths through villages, and weaving between huts and trees. Occasionally I took the wrong path, blocked by a wooden fence, and was forced to backtrack and try another route. When I saw some young men speeding along on lightly loaded bikes, I furiously pedalled to catch them up. They knew the route, and we travelled fast like an unstoppable steamroller. Usually, I was at the back struggling to keep up, but when the children saw me and took up the chase, one of the guys let me pass and became the rearguard defence, shouting and swiping at the children with a branch he had picked up for such an occasion.

After three hours of non-stop racing, I was exhausted and stopped at a village. Roman might have been a young chief, but he was confident, charismatic and intelligent. He and Jeremy, his friend, translated for the benefit of the curious crowd. There was complete silence when I talked and those at the back crowded closer to see better, and when Roman translated they crept closer to hear. When there was no room left to move, one of the older men jumped up, 'Get back all of you,' he shouted. 'Give the lady some space. She is our guest. Treat her with respect.'

At this, the adults stepped back, but the children wriggled into the spaces. So he picked up a branch and threatened to beat the next one who came too close, but as soon as he sat down and the talking resumed, they inched closer again. Suddenly, he leapt up like a madman brandishing a stick, and all the children fled except one who lingered until the stick was swiped at his backside, and then he, too, raced off unhurt with a cheeky grin on his face.

When there was space, I put up my tent and lay on my back in the darkness, listening to the men nearby talk deep into the night. I was awoken abruptly, not by the storm that was raging outside or the water collecting by my feet, but by Jeremy calling, 'Maman Hélène, maman Hélène, ça va?' Three times that night he came out into the rain to check on me. 'Please, Maman Hélène, come and sleep in the house with us.'

'Thank you, but I'm fine here,' I lied. I suspected my tent would blow away if I were not inside it.

The next morning we sat in the main room of the house where two children were still asleep on a rug in the corner. I talked with Jeremy while his wife breastfed their youngest son in the kitchen.

He told me about life in the village. It was simple: there was no work, only diamonds to dig for. He went to the dark corner of the room and searched among a pile until he found an old leather wallet. He opened it, pulled out a bundle of tissue paper, which he unwrapped carefully, and emptied the contents. A pile of tiny, rough diamonds lay there in the palm of his hand, unassuming nuggets like dirty pieces of glass tinged yellowish-brown.

'I will sell them when I need money to buy food,' he said and carefully placed them back in the wallet and put it on the table.

Two policemen sat under a makeshift shelter and directed me along the track that crossed the recently smoothed main road.

'The path to Kananga?' I asked.

'Yes,' they said, and so I continued.

An hour later I was back on my feet, pushing, in the sand. A tunnel had been carved through the thick branches, vines, and leaves. I was surrounded by the forest and should have felt trapped. On the contrary, it was a serene feeling to be guided along the path. If felt as though I was supposed to be going this way.

I was distracted occasionally by a swirling, fluttering multitude of colourful butterflies and by a thick black line painted across the sand as an army of ants marched five abreast and two high, and by a local who asked, 'Where are you going?'

'Kananga,' I said.

'No, you're not.'

'Yes I am.'

'No, you have come *from* Kananga.' He pointed back down the tunnel I had just walked through.

'What! So where does this go?' I pointed along the path in the direction we were headed.

'Luebo.' I was not supposed to be going this way. Without the sun for reference, I was going north, not east. *Shit.*

We agreed that I should continue. I could get to Kananga this way too. It would not be on the new smooth fast main road that I had inadvertently crossed earlier. It would take me deeper into the equatorial region along paths not shown on my maps and through unmarked villages. It was further, but I was determined not to retrace my steps through the sand and back up the hill. Besides, I had time and food and could always get water. I didn't need anything else.

It was several kilometres between villages, through more overgrown forest tunnels and along more sandy tracks. Occasionally I passed a clearing where subtle shades of the late afternoon sun streamed warm glows over me. They would have been lovely places to camp, but I had not filled up my water-bottles and had been warned several times of many deadly snakes in the area. I played it safe and continued.

Considering that it was not marked on any map, it was a surprisingly large village with radio mast and even a couple of motorbikes. Directed to the police headquarters, I asked where I might camp. The Commandant said I could stay at his home.

Before I put up my tent on the veranda of the old Belgium colonial whitewashed building, the Commandant showed me to a spare room with a motorbike parked in it where he had placed a thin mattress raised from the ground on a bamboo-frame.

'You can sleep in here if you would like. My home is your home,' he said. It was a sentiment I heard often here, as I had in Morocco and many places between.

The Commandant's house, with an aura of past grandeur, still had a large wooden dining table and cabinet alongside one wall in the bare main room. Now, though, there were no light bulbs because there was no electricity, and there were no taps because there was no running water, and there was no glass in the windows because it broke a long time ago and was never replaced, but bricked up instead to keep the mosquitoes out. There was no longer a bathroom because the back of the building had fallen down, and all that remained were some half-walled ruins and a concrete floor. I took a bucket and had my shower among the rubble, under the skylight.

While dinner was cooking, we sat on the veranda and watched the sun set over the village of Kabemba as people returned to their homes on this beautiful hilltop. The six o'clock pink-and-purple sky faded over the endless blanket of trees unfurling as far as I could see – to the sea, I conceived. It was the same pink and purple of every equatorial evening where the sun sets as regular as clockwork, the only thing that keeps a schedule here.

There were no lights glimmering through the trees or orange glow of a city hidden beyond the horizon, and it would have been peaceful and still with only the cicadas call if there hadn't been the incessant hum of a generator to power the bright floodlight, which illuminated this village that was not on any map. This village was here because of diamonds. Large mining companies can afford to provide their own power. I am sure there were some people happy that this village remained unmarked on most maps.

The commandant asked for my contact details, and I explained that I didn't carry a phone.

'What if you get into trouble?' he asked, clearly concerned. 'What if you fall off and are injured?'

My mind flicked back to earlier that day when I had been freewheeling fast down the rutted road through a small village. Momentarily distracted by some women's calls, I was too late swerving a rock and the front wheel rammed deep into the ground. The bike stopped abruptly, and I was catapulted straight over the handlebars. The hill was steep enough that I cleared them with unintentional ease and hit the ground with a heavy landing at a run. *Not a badly executed acrobatic manoeuvre.* The left pedal was dented from the impact, and I had jarred my knee, but that was nothing serious.

I reminded myself to be more careful cycling in these remote places. There would be no rapid emergency evacuation if I were seriously injured. Most likely, a bike would be converted into a stretcher and slowly pushed to Kananga, 150 kilometres away, where I could be flown to a hospital. It would be like the ill father I saw being taken by his three sons, covered with a blanket to shade him from the sun, carrying with them buzzing black flies and a sombre shadow that followed closely behind. He would be dead before he saw a doctor, but what else were his sons to do?

'I'll be careful,' I said thoughtfully. 'Perhaps I will buy a phone when I get to Kananga.'

I made an early start the next morning as the sun slowly warmed the forest and melted the blankets of cloud in the valleys. I cycled down to the river and removed the panniers from the bike and shoes from my feet and waded through the muddy water.

There were always people washing down at the river – washing themselves or their clothes or the cooking pots. It was where women gossiped and children played. They smiled and nodded at me briefly when I stopped to wash and clean my teeth before going back to their chatter. It was a long time since I had seen water run from a tap, but water runs freely in the open countryside.

There I met Sylvan. He too was cycling home to Kananga, so we agreed to cycle together. Sylvan bought goods in Kananga and then carried them on his bike to these rural outposts to sell for a small profit. There were many men doing this. It was the only way to stock the markets and shops since nothing larger than a motorbike can pass through on these tracks. Bicycles are cheaper to run and can carry heavier loads though.

Kananga was a surprise – concrete buildings several storeys high and tarmac roads. This was a real town. It even had enough distractions to keep me occupied for a couple of days – cheap local food and beer and an Internet cafe. It was still the same country though, and many things were the same.

When I enquired about a hotel, I was told about the most expensive one. When I enquired about a hotel for ten dollars, I was directed to the best of the brothels. The owner even suggested the expensive hotel might be better for me. I said I would decide for myself after I had seen the room.

I took the room. Brothels are not the worst places to sleep. At least it is easy to tell if the sheets are clean. Rooms are all the same when you are lying down with your eyes shut, so long as they are mosquito-free and not too hot. Besides, the owner gave me the key to the one flush toilet he always kept locked for himself. Of course, there was no running water, so it didn't flush, but it was clean. He provided candles for when there was no electricity, which was often, and soap and toilet roll as was customary. One of his men cleaned my bike for my plastic water bottles and one of the ladies did my laundry for a beer. We all won on these exchanges. Money is not the only form of currency.

Immigration quickly tracked me down. Two officers knocked on my door early the next morning and dragged me, and two Tanzanians who were also staying at the hotel, down to the station to complete paperwork, which was the antecedent to asking for money. This took most of the morning. I sat and wrote my journal. The two Tanzanian's got irate with the inefficiencies and formalities. They said they couldn't believe it; they had never come across such a ludicrous process before. I found that hard to believe. It was just another day of life here. My passport was returned a good hour before theirs – probably because I was a white girl or because I was patient. They joined me in the bar opposite the hotel afterwards. A standard bar-restaurant that was no more than wooden tables and plastic chairs, under a thatched open-sided *paillote*.

We poured beer from the big bottles into our small glasses, and whenever a glass was nearly empty someone filled it up, and when the bottles were drained someone bought another. There were always beer mats on the tables, and I used to wonder why you didn't put the glasses on the mats but the mats on top of the glasses. Was it just another Congolese logic that I would never understand with my European mind? I understood soon enough – you don't want flies in your beer.

The rest of the first day I spent drinking. One of those hazy days of dazed happiness where you laugh a lot and share stories and everything is so crystal clear at the time although you remember nothing of what you said later except you know it was important when you told it – carefree days when there is no need to consider tomorrow. Perhaps that is why the Congolese like to drink: they live only for today. Tomorrow is another day and may never come.

I also spent much of the day eating. To get here, I had been spending over ten hours every day on the road, and the fruit and nuts I snacked on never compensated for the energy I was burning.

I was as fit and strong as ever, but I was losing weight and hungry most of the time.

The rice and beans were boring, but I devoured them nonetheless. The chicken was delicious. It used to amaze me how the locals would strip a chicken thigh and leg down to the bone with their teeth, never wasting a morsel of meat, skin, fat, or gristle. Now I too did the same thing. The craving for calories and protein was great. I drew the line at breaking the bones and sucking the marrow out. My teeth are not strong enough for that.

I was always conscious of eating differently to the locals. It was not what I ate, but that I couldn't manage with only one or two meals a day. So in the afternoon, back in my hotel room, I ate huge bags of peanuts and whole pineapples.

There were many things like this that made me feel like an outsider, such as when I chose to sleep in my tent rather than in someone's hut in the villages or drank the expensive bottled beer rather than the local palm wine. It is surprising, when I look back now, that I never felt as though I was treated as a foreigner because I was white, or a girl travelling alone.

There was a poorly stocked supermarket in Kananga. I went there often because they sold greasy fried plantain that I loved. Matthieu was a teenager who worked there. Young and impressionable, but not shy, he sat down at the table while I ate and we shared my food. He asked for my phone number, so that we could stay in touch. When I explained that I didn't have a phone, he wanted to buy me one.

'No. If I really needed a phone I would buy one.' I considered it briefly and thought about my conversation with the Commandant in Kabemba. I decided I would continue to manage without.

'Have mine then.'

'I can't do that. You need yours.'

'I will buy another one.'

'Really, thank you, but no. It's very kind of you to offer though.'

'If you want, you can have my phone for your sunglasses. I really like them and don't have a good pair.'

I had already given away most things that I didn't absolutely need and the sunglasses I couldn't really do without. My eyes had suffered badly from the glare of the sun and dust in the air when I didn't have any in the Sahel. Some nights I woke up and if I opened my eyes, it would feel as though there was burning hot sand in them and I wanted to rub them, but the only thing that lessened the pain was to close them tight, let them stop watering and then fumble to do whatever I needed to in utter blindness.

The day I left Kananga, I bought some fried plantain for the road. Matthieu was there and when I said goodbye, he gave me his sunglasses.

'Thank you, but I have a pair already.'

'It doesn't matter. Take them. They are a gift.'

'But …'

'Take them. You can always give them as a gift to someone else who may need them more.'

22

Lazy Days at Lac Mukamba and in Lusambo

DRC

Lac Mukamba lies halfway between Kananga and Mbuji-Mayi, the capitals of West and East Kasai provinces. There used to be a village here until 120 years ago when the land collapsed and filled with water. Now there is a lake. It lies in a shallow depression, barely visible from the road through the trees that conceal a small, quiet village. On its shores are a few grand houses – relics of days gone by when the lake was a weekend holiday spot for Belgians from the towns.

The police directed me to the Catholic mission guesthouse.

'I was wondering, is it possible for me to camp here?'

'No.'

'Oh, OK. Do you have a room?'

'No, we are full. It is a busy day.' It didn't look busy.

'Are you sure I can't camp? I have a tent, everything I need.' There was ample space within the grounds. 'I wouldn't be any trouble and I'm leaving tomorrow anyway. I could camp just round the side there, out of the way …'.

'No, you can't camp.'

'Really?'

'No camping.'

'OK, is there anywhere else I can stay?'

'There are hotels in Kananga.'

I laughed. 'I know. I've just come from there. It's 100 kilometres away, and I'm on a bicycle.'

'You will have to go to Mbuji-Mayi then.'

I laughed. 'That is also 100 kilometres away. It has taken me all day to get here. How exactly do you expect me to get there with the bike?'

'I don't know.' That was clearly my problem to solve. The lady, realising that I wasn't going anywhere said, 'Come,' and walked off. She took me to the other white person who was at the mission.

'Bonjour,' I said and held out my hand.

'Hi.'

'Oh, you speak English. Hi, I'm Helen.' I hadn't spoken English in weeks.

'Dustin.' He sat back down and took up his beer.

I was stunned. This was so completely unexpected I didn't know what to say. 'So, do you work here?'

'No, I'm just staying.'

'Oh.'

'Want a seat?' he nodded towards the spare chair.

'That's a good idea.' I was looking towards his beer, 'One moment.'

I came back with a bottle of Skol and sat down. He was a polite, quiet American man from Montana and worked for the Wings of Hope charity, which focuses on providing medical air transport around the world. He was flying a delegation of people for a conference here and now had nothing to do until the following day. He was nothing like the many bush pilots I later met in Africa, who could be generalised as alpha-male extroverts on the verge of a drinking problem.

'So where are you going to stay?'

'Oh, I'll just take my bike and find a place to camp in the bush somewhere. It'll be fine. That's what I normally do. I think there was a small track I passed; it probably goes round the lake. I'll just follow that. No problem.' It was late afternoon, and the sun was going down. If I was going to find a place to camp, I needed to go soon. But I was reluctant to leave. There was beer and good company here, and I could talk in English.

We sat in the shade looking out over the lake and saw a small rubber dinghy heading towards us. This was no local villager out fishing in a wooden dugout canoe. As it neared the shore, we looked closer and saw that one of the men was white. I had seen only one other white person since I left Kinshasa. Now there were three of us, like buses. We watched them step out into the shallows wearing board-shorts and bare chests, and then Dustin said, 'Hang on, is that …' and he stood up to take a better look, 'it's Charlie. I might have found you somewhere to stay tonight.' He walked off towards the shore giving a quick glance back to me, 'Don't leave just yet.'

Well, I had no intention of leaving just yet. This was far too intriguing and besides, I hadn't finished my beer. I followed Dustin down the concrete steps and along the sandy shore to where the four men embraced each other and shook hands with smiles and hearty laughs like good friends make when they haven't seen each other in a long time.

They had only met once before. You make friends quickly here because it is friends who you ask for help when you need it. That is how things get done. It is whom you know and that is how you survive. More important than making friends though is not to make enemies, of anyone. The taxi-driver you meet today could become the president tomorrow. Improbabilities lie in the realms of the likely here. This was only the second time Charlie had been to the lake in years, and it was the second time Dustin had been to this lake ever. Those first times were the same times, and they met by chance. Now here they were again.

I stood a little awkwardly beside Dustin, quietly waiting for an introduction. I took another swig of beer and wondered who these three guys were and what it was that was so familiar about Charlie who was tall and slim with curly blonde hair. He was wearing a black and white headscarf, like the one Lars used to have, wrapped around his sunburned neck; it wasn't that. It was something about his smile or eyes or the way he walked or stood. I couldn't place it. Perhaps it was just that he was white. My thoughts were interrupted by Dustin, 'This is Charlie. He has a place just around the lake.'

'Hi, nice to meet you,' I said and shook his hand in the formal stand-offish English way. Introductions I always find awkward, second only to goodbyes.

'Hi, you too,' he replied.

Then I shook hands with Stephan and waved to Kambi, who was quietly setting up a couple of chairs on the beach.

'We were just on our way back to my place, but because we've had a long day and it's nearly the end of our trip, we thought we would celebrate with a couple of beers. Want to join us?'

Dustin asked Charlie if I could camp at his place because I wasn't allowed at the mission.

'Sure, that's no problem. I mean, why would it be? You've got a tent, yes? Don't worry, it's perfectly safe. We'll be in my place, and you can put your tent up outside, and if you need anything we'll be there.'

'Great. Thanks.' It hadn't crossed my mind that I wouldn't be safe. I trusted my instincts to trust these guys.

'I can't believe they wouldn't let you camp here. They call themselves Christians, but all they're really interested in is money these days. And they've got plenty of it. You know, they're buying up the land, growing plantations and selling the produce for biofuel. The local people barely grow enough food to feed themselves, and then you see this stuff being sold to big companies from their doorstep. I could tell you so many stories. But let's have a beer. What are you doing here?' I glossed over my story that I had told a thousand times before.

Then we went for a swim in the lake. It was good to get out of my sweaty bike clothes, and the water was cool and calm, and the painted sky was that six o'clock pink-and-purple. We got out and sat on the beach and drank cold beer that made me shiver with my wet hair, so I put a top on while Dustin and Charlie chatted, and Stephan joked, and Kambi sat quietly. Stephan always joked and smiled and laughed, and Kambi was always quiet and thoughtful and listened. Right then we were all content.

Once we had finished the beer, we loaded my bike and bags and a couple of extra drinks into the dinghy and walked it, splashing through the shallows, around to Charlie's place. A single room hut of mud brick and corrugated roof, a hundred metres from the shore in a clearing, it was more like the huts in the villages than the colonial mansions that white people used to own. Charlie might have looked European to the eye, but he was Congolese at heart. With a roof over your head, surrounded by friends, you don't need anything else. Other things just get in the way.

The lake provided water to drink and wash, and we could buy fish and rice in the village, and get fruit from the trees. What more (except beer) do you need? They had a spare car battery too, so there was power for light and a laptop for some of the evening.

When we had finished the last beer and local spirits and shared what little food we had that could be eaten without cooking, Dustin said he had to go back to the mission and sleep. Charlie and I went with him in the dinghy, and we paddled slowly over the lake that rippled in the moonlight, and under the stars that sparkled like diamonds. They sang songs and I listened, and we all laughed like happy drunk three men in a boat.

We drank another beer, said good-night until tomorrow, and then me and Charlie paddled back. It was much further the second time, made longer by the silences that Dustin had filled before and were interrupted now only by the unrhythmic splashes of our paddles in the darkness and our mutual agreement that this was a beautiful lake and a wonderful night.

'You know, there's another lake nearby that is more beautiful than here. It's a paradise where the water rises up from the ground and is crystal clear, and trees grow thickly all around. If you could delay your ride to Mbuji-Mayi for a couple of days, I'll show you that lake. You should see it; I think you would love it. We're going that way anyway. We could put your bike in the truck and bring you back …'.

'OK,' I said.

'Really?'

'Well, why not? I'm in no rush, and the reason I'm here is to see places and people I wouldn't otherwise. Oh, but only if you really are going there anyway and it's no problem. Don't go out of your way for me.'

'That's great. We'll go to Lac Fwa. You'll love it; I promise.'

'OK.'

There was not a single building here or road to the lake. I went for a swim while the men cleared some ground and began making their shelter from wood to cover with tarpaulin.

Lac Fwa reflected a colour that changed from deep blue to turquoise to pale green as the sun moved across the sky, and then, finally, to a dulled grey as the dark clouds gathered for the late afternoon storm.

I waded out into the water and stood with my toes pressed into the sand and felt the smooth pebbles under my feet. The surface of the lake was perfectly still except for the ripples I caused and the gently undulating wake of a pirogue in the distance, yet beneath the surface I felt the clear water rushing past my legs and the thick weeds by the bank, where the fish sheltered, waved and rippled in the current.

The lake is actually the start of a river, widened where the water gently bubbles up from beneath the rocks, rises to the surface, and spreads in swirls before beginning its journey downstream into the Lubi River that flows into the Sankuru that joins the Kasai and, as with all rivers in this country, eventually flows into the Congo River and past Kinshasa.

Several villagers were now watching silently from the banks. So I went and put up my tent in a small clearing and tried to ignore the boys who were staring and laughing and made me feel self-conscious. But all they were saying was, 'She is a woman and in just a few minutes, she has put up her tent and it is ready to sleep in. Tick-tack-quick-done. And it has taken eight men two hours of hard work to put up their shelter, and it still won't keep the rain out.'

Lac Fwa may be beautiful, but paradise is a personal perspective. My paradise does not involve mosquitoes or palavers with paranoid locals and drunk village chiefs who could not accept that we were simply tourists and had no desire to dig for diamonds or steal their fish. Tourism was a foreign concept.

Instead, the following day we drove north towards Lusambo. The town used to be the administrative centre before Kasai province split into two. From a thriving town on the Sankuru River deep in the forest, it is barely a shadow of its former glory. Large colonial buildings, still inhabited, have never been repaired. Where once there were beautiful gardens and tree-lined avenues, the space is now used to grow maize. Everywhere else, the forest is slowly but surely reclaiming the land; the march of nature is measurable and unstoppable. Just as Timbuktu is being lost to the sands of time, Lusambo will one day be lost to the forest forever.

When travelling, you can go by any name or persona you wish, embellish parts of your life or hide certain characteristics. Neither Stanley nor Brazza was born with the names they travelled with. It is liberating. It strengthens the insecure and emboldens the introvert; it removes barriers and levels the playing field.

It is also easy to be truthful to a near stranger because you know that once you continue your journey you may never see them again. Charlie made me want to be exactly who I am, and it was easy to be honest with him. On the rough and rutted road to Lusambo, we talked of our lives and hopes and told a lifetime of stories in the space of a day.

Despite my protestations, I sat in the front and Charlie drove. Stephan, Kambi, and John and Alexi who worked for Charlie, squeezed on top of all the baggage in the back of the open-topped Suzuki Samurai, and my bike was roped to the rear. They were content with the container of palm wine that was steadily emptied on the journey.

We arrived late at the village on the southern side of the Sankuru River because we had got low on fuel and had to find a village with some to sell. In every village we stopped, people crowded around the vehicle and peered through the open windows. They always asked for cigarettes, and Charlie always gave them a couple. Sometimes we stopped long enough to share our palm wine, and the children asked for food, but we didn't have any to give.

I was slowly beginning to understand that this was the way things were done here. Everybody helps each other out. You have something I need, I ask for it and you give it. It had nothing to do with me being a relatively rich white foreigner. It had everything to do with Article 15, *Débrouillez-Vous* – fend for yourself.

During the Mobutu era, Article 15 was an unofficial and unwritten addition to the constitution, and it is joked about today. It allows, even encourages, thievery and bribery to make ends meet – it means do what you must.

So I had given away my shirt to a lady who asked for it. In return, from someone else, I was fed and provided shelter for the night when I asked for somewhere to stay. When I thanked one village chief for letting me camp, I asked if he wanted anything. He said there was nothing – it was his duty to ensure I was safe. It was a poor village, and the people had little, so I offered my machete. That, he said, would be of great use. He would use it more than I. And so it continued. There was a little of a Robin Hood in everyone I met, of stealing from the rich and giving to the poor. There are worse things than doing the wrong thing for the right reasons.

We camped in the chief's compound until we could take a pirogue across to Lusambo the next morning. A projector had been put up in the yard, and a group was watching a film in French. One young man with a microphone translated into Tshiluba, so that everyone could understand. There is little variation in sources of evening entertainment in these remote villages. That was why the children loved it when we played films on the laptop although they understood little of the language, and it was why I was always surrounded whenever I camped in a village and watched while I cooked my dinner and put up the tent.

There was not much to do in Lusambo: sit and wait, sit and talk, and sit and watch the world go slowly by. So we took a dugout canoe down the Sankuru River to where Charlie's family owned a small farm that now lay empty and decaying. There was not much to do there either. Yet there are many ways to pass the time where there is nothing to do:

Sit.

Relax.

Eat.

Fish.

Eat fish.

And watch the sun rise and the dark clouds gather and the rain fall in heavy drops and the clouds dissipate and the blue sky return and in the setting sun watch the mirror-image reflections on the calm river of the trees and sky turning from blue to six o'clock pink-and-purple and watch the fishermen pole *pirogues* up the river and down the river and throw nets over the side to collect fish, and eventually the stars come out and the mosquitoes too and then it is time to take refuge beside a fire on the sandbank wrapped in a blanket, and when you have seen enough for one day and your eyelids are heavy, then is the time to crawl into your tent and fall asleep to the symphony of crickets.

That was how one day passed into the next, so that I didn't know what day it was because each day was only subtly different from the last, and I only knew the time of the day by the position of the sun and colour of the sky and the rumbling of my stomach.

I was happy those days. That we slept on the floor of an empty derelict house and sat on the moth-eaten upholstered chairs or crumbling brick wall and ate simply and little and were ravaged by mosquitoes in the early evening until we lit a fire, it was enough just to be happy. I could have stayed longer. With a shelf full of books, I could have stayed indefinitely. I had found a corner of the world I was content in, and it made me dream of what could be. It was the first time on the journey that I let myself consider what I might do once I reached Cape Town.

Throughout the journey, I had promised myself I would make no plans for after the trip. I had always felt that my life had been planned out several years in advance; go to school, so you can go to university, and then get a good job and work towards a career. It left little room for spontaneity. That was when I had decided to quit my job and travel. Otherwise, there was a risk that I would wake up in twenty years with a mortgage and possibly marriage and children and realise I hadn't done any of the things I really wanted to do. If I wanted these things when I reached Cape Town, I could still achieve them. I purposefully left the door to my options wide open, and it was liberating.

Until now, this had let me enjoy every day in Africa with no thought to the future. Perhaps that was why I felt so at home on the continent. I was surrounded by people who, by their experiences, had learnt to live only for today. It is not easy to live like that in England.

A few days later we took a dugout canoe back up the Sankuru River to Lusambo. There was still not much to do there. The main distraction was to drink. We drank palm wine or *tchichampa*, a potent home-made distilled clear liquor, or the more expensive but palatable bottled beer. We could drink at any time of the day. So we would sit and talk and sit and drink and then drink some more.

Palm wine comes from the sap of the oil palm tree. It is the lazy man's drink. Fermentation occurs naturally, immediately, and rapidly during the tapping process such that within an hour you can be drinking the sweet beer-strength milky nectar. Unfortunately, it has a very short shelf-life and goes vinegary and that is a good excuse to drink too much in too little time.

A woman came round during the morning with a 25-litre jerry can full of palm wine and a plastic cup. For a few Congolese francs, she filled the plastic cup and waited until you emptied it. First I looked at the contents, took out any floating debris that came from the tree during the tapping process, such as ants, bees, or other animals that shouldn't be there, and then gulped it down thirstily before handing back the cup. She then moved on to the next person and repeated the process. If the jerry can was not emptied after one round, she came by again.

We drank and laughed until we took a dugout canoe back across the river to the 4x4 and the road. We spent several days back at Lac Mukamba. I was reluctant to leave the place and people I liked so much.

In the cooler hours of the day, the shores of the lake were lined with women washing clothes, small children bathing, and older ones fishing. When the lake was a Belgian holiday resort, people spent the day fishing and the evening grilling the large fish they had caught. Now there are few fish left. Girls waded in with empty wine bottles with a hole in the bottom for the fish to swim up and be trapped inside the funnel. Young boys worked together with nets to catch the small immature fish. If the UNICEF-funded mosquito nets were used for their designated purpose, not for catching fish and birds, there would probably be fewer deaths by malaria and more wildlife. If only there was some regulation, this lake would be teeming with aquatic life. As it is, the locals scrape by on the dwindling remains.

In the evening, the lake was turned into a huge drum. Girls stood in the water up to their waists and cupped their hands to skilfully slap the surface. The deep rhythmic beat resounded round the lake for all to hear. Music and the Congo are synonymous. I never spent a day without hearing music or the beating of a drum, and where there was music, people danced.

I remember, later, sitting at a roadside bar watching the few men drinking beer alongside me, some deep in conversation and serious business-talk, and others looking blankly ahead absorbed in the music that was crackling through the speakers, and the couple of women cooking and gossiping, and children racing around, and a crazy man in torn rags dancing in the middle of the road. He twirled and moved with knee-high steps and flailing arms and body bent. His long matted hair of dirt and filth was flung through the air as he shook his head, and he wore a huge manic grin of rotting teeth and laughed loudly, completely unaware of where he was or who was watching. Perhaps he was not so crazy because I swear he was the happiest man of us all – a crazed, carefree, harmless lunatic hearing nothing but the beat of the drums. We could all be a little happier if we danced more and cared less for appearances.

23

Diamonds and the Mai Mai

DRC

From the lake, it was a day's ride to Mbuji-Mayi, the main town in Kasai Oriental, a town built on diamonds. People come here in search of a fortune, so the town has spread outwards into a sprawl of rundown dusty streets where the hopeful hopelessly eke out a living any way they can.

Mbuji-Mayi means 'Goat Water' and is named because of the goats that once grazed on the fertile banks of the river. Now, though, I saw only people panning for diamonds. If found, they took them to the roadside. Here, sat behind wooden tables, were men with a stack of money piled up waiting to be exchanged for diamonds. These diamond dealer middlemen were like the street money-changers of Kinshasa, who made their money on the exchange rate differences between the US dollar and Congolese franc.

Charlie said that his friend, Marie-Louise, would love for me to stay with her in Mbuji-Mayi. The address he gave was nothing more than, 'Chez Dieu Soit Beni'.

'Really, that's it?' The 'Home of God Is Blessed' sounded less like an address and more like a joke.

'Ask anybody in town, everyone knows who she is.'

Mbuji-Mayi is the third largest city in the DRC with a population of anywhere between 1.5 million and 6 million depending on whose estimate you believe. It struck me as unlikely that all these people, however many they were, would know the same Marie-Louise.

'Can you give me some directions of where to go?'

'I told you, just ask for Chez Dieu Soit Beni when you get there.'

I left it at that. If I didn't find it I could always stay at a hotel.

As I approached Mbuji-Mayi, immigration stopped me and told me to go to their headquarters.

'Where are you staying?'

'With friends.'

'Do you know how to get there?'

'Do you know Chez Dieu Soit Beni?' I tentatively asked.

'Of course. I will get one of my men to show you. I know Marie-Louise very well.'

I thanked my chaperone, walked to an unsigned metal door and knocked. A boy opened it.

I wheeled my bike down the side of the house into a large dusty yard closed in on all sides by buildings. The house stood directly behind the market shops. There were lots of people, but mainly they were children of varying ages. One group of well-dressed men and a woman was sat at a plastic table drinking.

'Welcome. Join us. Come sit. Would you like a beer?'

'Hello. Thank you. But I am looking for Marie-Louise.'

'Over there,' said the woman as she pointed across the courtyard. I walked in that direction, towards two girls pounding millet. I had no idea what Marie-Louise looked like, let alone how old she was.

'Hello,' I said to the older girl. 'Marie-Louise?'

'One moment,' she said, and she scurried off into the house. Soon she returned with a short lady who walked slowly with a huge smile that showed the many creases on her face made deep by age as well as hard work and happiness.

'Are you Marie-Louise? I'm Helen, a friend of Charlie's …' and before I could say any more, she was holding me in a tight embrace as I bent down to reach her height – hugging me like a long-lost relative. I wondered if she had mistaken me for someone else.

'Welcome, welcome,' she was smiling and laughing. 'You know Charlie. You are my sister. This is your home.'

I wrestled myself free from her arms and looked at her wondering if one of us had misunderstood something. I went on to explain that I was from England and cycling through the country on my way south and that Charlie would be coming tomorrow. She went on smiling. I am not sure she understood everything I said as she had used all the French she knew in welcoming me.

'You are thirsty, no?' That's what I thought she said. She was speaking in Tshiluba now, but I recognised her hand signals.

'Yes, I am.'

'Come.' She took me by the hand and led me back to the people at the plastic table.

'This is Helen. She is staying with us.' I was glad to be welcome.

'Do you drink beer?'

'Er, yes.' *That wasn't what I had in mind when I said I was thirsty.* One of the men stood up and moved his chair round for me.

'No really, that's not necessary.' The man went off anyway and returned with two more chairs and glasses, into which he poured beer from the bottle of Skol on the table. We all shuffled around to make more space.

'Welcome Helen. *Santé.*'

'*Santé,*' we all replied, clinked glasses, and drank. I explained where I had come from, and Marie-Louise just smiled and occasionally took hold of my hand, squeezing it hard and shaking it.

Over thirty years ago, Marie-Louise's husband died, leaving her childless. She vowed never to marry again. Instead, she devoted her life to children who have nowhere to live. Her home was an informal orphanage. Any child who lived on the streets was welcome into her home, where they would be fed and have a safe place to sleep. Some had lived there for as long as they could remember. One teenage girl was brought as a baby when she was found abandoned in a skip. Some of the boys, who were almost men, had stayed to help Marie-Louise. They fixed her truck, and drove her when she needed to go somewhere, and any number of other jobs.

Dai, the youngest, was only six. She was brought here a few weeks before by her parents who said they could no longer look after her. She had put on weight since she first arrived, and still she was just skin and bones and protruding belly, so featherlight and quiet, I barely noticed when she sat on my knee. She always carried a big smile during the day and any time I took a photo she was there, in the front of the shot or creeping into the corner, always with that beautiful smile on her tiny face that looked much older than she was.

At night, though, she lay down to sleep by herself, and in the darkness her thoughts and dreams tormented her. She lay awake with tears rolling down her cheeks in sadness and loneliness and the inability to understand why her parents had left her. Then, when it got late and Marie-Louise lay down to sleep, Dai would creep over and lie down beside her and feel safe and warm and a little less alone. Finally, cuddled up like a pup, she would drift off into uneasy dreams. The next morning she was always bright and cheerful and you could easily forget her anguish that she hid behind her smile.

The other children who had been staying there much longer did not appear to be troubled by their past in the slightest. It goes to show how resilient kids are and that time is a healer for many wounds when they are given a safety net like this home.

Marie-Louise had her own bedroom in the house, but it lay unused on most nights. She slept outside on the floor with the children. It was only when it rained that she slept in her bed, and then all the children piled inside the house too and squeezed into the spare spaces, so it was impossible to move about until morning.

Marie-Louise is not rich, although the house that her husband left was bigger than most. She makes her money from the shop she owns in the market. With the profits, she feeds all the children who live there. There were about thirty on any given evening, although they came and went, and even Marie-Louise did not know how many there were. They ate only basic food, the same fufu and cassava every day, unless they had guests to stay, and only then did she indulge in some meat or fish too.

Marie-Louise gave me one of the guest bedrooms with the luxury of a bed. I would have preferred to sleep as everyone else did, outside on the floor where it was cooler. I was, after all, no stranger to sleeping under the stars. I always detested special treatment, but I gratefully accepted Marie-Louise's kindness, which she handed out thoughtlessly.

We sat down at her dining table for breakfast, surrounded by posters of the Virgin Mary and statuettes of the crucifixion of Jesus, and someone always said a prayer before we ate bread and drank coffee. Once everyone had finished, we moved outside, and Marie-Louise fed the two pigs and all the birds. Taking a handful of seed at a time from a plastic container, she bellowed in a deep slow monotone voice sounding each syllable with the same strength and hanging on to the last, 'Mes amies!'

Scores of pigeons swept down from the roof and rafters, and the chickens raced, clucking and wings flapping, from hidden corners of the yard and pecked at the floor where the seeds had fallen. Then she called a shortened, 'Mes …' and then, 'mes amies,' and after each call came an echo in the dainty high-pitched voice of Dai.

Anybody you speak to in the Congo can tell a story of someone who got lucky and rich, because living here is one big lottery. Everyone is tumbling through life in the hope their number is drawn. There are the unlikely stories of the pauper becoming a prince, of the miner finding the million dollar diamond, or in Joseph Kabila's case, of the taxi-driver becoming the president. Although in the latter, as with most political manoeuvres, there is usually a western government plot behind the luck.

It is these stories people cling on to because it keeps alive hopes that their situation, however hopeless it may seem, could change overnight. You see these stories on street corners if only you look. On the corner of the street that Marie-Louise lived on in *Marché* Simis was a big shop. Besides the size, it was distinguishable because, unlike most of the shops, it had a name: *Dieu M'a Donné*.

There was a lady who used to sell second-hand clothes in the market when one day she discovered five thousand dollars in the pocket of a jacket in the jumble. That is a fortune here, but like any entrepreneurial business-minded lady, she invested the money in her own store. With the profits she bought trucks to import goods, and slowly she transformed her find into a million dollar business. What I call luck and entrepreneurial flair she knows as the Lord that provides.

My walks in the market, through several blocks of permanent open-fronted stores whose contents spilled into the streets, became a slow affair. People called out, '*Muoyo mutoké.*' I knew they were saying hello to me because I was the only white one there.

I replied, '*Muoyo.*'

'*Biche?*' they asked.

So I answered, '*Bimpe.*'

Never in the whole of Africa in any language did I ever hear someone say they were not fine. You always answer that you are OK. That is the way it is done. Only once these formalities are over, do you go into details and say whether it has been a bad day and find out from someone else that their sister has died or whatever else has happened. Just as there is little room for planning for the future, so there is little point in dwelling on the past. What has been is done and what is to come will be. You can tell a lot about people by the way they greet each other; not only in what is said, but how it is said.

In some cultures, greetings have a great importance, no more so than with the Dogon of Mali. They not only say hello and ask if you are OK, but then they go on to ask how the family is, and the children and house and village, and to each question you reply that they are fine until the questioning stops. Then it is your turn to ask after all and sundry in a slow melodious rhythm, never a tedious drone. If anything is worth saying, it is worth saying fully and slowly and respectfully, and this mimics how the Dogon go about their lives with honour and grace.

My favourite of all was the Krio greeting in Sierra Leone. 'Ow de bodi?' they asked. It was short and sweet and to the point in an accent that could be mistaken for coming from the Caribbean. After all, Sierra Leone was settled by freed slaves brought back across the Atlantic, and they spoke this pidgin English that was common between them and the slavers because it was simple and understood by all. It has not changed, like many things.

'De bodi fine,' I replied.

* * *

One indolent day gently rolled into the next until nearly two weeks had passed. I had lost the momentum of always being on the move and the inertia was too great to overcome. I seriously considered staying longer. I liked it here, I liked Charlie and was happy. The idea to write a book had been on my mind for a couple of months, and I could write here as well as anywhere. It would be easy to extend my visa for a few months, and then I could continue to Cape Town later, although I suspected I wouldn't. I was torn between a deep-rooted desire to finish what I had started and to skip right ahead to the next part of my life, whatever that might be.

At night, I lay awake dreaming. My mind conjured up all the possibilities of life, and on some nights I was convinced I would stay, and I decided to get my visa extended as soon as the day broke. But with daylight the dreams faded, and I never kept the courage to do it. My heart implored me to stay, but my head screamed, '*You must go*!'

So I set a day to leave and packed my panniers the night before. It felt as though a weight had been lifted from me. Deep down, I knew that once I hit the road again, I could clear my head and think rationally.

That last night in Mbuji-Mayi I was plagued by gut-wrenching, stomach-churning feelings. I feared I was turning my back on something good. The benefit of having only one life, however, is that there is no right or wrong choice, only the one you make and that is always better than making no decision at all and lingering eternally on the edge of *what if*.

It had taken all my emotional energy just to make this decision. Now, I felt drained and my stomach was reeling. I got up when it was too hot to stay in bed any longer. Charlie was already sat outside in the courtyard.

'Morning.' I pulled up a plastic chair and sat down.

'Morning. Have you heard the news?'

'No.' *Of course not, I've been in bed. How would I have heard?* I was in a bad mood. 'What news?' I asked.

'On the radio this morning. The Mai-Mai has attacked one of the villages east of here. The way you are going to Kalemie. They've just said that the government is sending in troops.'

'Oh, that's not good.' I didn't know what else to say, but my mind was already thinking about the options for me to continue and whether it was really that bad. I sat quietly, knowing that Charlie would carry on talking. If I listened long enough, my questions would be answered without having to ask them. Presumably, I didn't look perturbed enough because he stared at me, trying to see through my wall of silence to what thoughts I was hiding. He could see straight through me.

'You do know who the Mai-Mai are, don't you?'

'I've heard of the rebel group, but don't know much about them. I thought they were mainly up in the north-east.'

'They are near here too. I wouldn't call them rebels though. They are just local militia groups that were formed to defend their villages during the last war. They never disbanded though, and now they periodically resurface a couple of times a year and cause trouble. They can be dangerous though. What will you do?'

I wondered how I could find out more about the situation. I trusted Charlie, but I also knew he could play people and get them to do what he wanted while thinking it was their decision. He was smart and understood what made people tick. He knew I could see this, but he made the mistake of thinking that I was smarter than I am, and that I was capable of rational, logical decisions that involved him. I knew he didn't really want me to go that route. The problem was that there was no one else to ask. I didn't understand Tshiluba, so listening to the radio was pointless. This kind of news never made it into the international papers. No one in Mbuji-Mayi knew exactly what was going on anyway.

I was reluctant to change my plans again. 'I don't know what to do,' I said and shrugged my shoulders dejectedly. It was another punch in the gut.

I put up one final assault. 'Well, where exactly are they? I mean, maybe I can reroute around them if things don't settle down when

I get closer. Knowing immigration and the police here, they won't let me go anywhere that is really dangerous. Or I could just head to Lubumbashi, I guess.'

'Well, why don't you go to Lubumbashi then. It is safe that way. There'd be no problems. I could even come with you if you wanted me to. Not on a bike, though, but I could take the train or a truck and meet you there.'

I sat quietly and thought about it. I really wanted to go east and see Rwanda and Burundi. However, I had no desire to be caught up in any fighting or trouble, although I suspected it might not be that bad and all would be calm when I passed. Lubumbashi was the sensible option though. As usually happened, Charlie continued talking before I had finished with my thoughts. He was too quick for me.

'Why don't you stay another day and see what the news is tomorrow?'

'No, I can't stay longer.' That was the only thing I knew.

'It's only one more day.'

'I know, but …' and I took a deep sigh and looked into Charlie's blue eyes that were boring into me, 'I can't stay. It's taken two weeks to finally get round to leaving. It will only be harder tomorrow. You know, I felt sick all last night I hardly slept. Sick at the thought of leaving you and leaving here and …'

'So stay.'

'I can't!' I exclaimed and then was silent. I wanted to make him understand how I was feeling, how I was torn between staying and going, how every time he suggested I stay was like having my insides ripped out from where I stood because in my heart I really wanted to, but I also couldn't give up on getting to Cape Town, which now had become a euphemism in my mind for not only finishing this trip, but also for my whole life and family and friends in England, and everything I knew that had no place in the Congo, and was my voice of reason.

Charlie read me like an open book. I often think he understood me better than I did myself and had even read pages I had not yet reached. For once he didn't say anything.

'I'll go to Lubumbashi. It doesn't really matter which way I go, and I'd like to take the train anyway.' I felt defeated and relieved in equal measure. The decision was made; at least I would be on the move again. There would be adventure and stories to tell whichever way I went.

'I'm glad. I think it's the best thing.'

'I know.'

'East Africa will always be there.'

'I know.'

'Do you want me to come to Lubumbashi?'

'Yes.'

I should have said no. Sometimes it's hard to let go. This was smoothing down the plaster I had been slowly and excruciatingly removing. I should have ripped the damn thing off in one and been done with it. Just as I flit seamlessly from obsessive bouts of energy and activity to sunken lethargy, so I can fall from being fiercely independent to being downright reliant on another person.

'OK, let's make a plan.' He always said that. It was a phrase he had picked up during his time working in South Africa. South Africans always 'make a plan'.

'You know, you are a lot like an African woman.'

'It must be my skin tone,' I joked. 'What do you mean?'

'I mean that you are always saying "I don't mind" or "I don't care" when I ask you about inconsequential things like what to eat for dinner or whether to take the bus or taxi and you let other people make those decisions. You're very easy-going – most women aren't – until the question is important or something you really care about, and then you're very sure and there's no persuading you otherwise. When an African woman has made up her mind, there is no point trying to change it. I'll come to Lubumbashi.'

The plan was simple: I would cycle to Kaniama, he would take a motorbike or truck and meet me there in a few days, and then we could take the train to Lubumbashi.

He gave me the names of two brothers I could stay with. 'Ask anybody in town; everyone knows who they are.' *Déjà-vu*. If everyone in Mbuji-Mayi knew Marie-Louise, it seemed likely that I could find these brothers in a small town.

It took two very long days to cycle to Kaniama in Katanga province in the south-east of the country. Katanga was a break-away state that was briefly independent in the 1960s, and many people here still see it as separate from the rest of the DRC. It is the richest of the provinces, with most of the wealth generated from its copper and cobalt resources. It is no surprise that many people resent the wealth being taken by the Kinshasa government 2,000 kilometres away when they receive so little in return. It is left to the large mining corporations who control the power in the region to maintain much of the infrastructure, weak as it is. Without the roads they build, mining and industry would be impossible.

So the earth roads were in good condition, and now I could cycle rather than have to push. Rivers had bridges over them and because of the rail line, the larger villages' markets were well supplied. I even saw a standpipe churning out fresh water. It was the first running water I had seen since Kinshasa, two months earlier, that was not a river.

Rain was another matter. Further south now, I had left the forests behind and was cycling through savannah. Under the blue sky of morning, there was no shelter from the burning sun. However, over several hours, clouds amassed until there was a grey blanket of humid oppression. By late afternoon the wind had picked up and a threatening black sky edged ever nearer.

I was going to stop at the next village, but the other men on bikes were going to Kaniama too, and they had also started the day 100 kilometres away, although they had started four hours before me. If they could reach Kaniama, there was no reason why I couldn't. The strength and stamina of people here were astounding, yet they didn't recognise it because it was expected.

The appeal of knowing there was a place to stay, rather than camping through a storm in my leaky tent, drove my aching legs to pedal on. The men stopped for a break, and I continued until, after an hour of cycling, I came to a village where the road petered out into a patch of hard dusty earth surrounded by simple houses.

I stopped to ask the way and was soon surrounded. Everyone wanted to know what I was doing and where I was going, and all I wanted was to know the way, so I could get to where I was going before getting wet. The black clouds were almost upon us, and every time I saw the lightning strike in the near distance, I got more irate at the inane questioning. I knew Kaniama was close and somewhere east of the main road. The problem was that the men were directing me down a road that headed south-west. It didn't make sense.

I focussed on the older man, who commanded most respect. 'Are you sure this is the road to Kaniama?'

'Yes, follow it straight.'

'I said Kaniama, the road to Kaniama. But that road turns right and I need to turn left, don't I?'

'Yes.' Someone tugged on my arm from behind, and I spun round to look at him.

'Come. Come this way. You stay here tonight,' he demanded. I yanked my arm free because I needed it to hold up my bike and because I didn't like being ordered.

'No, I am going to Kaniama.'

'But it is far,' someone else piped up. 'We have a place here for you to stay.'

'No, thank you.' I would have gladly stopped for the day. My tired body and aching legs willed me to, and my mind was ready to give in. But a little voice in my head said *Trust your intuition – it's not safe here*. I felt uneasy and didn't trust anyone I saw. Perhaps it was only the brewing storm and the darkening skies that lent a sinister touch. Darkness magnifies fear in us all. It was probably all in my mind, but I couldn't ignore my gut feeling that had got me safely this far. I had to put my trust in it above these people I didn't know.

I turned back to speak to the older man, but I was distracted now. 'So that's not the road to Kaniama?'

'Yes.'

'OK, so where do I turn left?'

'Just follow that road to Kaniama.'

'OK, if that is the road to Kaniama, where is the main road?

'That is the main road.' *Sigh.*

'So it's main road to Lubumbashi?'

'Yes.'

'Well, it can't be the main road and the road to Kaniama, they're in different directions.' *Help me. Am I going crazy?* If I'd had the energy, I might have started jumping up and down and pulling my hair and dancing like a madman to the Congolese drums.

I looked to the land for help. There was one other track beside the one I had come down. I had assumed it was just an older track. Then again, the other man had been pulling me in that direction. I asked, 'Where does that road go then?'

'Kaniama.'

'What?' *I am going crazy.* 'But you said that road,' and I pointed west down the main road, 'goes to Kaniama.'

'Yes. They both do.' *Finally, we are getting somewhere.*

'OK, so which road is shorter?' They pointed to the second track.

'But the main road is better. That track is very bad. It is better you go on the main road. That is the way the vehicles go.'

'Yes, but I am on a bicycle. Which way would you go if you were on a bicycle?' Everyone pointed to the track. *Finally, an agreement.*

This was always the problem: people heard me speak, but they didn't listen. They don't answer the questions you ask, but give you the answers they think you want to hear. It is all about asking the right question. The problem is knowing what that is.

'How many kilometres is it that way?

'About fifteen.'

My heart sank briefly with the thought of another hour of cycling and bounced right back as the thundered cracked and the adrenalin kicked in. I thanked the men for their help and pedalled off.

Downhill and then winding through forest trails, I would have got lost were it not for the two other locals on bikes I followed. Weaving between trees and dodging roots, swerving to avoid someone coming the other way, and never knowing what was ahead or when I might hit the floor was the kind of riding I liked.

It was almost dark. The men on bikes got further away, and eventually I lost sight of them. Left alone I emerged from the forest and pushed the bike across an open sandy track. The air was saturated and a fine drizzle on the wind was cold through my damp clothes. Palm frond shadows thrashed in the wind and the thunder clapped and roared, and I felt the earth tremble through the tyres. Streaks of lightning shuddered and bolted across the sky overhead and lit up the pink-tinged clouds, and for a few seconds I could see the route ahead before being plunged into darkness until the lightning forked from cloud-to-cloud again.

I came to a stream, crossed it and went up the other side where there was another bedraggled soul pushing his bike up the slippery mud slope. When we crossed a train line, I asked him how far it was to Kaniama.

'This is Kaniama,' he said. I couldn't see anything. We walked on together.

'Where are you going?'

'Kaniama.'

'Me too. I don't suppose you know Guy or Lambert?'

'Yes.'

'Really?'

'Yes.'

'Do you know where they live?'

'Yes, I will show you.'

We came to a wide river, lined with houses, which was the main avenue through town, flooded and flowing with muddy water. We cycled along it, mud spraying up our legs and rain pelting down in big heavy drops. Kaniama was drowning in the storm. Down smaller sodden streets, we slipped and slid on unseen stones and sandy gulleys carved out by the water, and when we couldn't pedal we pushed instead, and the water flowed over my feet and squelched in my shoes.

'Is it much further?'

'Not far,' he always gave the same reply. On and on we went and the rain was relentless. All was dark and I had no idea where I was going, and then suddenly my guide through the night said, 'We are here. This is Guy's home.'

My guide knocked on a door. When it opened, he spoke quickly with the man standing inside, and then he turned to me and said to be safe, and with that he was gone. I called out thanks through the blackness, but there was no reply. I never saw him again.

'You have cycled from London. Come, come, Charlie's friend.' *What?* News travels fast with mobile phones.

Soon I was washed, in dry clothes, supplied with beer and being fed and treated like one of the family. Here was a beautiful home with soft furnishings and lighting, warm and comfortable, lived-in and loved. I could relax here.

There was not much to do in Kaniama, but as in Lusambo and Mbuji-Mayi a week passed quickly. Charlie arrived the next day. He had known Guy and Lambert since they were children. Now they have their own children. We would sit and talk and drink at the house and then walk into town and do the same in the shade of a *paillote* and wait until dinner. Then we would eat fufu and fish or fufu and chicken or fufu and duck or guinea pig or snake or any other animal that was living a few hours earlier, but ended up in the pot. We would sit outside under the stars and drink beer late into the evening and talk and laugh and when we started yawning, go to bed and sleep deeply until the sound of the rooster woke us up and then lie half-awake half-dreaming until my stomach said it must be time for breakfast, and we would drink coffee and talk and sit in the shade of the house as the sun heated the dusty earth and the children went to school or to play in the fields absorbed in their games, and then it was time for beer, so we drank some more and realised that another day had passed, and I wondered which day the train would arrive.

24

Malaria in Lubumbashi

DRC and Zambia

There was no train timetable. The train would arrive when it was ready – thinking or worrying about it wouldn't make it come any faster. The only thing to do was make sure I was on that train when it left. Since the train only stopped in Kaniama for about thirty minutes, I had to keep an ear out and never be too far away.

I asked Charlie if he could find out when the train was expected. Charlie asked Guy, and Guy asked his friends while they were sat drinking in the *paillote,* and one said the police chief may know, who was then asked, and he said he knew who could find out with a phone call. Everyone always knew someone in the know. If that person didn't really know, he made up an answer anyway because any answer is as likely to be right or wrong where nothing is certain.

The phone call was made, and the train's scheduled arrival was narrowed down to a 'not before' date. When that passed, it was expected on Tuesday. By Tuesday night they said it would not arrive tomorrow, but probably on Thursday, although it could arrive anytime, so to be ready just in case. Finally, on Thursday around midday, while we were drinking like every other day, Guy said to be quiet and listen and yes, that was the sound of the train and to go get our bags immediately if we were not to miss it.

We walked down the laterite track, past the defunct dairy farm full of abandoned machinery that would work if only someone tried and past the derelict gas station now entirely overgrown, so that the only visible sign was the Fina logo peeking through nature's wall in final protest.

Guy and Charlie always talked about how things once worked. When the Belgians were here things worked, now they don't. They may be biased as there is Belgian blood in them both. No doubt their grandfathers talked of better bygone colonial days. But I heard the same from other Congolese, and while they would not wish to give up their country's independence, none of them denied that things worked better then.

They also talked of how things could work again. It was just talk though, of hollow dreams that faded into thin air and what might have been. People here have spent so long living through uncertain times that they have learnt to live only for today. If you ask a man who is struggling to feed his family why he doesn't plant seeds, so that fruit trees will grow on his land and provide food for his children, he will ask if they will feed his children today – they won't and he knows it. Well, then that is not a solution to his current problem. Why would he spend money on seed he cannot afford for trees that may never even provide food for his children in the future? His history tells him there are many things, beyond his control, that can happen to prevent those seedlings growing into mature fruit-giving trees. He would think that you are the foolish one for suggesting such a thing.

The train was powered by a Sheltam locomotive run by South Africans. It was green with yellow and red reggae stripes and looked out of place: it was working. Charlie asked if we could ride up front with the South Africans. It is the advantage of speaking many languages, and Charlie spoke six, that you can converse with almost anyone you meet. A common language is a good basis for friendship.

I waved to Guy and his family, and we called out, 'Bye-o' and 'God-bye'. Finally, the train was ready to leave, and when it began rolling down the tracks, we went inside and made a space to sit and peered through the grating in the window.

'I love it how they say God-bye here,' I said to Charlie.

'I don't. It sounds so final like it's the last goodbye ever and you'll never see them again.'

'I don't know about that,' I said.

The train stopped in Kamina to change locomotive and then was not allowed to leave. There was news that the Mai-Mai rebels, having been driven out from near Mbuji-Mayi, had come south and now attacked a village further down the rail line. Despite changing my route drastically to avoid encountering them, it was ironic that they had chosen here and now to resurface. Some things you cannot foresee or plan for.

Eventually, the train was allowed to continue. After all, the Mai-Mai had no interest in a passenger train or a white tourist; they were only interested in money and mines.

The second half of the journey was much slower, run by the Congolese. Most of the time the train was stationary. It stopped in the bush because there was not enough power to pull all the passenger carriages up the slight incline.

Two men were uncoupling the carriage ahead of the one I was in when they saw me peering out of the window; work stopped, shouting commenced, and finally the carriages behind were uncoupled instead – the white girl was not going to be left waiting in the bush. So we waited at the next station while the engine went back to relay the stranded carriages. There was time to use the toilet and wash, which was much needed on a five-day journey.

I walked to the small building standing isolated in a field. There was a queue of women waiting outside the toilets – that's normal anywhere in the world. The men's side was free – same as always. I lingered at the back of the queue contemplating whether to use the men's side. I peered round the women and looked through the door. Inside, the walkway was crammed full of naked women of all shapes covered in soap. There was water everywhere. This wasn't a toilet; it was a shower.

'Toilette, non?' I asked the women near me. They looked at each other and said something I didn't understand. Some pointed away and another pointed inside, and they spoke quickly.

'I'm sorry, I don't understand.'

'You, pi-pi or ka-ka?' one lady shouted out to me. That I understood. I hesitated to reply – English prudishness at play.

'Me? Ka-ka,' and they laughed because I understood, and I laughed because I couldn't believe I was shouting out in the middle of a field to a group of women that I needed to take a shit – that is not normal anywhere in the world.

I was led to the front of the queue where I squeezed my way past the large black naked soapy bodies being rigorously scrubbed. Behind the door at the end was the hole in the ground. The door was glass panelled although some of them were missing, and when I squatted down I could see the suds running down the back on one lady's thick calves. The other gaps were higher up and blocked by a butt or other body part, so that no one could see in. Then the owner of the large naked butt bent over and peered between her legs, so that suddenly I was confronted with a big smiling face at my squat-height eye-level.

'*Ça va?*' she asked.

'Yes. I'm fine,' and with that the head disappeared again. Privacy, like tourism, was a foreign concept here.

The next stop was longer. The police searched up and down the carriages looking for alcohol. It was illegal to sell and drink it on the trains although that stopped nobody. Anyone too drunk was rounded up and arrested until they paid a fine or sobered up.

* * *

Lubumbashi was a large modern city and came as a shock after two months on the road and in the bush. There were supermarkets, imported electrical goods, many restaurants, and a large ex-pat community. We stayed with Charlie's brother in the Bel Air suburb where, instead of the Fresh Prince, there were potholes, dirt roads, and corner kiosks selling one dollar phone top-up cards.

After two weeks in Lubumbashi, lapping up the luxury of choice restaurants, bars and clubs, it was time to return to the road. Life was much simpler there.

Leaving was not easy. My fight of head over heart on whether to stay or go had ravaged on. My head finally won the struggle – I resolved to leave.

'I'm going to go see my friend, Philippe, for a couple of days about work. You should leave while I'm gone. I don't want to watch you go,' Charlie announced one morning.

'OK.' I was happy with that. 'I'll go the day after tomorrow. I could do with popping into town to get some things first.'

Charlie left that evening. I went straight to bed. I was too tired to feel much or do anything. In the short time between our farewells and when my head hit the pillow, there was only a fleeting loneliness that swept over me before I drifted into a deep dreamless sleep until I woke with a churning stomach. I put it down to the meal we had eaten at a restaurant in town with some friends.

As we had dug into the grilled chicken someone had commented that it tasted bad. We all said we would suffer the consequences because we were too hungry to complain or care. That was the only time I got food poisoning on the trip, and it was at the smartest, most expensive restaurant. Street food was always safer.

After an unusually late wake up, I took the bus into town, but wandering around was exhausting. I gave up and took a taxi straight back. There was nothing I needed that I couldn't get on the way. I spent the afternoon lying listless in bed.

It was cooler now that the rains had started, and I stared mindlessly through the window as the sky turned grey. To think that I had been washing outside in my bikini during the afternoon storms, standing under the water streaming from the roof that had no guttering because I was fed up with bucket showers in a bathtub – it made me shiver.

I pulled up the sheet around my chin, but I still felt cold, so I grabbed the blanket too. It wasn't enough, and finally I overcame my laziness to put on all my warm clothes in an attempt to stop shaking. My skin was clammy like those sweaty nights camping on sun-soaked rocks of the Niger River. I tossed off the covers, but then I was too cold, so I replaced them, and I shivered and sweated, and I couldn't decide if I was hot or cold. I wondered if I might have malaria, and I considered the symptoms and what I should do, but I didn't have the energy or willpower to move from my foetal position buried in the blankets.

Time passed. I don't know how long I had been lying like that when I heard the door open. When no one spoke, I looked up to see who it was.

'What the hell happened to you?' said Charlie who was stood at the far end of the room staring at me.

'What are you doing here?'

'I leave you for a day and look at you. My God, what's wrong?'

'Nothing. I just don't feel too good.'

'Have you got a fever?'

'I don't know … er …'. I touched my forehead with the back of my hand, 'I don't know. My head feels a bit hot, I suppose.' It was very hot.

'Get rid of those blankets. You don't need them.'

'I'm cold. Do you think it could be malaria?'

'Maybe.'

'Should I take the treatment?'

'Have you got some?'

'Yes.' I had been given one pack along with some antibiotics by Emily, an English doctor volunteering in Freetown. I had bought a second pack in Abuja at the Sheraton Hotel pharmacy, which I figured was the least likely place to be selling counterfeit drugs.

'Then yes. Where is it? I'll get it.' I took the first dose. I wondered what my doctor would have thought about this self-medication.

'So what are you doing here?' I asked Charlie again.

'I felt awful running off and leaving you, so I came back and will say goodbye when you leave.'

'You didn't need to.'

'It looks like I did. Why didn't you tell Gaston you were sick?'

'I hadn't got round to it yet.'

'OK, well, you should rest.'

Later that evening, I got up and joined Charlie, Gaston his brother, and Phillipe sat outside on the plastic chairs that were the only seating in the house and got moved inside or outside as the weather demanded.

'Are you feeling better?'

'Yeah, a bit. I've stopped sweating and shivering at least.'

'You look better,' Charlie said.

Want some beer?' Gaston asked.

'No thanks.'

'You're not that much better then.'

'I'll be fine. I'll still leave tomorrow like planned.'

'No you won't. You must rest,' Charlie said, his eyes locked on me.

'No, it's fine. I'll be OK. I'll take it slowly,' I replied adamantly, holding Charlie's stare.

'Listen to Charlie.' I broke eye contact and looked at Phillipe. 'If it's malaria, it's very important you rest. Any exertion or stress will weaken your body and the malaria will come back. You need the energy to fight it. Physical exercise like cycling is a very bad idea,' he added seriously. He was Charlie's friend and would always back him up, but he did have a point.

'I don't know. I'd rather go.' My resolve was starting to waiver.

'Look. Stay a few days, until you finish those pills and then go. You could go and stay at Phillipe's where it's quiet. He's got Internet and TV and lots of movies. You can sleep, catch up with emails and stuff you can't do here, and then head off when you're well,' Charlie suggested.

'You're welcome at my house with my daughter. She would love you to stay. You can have your own room and we'll take you out for pizza or whatever you want to eat.'

I conceded. *Am I ever going to leave the Congo?*

Three days later I cycled out of Lubumbashi. I said goodbye to Charlie again.

'Will you come back?'

'I'll come back. I need to finish what I started first, but I will.' I meant it too then. I don't say things unless I mean them.

'Really?'

'I said I would.' The only problem was that I had the idea to return for a few months, Charlie thought I meant much longer.

'You won't, but it's OK.'

We hugged until he whispered, 'Just don't say God-bye,' and with that he let go.

I raised my hand to wave but lowered it again, 'Bye-o.' I feigned a smile and the corners of my mouth creased briefly before I gave up and just stood staring.

'Bye-o,' he said as he turned around and walked away. And that was the saddest I ever felt, and it was for Charlie, who looked back through tears and a look as though it were the last time he would ever see me with his blue eyes piercing like arrows.

* * *

It was a full day's ride to Kasumbalesa, which had all the noise and dirt and dubious characters that a busy border town breeds. Unwilling to get an exit stamp, I stumbled into a bar instead. I half-heartedly considered turning around and going back. Everything I did was half-hearted now. *Might as well put those last grubby Congolese francs to good use – a Simba for old-time's sake.* It never is just one beer.

It was dark and about to rain when I thought to find a hotel. There was no shortage of cheap brothels. The nightclub music grated and reverberated round the four whitish walls of my room, and I could still hear the mosquitoes' high-pitched buzzing round my head. For each one I killed, smearing blood over the sheet and walls, another took its place. I couldn't sleep anyway: my heart was racing like a runaway train. *Perhaps I should have rested longer in Lubumbashi.* It was too late now.

I lay awake until morning, packed my bags and walked to the border. Summoned to the front of the queue, I soon had an exit stamp. There was no going back now. So I pushed my bike through the mud, between the endless queue of lorries. The narrow spaces between them were filled with bikes loaded with goods. There was deadlock, with nobody going forward, and nobody going back – nobody, that is, except me. My fully loaded bike was moving through the air by two boys carrying it above head height. I followed behind, bike- and bag-less. All I had to do was answer the endless flow of questions from the motionless transporters.

'You come from Congo?'

'Yes.'

'You go to Zambia?

'Yes.' I thought that was obvious.

Past Zambian immigration, I cycled on the smooth tarmac road past the ten-kilometre line of stationary lorries waiting to cross the border. Unless they bribed their way to the front of the queue, they would be waiting months. It was no wonder imported goods in the Congo cost so much.

Sometimes when you cross a border, you instantly know you're in a different country: a new language, a new uniform, driving on the other side of the road. With Zambia, it was the birds. The air was filled with sweet happy chirps and deep soulful calls. Zambia was alive with wildlife. In Central Africa it had all ended up on the dinner plate.

I arrived in the first town after the border with a lacklustre attitude and my heart still racing. I checked into the first hotel I saw and slept. The next day, fuelled on only by my stubbornness, I crawled to the next town. My heart pounded, and every exertion was exhausting. I checked into another hotel, slept and stayed another night. Gradually, I gained strength, and I felt life returning to my body and with it, some enthusiasm.

The first major town in Zambia was a shock. There were traffic lights and pedestrian crossings. I was shouted at for going through a red light. *Wait – I thought I was in Africa! No one cares about traffic signals.* Now I was in southern Africa, and that, I found, made a big difference.

There were supermarkets too – huge, air-conditioned rooms with aisle upon aisle of imported goods. Choose fresh foods. Choose tinned foods. Choose cold drinks and hot meals. Choose kitchen wares or toilet products. Shopping was much simpler when I could only buy spaghetti and sardines from a wooden shack. Me, I chose chocolate. And crisps and cheese and meat and yoghurt and fresh milk and very tasty pastries and my new favourite Chakalaka tins of spicy vegetables. Soon I was fully loaded and my panniers were overflowing too.

The copper belt with big mines, dusty tracks, and trundling trucks eventually gave way to huge tracts of farmland where the savannah had been fenced and flattened – wilderness tamed. Farming was now on an industrial scale with huge machinery and massive irrigation systems. The farms were mostly white-owned; the poorer blacks made do with the wide roadside verges and simple hoes. According to the small wooden signs staked into the ground, this was 'Community Farming and Conservation in Action'.

Zambia was all too easy. I missed listening to conversations in French intermingled with Lingala, Tshiluba, or Swahili. I found myself looking for cheap restaurants that served *fufu*, except now it was called *nsima*. Deep-fried chicken and chips in fast-food chain restaurants were more common though. People asked if I needed a knife and fork and were surprised when I ate the *nsima* with my hands like the locals and drank water that wasn't from a sealed bottle.

In Lusaka, Zambia's capital, I found a backpackers hostel, the first on this trip. After four night's camping in the bush, I needed to wash. Directed to the shower block, I was perplexed. *Where's the bucket? Where's the water?* Instead, I was confronted with two taps. I tentatively turned one of them. *Ouch! Hot water!* This was not the Africa I was used to. I could count the hot showers from the last year on one hand. The number of cold showers wasn't many more. For months, it had been only buckets of water or rivers to wash in.

After the shower, I seated myself on a stool at the bar and drank Mosi beer. Soon the other barstools were occupied too. It was Friday afternoon, the end of the working week. Guys in shirts and smart shoes bought drinks and got drunk. I vaguely remembered that was what you did when you had a regular job and always knew the time and the day. This was not the Africa I was used to. It was more like home. It had been a long week for me too, only mine was measured in kilometres rather than emails.

Ryan came and sat down next to me at the bar. He was a local Zambian whose family had a farm. He had travelled in Africa on business and always stayed at this hostel when he came to Lusaka.

'You aren't like most of the tourists, white people, who come here.'

'What do you mean?' This was not a common line of conversation. I had not seen many tourists or white people until now. The girls in my dorm were all British gap-year goers and ten years younger than I. They seemed so vibrant and naive, and I felt worn and faded like the clothes I was wearing.

Ryan considered this momentarily and looked like he had many thoughts and was trying to choose where to start. All he said was, 'You've been sat quietly at the bar all afternoon, talking with these guys.' He nodded to the young men at the bar.

'Well, why wouldn't I?' It had been good to talk with educated young men about things other than the possibility of sex or marriage.

'And you're talking with me now.'

'Should I not?' I asked with a mock-coquettish grin and a raised eyebrow. But he didn't see the sarcasm and continued seriously. The subtlety of British humour was the one thing I always missed wherever I travelled.

'No, it's just that most of the white tourists only talk with other white tourists.'

'I suppose so.' I could not think of anything I wanted to hear from the gap-year students whose primary concern seemed to be to tick the guidebook checklist of top things to do in Africa.

Have you done the falls yet? Oh, why of course! And today I'm doing the rafting before I do a safari in Botswana. You just HAVE to stay at the backpackers camp in Kasane, I've been told. I did Tanzania last week, but apart from Zanzibar there's not much to do, and the safari is cheaper here.

I could not fathom how you could 'do' a country within a week, have any understanding of the cultural complexities that tie it together like a patchwork quilt, and have time to see the diversity of nature that exists there.

'You're much more interesting to talk to,' I said to Ryan. 'Besides, why would I come to Zambia and spend all my time talking with English people? I can do that in England.'

'You have a point. They will go home soon and tell their friends how they have travelled and seen Africa. You can't know Africa unless you talk with Africans.'

'Perhaps. But they are still young,' I defended. I saw flashes of an eighteen-year-old me in them. The only difference was that I had gone backpacking in South America. 'We all need time to grow up and learn for ourselves. Anyway, I don't think you can truly know Africa unless you have lived here, and I have not.'

'So what are you doing?' *Sigh.* I gave the abridged version of the last eighteen months.

'What are you searching for?' *That question again.*

'I'm not searching for anything.'

'You are. You don't undertake such a journey unless you are searching for something.'

'Maybe I have found it.' I was thinking about how I was missing Charlie and the Congo and about going back.

'No, you have not.' Ryan was adamant.

'I think I have.'

'Believe me, you haven't.' He sounded like Charlie, so sure. *How dare he presume to know me after only ten minutes talking! But maybe he has a point.* I didn't entirely believe what I was saying. It annoyed me that he could give a straight answer when I could not.

When the road was easy, and it had been, and with only myself for company, my deliberations were my only diversion. I had spent hours in the saddle with one track on endless repeat – what did I want in life? Now, my attempt at scratching this record from my thoughts with beer, for just one night, had failed. Ryan had got me thinking again.

'You don't know me. Why are you so sure?'

'Because you wouldn't be here, talking to me, if you had. When you find what you have been searching for, you don't then leave it behind.' It was that simple.

The rest of the weekend was an alcohol-fuelled haze, and by Monday morning I was back to work on the bike. Ryan said goodbye, 'I really hope you find what you're looking for.'

Was it not possible to undertake a journey without searching for anything? Was it not enough to simply enjoy each day and everything that came with it, and to be free and happy?

I realised that it was a search for happiness that set me on this journey, and I found it everyday in the freedom of life on the road. Happiness, for me, was not settling down in one place, the Congo or anywhere else, not yet. For now, I was most content living only for today.

A couple of weeks later, when I had built up the courage to email Charlie, I explained that I would not rush back once I reached Cape Town. A huge weight was lifted off my shoulders as I dragged myself out from the avalanche of self-imposed commitment. There was now no rush to reach Cape Town and after that was a blank slate again. It was liberating, and I relished the possibilities that lay ahead.

I conjured up outlandish plans for my immediate future and planned them down to the finest detail. When one idea was perfected, I thought up another. There were so many things I wanted to do that enjoying each day with little thought to the future was going to be a full time occupation.

Part Four
Southern Africa

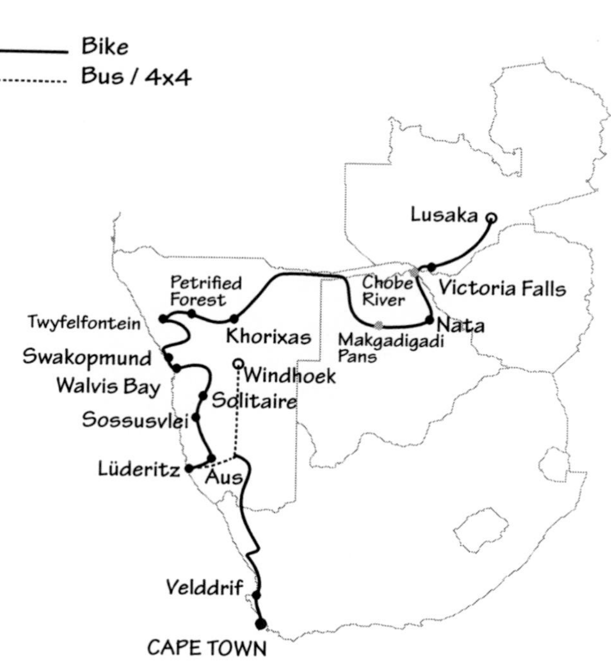

25

Living Among Lions

Botswana and Namibia

'You must pray to God every night.'

'No.'

'You do believe in God though?'

'Hmm ...' I decided to be honest, 'no.'

'You must believe in God. You cycled here from England and you're still alive!'

'Well, no I don't. But yes I am, clearly.'

'Then what do you believe in?'

There was not time for a long philosophical debate. I was waiting for the boat to cross the river into Botswana, and it was already on the way.

'I'm not sure. I suppose, I believe in sound judgement,' I smiled, 'and a spot of good luck.' I was thinking back to when I swam in the Sankuru River in the Congo and was later told there were many crocodiles lurking in the murky depths. That was definitely not one of my smarter moves. It is easy to forget about unseen threats. *Perhaps just a lot of good luck.*

The young man in smart trousers and polo shirt tucked in at the waist studied me and shifted his bag uneasily on his shoulder. He was not sure what to believe now. We both stood in silence until the platform ferry reached the bank and then walked on.

'But aren't you scared?'

'Of what – people? No.'

'Scared of animals?'

'Not so much.'

'But the lions. You must be scared of lions.'

'Not really.' There weren't many lions to worry about the way I had come. They were on my mind though. I often thought about what was down the road, and lions were definitely there. 'I have been thinking about them,' I admitted.

'What are you going to do about them?' *Good question. I had been wondering about that too.*

'Well, unless I hear better advice, I guess I'll cycle in the daylight and stay in my tent at night when they'll be hunting. And trust to luck.'

'Man, I can't believe you're still alive. I mean, this is Africa.' As I pushed my bike down the ramp into Botswana, he called after me, 'I shall pray for you tonight.'

Those words were ringing in my ears as I started south towards Nata. The road passes through game reserves, which means fewer people and more animals.

Initially, my main concern was water. I bought an extra bottle before leaving town. Barely two kilometres later, the water bottle rattled loose from the bottom cage, rolled under the back wheel, split open, and deposited the ice-cold water over the tarmac. Another two kilometres further on, the water bottle strapped to the front pannier slipped out. It, too, rolled under the back wheel and punctured. Water spurted from a hole in the plastic. I dropped the bike in the road and rushed to save what I could. This had never happened in 20,000 kilometres, and now it had happened twice in four. I checked the remaining water bottles were secure and wondered whether my good luck had run out at last.

I kept a lookout for any unsavoury wildlife that might consider me a savoury snack. *Perhaps I have been lucky until now. I'd better not push it.* My field of view was limited by dense green bush to my left and right. Only the grey asphalt continued ahead endlessly to the horizon.

It was a grey, dull day and certain to rain. I intensely scanned the bush looking for lions. My plan was to cycle only once the sun was well up, when any lions would be resting from the heat. This didn't account for cool, overcast days like today. Hopefully, they wouldn't be hunting me. Elephants, I had been warned, were also numerous on this road. I figured they would be easy to see.

It was not long before I sighted the first elephant, surprisingly well camouflaged by the thick bush and grazing on a tree by the roadside. I was almost on top of him before we both saw each other. He immediately stopped eating and turned to face me. I pedalled faster.

I was still wondering how I managed to miss seeing the elephant when I saw a herd of them ahead. I had slowed down to consider the options when a white 4x4 pulled up alongside me. It was the police from the checkpoint I had passed earlier.

'Are you OK?' one officer asked, as you might to someone who looks lost.

'Fine,' I said.

'You do know there are wild animals on this road, don't you?'

'Yes.' *I'm not stupid.*

'Do you know what to do if you see a lion?'

Is this a test? 'I would like to know what you advise,' I said tentatively.

'Well, we haven't tried this you realise,' and the officers exchanged glances, 'but this is what you are supposed to do if you see a lion: you stop, face the lion and don't move. It's very important that you don't run away.'

I stood silently, expecting to hear what I should do next, but nothing more was offered. 'OK,' I encouraged and waited for the officer to continue.

'Well, if you are OK, take care and be safe.' The driver turned on the ignition and started to make a U-turn.

That's it?

I pedalled away, confused, wondering how any wild cat staring contest would end. Then I remembered the elephants. One had seen or smelt me. It turned, with trunk in the air and huge ears agitated, and then the others reacted too. *Uh oh.*

Fortunately, the police saw and drove up alongside to shelter me. Now that I was hidden from view, the elephants went back to grazing. Then the police left.

Alone once more.

This whole time, I was cycling faster than usual and didn't stop for breaks. It was a completely irrational response to the lion threat. I would only be more tired if (and hopefully not when) there was a problem. Adrenalin fuelled me on, but that could not last.

My mind wandered, and the next thing I was aware of was that the bush had gone and I was cycling through open savannah. I wondered how long I had been lost in my own thoughts, not thinking about lions or elephants. Since I was failing to see huge elephants that didn't even try to hide, I was unlikely to see a lion stealthily stalking me. I decided to stop thinking about it, turned on my music and tuned out. Ignorance is bliss.

I couldn't ignore the little Metro with three young girls and their luggage crammed inside. It pulled up alongside me.

'Hi. We thought we should warn you that there is a lion ahead.'

'Oh. How far ahead?'

'Um. Not far.' *Not helpful.*

'Just roughly. Is it 100 metres? One kilometre? Five?'

'You see that tree over there? Near there,' the girl pointed. *About 500 metres then.*

I clearly didn't look too concerned because the blonde girl in the passenger seat leant over and went on to clarify, 'It's a rather, um, aggressive lion.'

'Really?' *What's that supposed to mean?*

'Yes, it's rather aggressive. It tried to climb on the car.'

I looked at the little blue and white metal box they were crammed in and thought that wouldn't be hard. I thanked them for warning me, thought quickly, and concluded I should wait for the next sizeable vehicle to come and ask for a lift.

It was the end of the South African Christmas vacation time, and many families were returning to Johannesburg. While loading my bike onto the roof on one couple's vehicle, another stopped. The driver leant out to ask what the problem was.

'There's no problem. Apparently there's an angry lion ahead, so I'm going to get a lift past.'

'A lion!' The lady passenger exclaimed.

'We'll go and check it out for you,' the driver said, already swinging his Land Cruiser around in the road. They just wanted a photograph.

When we passed, the couple were out of their vehicle on the other side of the road. That didn't strike me as a sensible thing to do. We slowed down, curious and concerned.

You know that feeling when you have spent the morning cleaning the car only to have your pet cat jump up and leave a trail of paw prints over the bonnet? You might even want to strangle the cat. Now imagine you are driving through Botswana in your shiny white, brand new Land Cruiser, and you stop to take a photograph of a lion, and it leaps. Now you have huge muddy paw marks smudged down the side of your vehicle along with deep scratches and a hole where the rear side window used to be with glass shattered over your luggage in the back. If that happened, you would be really pissed off.

Every person who travels through southern Africa has a lion story to tell. It is usually about someone they know of, a friend of a friend or their brother's wife's sister. The stories are always recounted, embellished and romanticised until they assume a mythical status. Even Livingstone had his own lion story. He was attacked and lost the use of his left arm. And as long as lions continue to roam the African landscape and tourists come to see them, there will always be new tall tales to replace the old.

For me, it was enough just to see one. I did of course tell of my brief lion encounter when people asked because it was the kind of story that people like to hear, and it was the one I knew best because it was mine, even if it wasn't the greatest.

There was also the story of the man who was eaten by a lion when he came back from the camp toilets during the night. The family found his remains the next morning. No one seemed to know this man. Instead, they told the story because it had happened only a few weeks ago, and they had since stayed at that very same bush camp.

There was the story of the jeep that wouldn't restart after the driver had switched off the engine while the passengers took photos of a pride of lions they had come across in the Kalahari. They had no means of communication and for three days were trapped inside their vehicle with little water and only the footwell to piss in. All the while the lions waited patiently. By chance, a ranger with a rifle happened upon them and guarded the driver while he repaired the vehicle.

My personal favourite was of the local man who used to cycle home every day from the farm he worked at. He did not worry about lions because he had lived and worked there all his life and had never had any trouble. Worrying would not help anyway, and what would be was God's will. It was a white-owned farm, like many large farms in southern Africa. When the family heard that their worker used to cycle so far without protection, they gave him a rifle.

'What use is a rifle when I need two hands to cycle? A lion will not wait while I stop pedalling, halt, hold the barrel up, take aim and fire.'

'Take it anyway. It may save your life one day.'

His solution was to strap the loaded rifle to the frame of the bike, so that he only had to remove one hand from the handlebars to pull the trigger. The day came when there was a lion on the road. The man was so surprised that he fired the rifle and because it wasn't aimed right it missed the lion, but the recoil was enough to send the bike backwards, and the man was catapulted over the handlebars and landed with a thump and broken arm on the earth. The lion was so surprised by the flying man that it ran off. So maybe the rifle did save his life, if not in the intended way.

There are many exclusive lodges throughout southern Africa. Upmarket camps where you can sleep in rustic cabañas, sip gin and tonics beside the pool, drink beer in the open-air bars and eat gourmet meals of fresh game served by black-tie waiters. These lodges regularly have a place to camp also. They cater for the numerous couples and families on holiday who arrive in their fully-equipped 4x4s carrying everything they need to camp in style. They are well-suited also to a cycle-tourer who is looking for a shower and safe place to sleep.

I had cooked pasta for dinner as usual and was sat beside my tent about to eat when one of the camp guards handed me a note on a scrap of paper:

> INVITATION! To join us for supper tonight as our guest. You spoke to our three daughters earlier – we are normal but pleased to hear about your trip. We are having bubbly in Chalet 23 now, but will eat about 7.30 p.m. Join us for bubbly or supper, whichever you feel like. JOLLY GOOD FOR YOU BIKING ALL THIS WAY! Fitzgerald family. (We'll recognize you if you come to where supper is served!)

They would recognise me, I thought, by the faint odour, even after a wash, that was engrained in my slightly ripped, dirt-stained shirt, which was my smartest (only) top I hadn't been cycling in for four days. I was not kitted out for civilised company and fine dining. I had not used a knife or fork or plate in months. I was used to shovelling pasta or oats straight from the pan with a spoon without a pause for thought until every last morsel had been devoured.

I put the lid on the pasta, which would keep for tomorrow's lunch, and wandered over to the chalet. They were all too polite to comment on my appearance. Anyone who says 'jolly good' has been brought up well enough to know what not to say.

To make up for the Fitzgeralds' generosity, I gave the only thing I had: tales from the road. I told my lion story because it was still fresh in my mind. Flea, the mother, recounted a story of a friend who woke up in their tent on a rainy night. He discovered a lion had crawled underneath to shelter and was lying down beside the man. The friend dared not move, and thanks to his intoxicated state, he fell back to sleep. When he awoke in the morning all that remained was some lion spoor.

With the lion episode fresh in my mind and recent warnings of more lions, cheetahs and wild dogs, I intently scanned the bush the next day. Anthills in the distant verge were easily mistaken for lions lying in the grass, just as rocks in the Niger River were easily mistaken for hippos' heads. *Stop being paranoid, just be cautious.* That was more easily said than done, when in the space of one day three different vehicles stopped to tell me there were lots of lions in the area.

'It would be better not to cycle, but if you must, then don't stop for long. Aren't you scared of the wild animals?'

'Not so much,' I replied, although by now I was thinking that maybe I should be.

'So you are in God's hands. You must pray a lot every night.'

'Something like that,' I said to evade a discussion on religion, but I was thinking that maybe I should start praying. I remembered the road safety officer who, the day before, had wished me, 'Have a safe journey to your destiny.' I had no idea where my destiny lay; I just hoped to reach my next destination.

That night I slept in the bush near a waterhole frequented by cattle. I retired to my tent before dark. Lions, apparently, aren't smart enough to realise a person might be inside the flimsy tent. As long as I didn't get out in the night, I would be safe. Besides, humans are not on a lion's typical menu. As long as I didn't threaten one, I would be safe. That is easy for someone to say from the comforts of their en-suite room in a luxury lodge. It is little comfort when alone in the bush with only a bike pump for a weapon. Hyenas, I was warned, are smarter (or hungrier) and will rip through the tent and drag me out head or foot first.

I lay in my tent and listened as the wind picked up and watched the sheet lightning in the distant dark sky. Most of the cattle had finished drinking a while ago and had wandered past my tent, stopping briefly out of curiosity before continuing further into the bush. A couple were still lingering, and I could hear them laboriously masticating the cud.

I must have drifted off to sleep because I was woken up by a howling wind. Sleepily, I forced my eyes open, wondering what the time was. The outer of my tent was flapping wildly in the wind, and I noticed that the zip had come undone. I could see past the clearing to the scrub and small trees. The clouds had passed now, and the bush was dimly lit by the starry sky.

Suddenly, I was alert – if I could see out, other things could clearly see in. I grabbed my head-torch and reached for the zip and that was when I saw it: the outline of a large body, sleek and powerful, moving through the bush with long loping strides. The head turned, and two yellow eyes reflected back at me. *Shit.* I quickly zipped up the tent and thought a thousand thoughts in a skipped heartbeat, and then my head filled with the beat of my racing heart. *Maybe it didn't see me. … Maybe it's not hungry. … Maybe my luck has run out.*

There was now something trying to get into the tent. *For the first time in my life, is now the time to start praying? Is it my destiny to be devoured by a lion?* No, it was two hunting dogs, and they were furiously crawling under the tent outer to get inside. I tried to push them out, and as one sneaked in there was an almighty yelp as the other dog disappeared, dragged into the darkness. *Shit. Perhaps one dog is enough cat-food.* I sat there, motionless, not knowing what to do.

After some time, I noticed that the dog inside my tent had calmed down. It turned round and round in a tiny circle, padding down the end of my sleeping bag before it curled up and closed its eyes. *If the dog isn't concerned about the lion, then there's no need for me to worry either. It's not like I can do anything anyway.* Overcome by tiredness, I too lay down with my feet against the warm body and fell fast asleep.

I woke in the morning, slowly roused back to consciousness by daylight flooding in. I felt exhausted. Before I even opened my eyes, memories of the night came flooding back to me in a tidal wave that shocked me into the present. My eyes flashed open, and I looked around – the tent zip was firmly closed and all was peaceful. The wind had gone and left only an eerie stillness. Something was not right – the dog was gone. My brain finally woke up, and I realised that there never was a dog, or two, or a lion, only a dream.

But it did make me wonder what I would actually do if there was a lion outside my tent. Or a hyena.

* * *

Africa's wildlife is not best seen from a bike saddle. The animal encounters were frequent, but often fleeting and occasionally fear-inducing. It was a game of who would see who first.

With any of the many antelopes – impala, kudu, gemsbok, springbok, and bushbuck to name a few – they are quick-witted and ever alert, flighty and fast on foot. It was only once they moved, because it is easier to see a moving animal than a stationary one, that I caught a glimpse of their bounding backside as it vanished into the distance.

Elephants, by virtue of their size, were easier to see and less likely to flee. They were dumb to my advances until they smelt me. If I was pedalling faster than the wind, I was upon them in a flash. When, suddenly, they saw me too close for comfort, they turned and threatened to charge.

The big cats surely saw me first. I could only hope they were not hunting me. Lions, like hippos on the Niger River, were one animal I really wanted to see and in equal measure didn't want to, at least not too close or be the last thing I ever saw.

However, cycling is great for seeing birds and smaller creatures that roam and run and burrow and build. But for the big game, it was better to travel by jeep or boat.

I took an evening cruise along the Chobe River that forms the northern border of Botswana. I watched hippos basking in the dying sun, a warthog racing along the shore, a family of elephants come hurtling down the hillside for an end-of-day drink at the river's edge and spotted the eyes of crocodiles hidden in the murky shallows lying in wait for the waterbuck or impala to step too close, so that they could feast. A fish eagle sat on the treetop with its white neck and golden beak held proud. Then it took flight and swooped with razor-sharp talons spread and swiped a fish clean from the river. Grey herons stood and pied kingfishers darted. There was no ignoring the many other cruise boats on the river, and there was no avoiding the feeling that this was little more than an open-air zoo because the animals were guaranteed. There were no fences – the river was their lifeline and chain.

I also went on a day safari in a 4x4 across the Makgadigadi Pans, large expansive salt flats. Just as the Sahara is made up of many deserts, so the Makgadigadi is made up of many salt pans. They are interspersed by sand and savannah and surrounded by the Okavango Delta wetlands to the north and the Kalahari Desert dry land to the south. The salt clay pans shimmered, and the whitened sun-faded earth was crisp and dry except for pools of water from the recent rain that sparkled and reflected the blue sky and white cotton-wool clouds.

There was no shade except a lone baobab, below which dung beetles rolled balls of manure and dragonflies hovered. Herds of wildebeest congregated on the plains and a thousands-strong striped army of zebra took flight when startled by the vehicle. When the searing heat was simmering towards sunset, I saw two bat-eared foxes playfully chasing each other, a jackal and a hare, ostriches on the horizon, and a meerkat peering banded-eyed through the grass. This was the Africa of Attenborough and my imagination.

I used to sneer if someone said they were a birdwatcher. It is easy to disregard things you know nothing of. My interest of birds extended little beyond a passing acknowledgement of those that frequented the garden where I grew up. With the curiosity that comes with youth, I had learnt to recognise the blackbirds, tits, robins, swallows, and house-martins that nested in the stables each summer, coots and moorhens with their chicks that came across from the pond opposite, and sometimes a pair of magpies, which were the only ones I really paid attention to because if I saw one I would search for a second in hope of good luck. Sometimes I peered through the kitchen with binoculars if my mum had spotted a woodpecker, or I saw the barn owl on a telegraph pole on the way home at dusk.

Otherwise, I paid them no attention. It is the constants in life that you end up taking for granted and stop noticing. I was too busy running around and playing games to stop and see the beauty of their finely crafted wings that have perfected the art and science of flight or to see the diversity in their many colours and characters.

The birds in Africa renewed my childlike fascination. They were exotic and colourful and chirped new songs from the bush, or they were big and powerful and gracefully glided in the thermals up high. They were the constant in my solitary life on the road, and I saw them as my friend. They watched over me throughout the day – the lilac-breasted roller on a telegraph wire, the weavers, a bee-eater or one of the many LBJs (Little Brown Jobs, which even bird enthusiasts have trouble identifying), until sunset when they left me to rest in my tent nest until morning. And their dawn chorus was my wake-up call.

* * *

I crossed the border into Namibia late in the afternoon and pedalled fast through the game reserve. Menacing black clouds loomed over the Okavango Delta. I made it to a lodge and put up my tent before the downpour ensued. Then, wet tent, wet clothes. But it would take more than rain to dampen my spirits. I was still dry though, so I went to the bar.

I spent two days cycling north and was now on the road that passed through the Caprivi, a narrow strip of Namibian land squeezed between Botswana, Angola and Zambia. The Caprivi Strip was acquired by the German chancellor, after whom it was named, in an exchange with the UK in 1890 for the island of Zanzibar. It turned out to be a bad deal for the German. The idea was that the land would connect German South-West Africa, as Namibia was then called, with the great Zambezi River, thereby enabling a trade route to the East coast. The Germans completely ignored the significant obstacle that Victoria Falls, with a drop of over 100 metres, posed for a navigable water route.

Livingstone was the first European to set eyes upon the great waterfall that he named in honour of Queen Victoria. It had been known by locals long before as *Mosi-oa-Tunya* meaning, more romantically, 'The Smoke That Thunders'.

When I visited, I heard the rumbling first. Then I saw the water rushing over the rocks and plunging into the depths of the gorge, crashing into a white frothy turbulent mass and billowing cloud of spray that rose on the air and dampened my clothes. Livingstone described it as, 'scenes so lovely must have been gazed upon by angels in their flight'. There was no denying that the falls were impressive, but I could not help feeling slightly disappointed. To pay to enter, and then be guided along wooden walkways along the fenced off waterfall, took away the power and raw beauty of nature.

Despite it being the rainy season, Botswana had been surprisingly dry. The weather was characterised by short sharp storms that refreshed and revived and were a most welcome break from the midday heat and heavy humid overcast days. Now in Namibia, it rained with a vengeance.

Drivers often stopped to ask if I was OK. One local pulled over and leant out of the window, 'Do you want a lift?' he asked. 'Oh … sorry … I thought you were a man cycling in the rain, but you're a girl … a woman … well, that's even worse,' he spluttered on.

A man would be no less drenched than I was, so I just said that I didn't mind the rain (a lie), that I couldn't possibly get any wetter (the truth) and that I had nearly reached the town where I could then get a hotel (another lie – my plan was to sleep in the bush).

The road gradually rose up through the mountains with rich, lush grass in the valley and huge cattle farms and fenced tracts of land. There was nowhere to camp. When it was almost dark, I cycled up to one of the farmhouses, hidden from the road along a rough track, and knocked on the door to ask if I could camp there.

My campsite was a spotless en suite guest room with king-sized bed and massive duvet to get lost in. There was no leaking water dripping on me during the night or puddles under my mattress. For the first time in a week, I put on dry clothes in the morning. Being the uninvited guest was an excellent strategy.

After a filling breakfast, I hit the road and even spied a porthole of blue in the sky. *Will I see the sun today?* No. It rained harder than any other. Fortunately, as I headed further west, the weather improved.

Desert Snow

Near a small town, after an increasingly hot long day on the road, I smelt food. There were two *bakkies* parked by the roadside with smoke rising from a barbecue. As I slowed down, a face peered out from behind one truck and waved.

'That smells really good,' I said, salivating. This introduction was a subtler version of the uninvited guest.

What else could they say except, 'Would you like to join us for some kebabs?'

And what more could I say other than, 'Yes please.' I was already licking my lips in anticipation. Hungry cyclists, not baboons or hyenas, are the scourge of the roadside picnicker. Two kebabs, a rack of ribs and a drink later, I hit the road towards Khorixas. The guys from Grootfontein packed up too and continued the return journey from their fishing trip on the coast.

It was time for some fun – time to hit the gravel and leave a trail of dust. With gravel roads came corrugations and they were not much fun. It was time to shake and rattle and roll on slowly with dust in my hair and grit in my teeth – it was time to grit my teeth and bear it.

Now the sun was out, and it was scorching. Last week life was green; now it ranged from golden yellow to a burned rusty red arid landscape of rocks and few trees.

I stopped in the shade and sat on a gnarled root that poked out of the ground and gulped down my water. I didn't care that it spilt from the corner of my mouth and dribbled down my chest. When I had satisfied my thirst and wiped the sweat from my forehead, I just sat there and looked at the vast emptiness around me and smiled. The desert was laid bare in front of me with nothing to hide. It showed only its simple beauty and my own insignificance.

Welcome back to the desert.

26

Fear of Hyenas and the Skeleton Coast

Namibia

It is easy to think of Central Africa before the Europeans arrived as being inhabited by disjointed pockets of primitive savages running naked and living in mud huts who survived by hunting in the forest and savannah. That was the story brought back by the first Europeans. It suited their ambitions on the continent to portray people in need of help and salvation. Sadly, that image still pervades today, no more so than in Central Africa.

We forget of the many kingdoms that once thrived. Simply because there was no written history does not mean they did not exist or were not great. Their history is a spoken one, passed by word of mouth through the generations – that does not make it less accurate.

Events are only true at the time they happened. After that they slide from fact into the realms of fiction, warped by our mind's fickle memory and subjective judgement. The truth of a history depends on when it was written, by whom and with what agenda. It is important to remember this, especially today when any man can be a self-proclaimed expert. From the Bible to Wikipedia, it has always been this way.

It is nature's way to migrate. Journeys covering great distances that push never-ending to a future that always lies just beyond reach. To stand still is to stagnate and you will not survive. Ever since the first humans migrated out of Africa, people have been crisscrossing the continent in the search for survival.

By the time the Portuguese explorer Diego Cão arrived, in 1482, at the mouth of the Congo River, the Kongo kingdom was the most powerful in the region. It had a structured government and an extensive trading network. Besides the natural resources of the country, they manufactured and traded copperware, iron goods, cloth, and pottery.

The Kongo, and the Loanda, Lunda and Luba kingdoms too, all formed as the Bantu people, who originated from the shores of Lake Chad in West Africa, travelled south through Cameroon and spread out through Central Africa towards the east and south. My own journey, in comparison, was nothing more than following an old well-trodden route.

This migration happened over centuries and as people settled, alliances formed, kingdoms merged and split, and rose and fell, as all great empires are bound to do. And as with any great movement of people who seek a place to settle in a land already inhabited, the weaker were marginalised and discriminated against.

First, there were the hunter-gatherer Baka people of Cameroon and Gabon. You may know them by their diminutive name as Pygmies. The Mbuti, Aka and Twa too, all short in stature, were shoved into Central Africa's remotest corners. They have survived the onslaught of the Bantu's migration south and the Arabs too, who invaded from the Indian Ocean in the east to explore ever deeper into the interior in search of people to enslave.

Then there were the hunter-gatherer San people of southern Africa. You may know them by their more common name as Bushmen. Also short in stature, with light skin and wide slit eyes more commonly associated with a Mongol, they were beaten into the driest depths of the desert. They survived the Bantu's continued migration from the north and the white man's invasion from the sea in the south as they searched for lands to settle. It is cruel irony that while the 'settlers' travelled thousands of leagues to find a land large enough on which to spread, the native nomadic wanderers were forced to settle on the smallest scraps of their homeland.

The desert defies death and decay, and is history laid bare – a museum and testament to the earth's powerful forces and enduring nature, to all it has weathered and survived.

The Sahara, like Namibia, was not always a suffering inferno where the struggle for life was strongest. It has its own ancient story told through the tiny calcified shells that crunched and crumbled underfoot as I walked over the sand, which was once an ancient sea in Jurassic times when dinosaurs roamed the land.

In more recent times, the Sahara has fluctuated from dry inhospitable desert to fertile savannah with freshwater lakes and great rivers and many mammals. Rock paintings found in the mountains of the Algerian desert show great animal migrations, not only of antelopes and gazelles, but crocodiles, rhinos, giraffes, buffaloes, and elephants too. The art, dating from 6,000 BC, spans millennia and shows that humans inhabited these rich lands until gradually they dried up as the climate changed.

My journey did not take me to Algeria, but I saw similar pictures in Namibia at a place called Twyfelfontein, meaning 'doubtful spring' in Afrikaans. There are thousands of engravings on the huge slabs of red rock that litter this giant's boulder field. The oldest engravings of animals were made by San Bushmen, who carved through the reddish-brown desert varnish of iron and manganese oxides, which coats the rocks where rain rarely falls, to show the lighter sandstone underneath as Africa's wildlife.

When Khoikhoi herders displaced the San Bushmen, they added their own images and marks to the collection. There are imaginary creatures too, and some say these are evidence of shamanistic rituals showing the transformation from human to animal form. That could, however, simply be academic insistence that everything must have a deeper meaning, when the reality is that these engravings are nothing more than expressions of man's creative nature.

But long before the turmoil that humanity on the move brought, there was a time when there were not seven continents – only one Pangaea – and the earth was under the frozen grip of the Great Ice Age. The southernmost parts of the continent were covered in vast ice fields and glaciers. Then, as the global climate warmed around 280 million years ago, the thaw began.

The glaciers melted, and torrents of icy water carrying rock debris rushed relentlessly, gouging out the earth, and swathes of forest that had lain like blankets were razed to the ground. Tree trunks snapped from their roots under the unstoppable fluid force and were carried with the flow over great distances until, finally, the waters slowed and they came to rest, scattered like the fallen after battle. The trees lay in their graves – buried under sand and dirt – protected from the ravages of rot and decay.

Over millions of years and under great pressure, silica-rich minerals slowly permeated the wood, dissolved the organic matter, and then crystallised into quartz. Millions more years passed and imperceptibly slowly the continent split, land surfaces rose and became separated by seas. Lesser Ice Ages came and went, and the earth was continually bombarded as melting glaciers formed rivers that flowed and eroded.

When the temperatures rose and the water was gone, great winds blew across the deserts and the land took on new shapes. Once deep-buried rocks became exposed above the ground. Now, they are smoothed and pockmarked, standing isolated in defiance. The fossilised trees are scattered in their open graves in the heart of Damaraland in the dry North-Central Namibia. These are the last remnants of those past turbulent times.

One small sector of open land where many fossilised trees lie has been sectioned off by the Namibian Tourism Board and called 'The Petrified Forest', so that you may pay to see these ancient specimens.

My guide was not like those I had encountered in other parts of Africa. He did not just walk beside me saying that *here is a petrified tree, that is just a rock* and *there is another tree,* and then having pointed out the obvious demanded money for his services. No, this guide was informative, and made no demands. Unfortunately, I could not get enthusiastic about a few chunks of dead tree, and I already knew how to tell the age of one by counting its growth rings.

He was patient though and humoured me by explaining more about the welwitschia that lay around the site. These alien-looking giant plants sprouting from the ground had the advantage of being alive and colourful, and being a girl of simple tastes, that was enough to capture my interest.

Endemic to Namibia and southern Angola the welwitschia grow in the dry arid areas within the coastal fog belt, which is rarely more than 150 kilometres inland. Unique in the plant world, they have only two leaves that continue to grow for as long as they live, which can be 2,000 years. The two large broad leaves get torn and ripped into tentacles by the wind and animals. They always grow outwards and curve down towards the ground, effectively capturing as much moisture from the fog and directing it to where their roots can absorb it. Nature is the world's greatest engineer, and you need to look no further than the harsh desert environment to see some of its most creative solutions.

Beyond the petrified forest of fallen stone trees, I cycled as far as possible until the light began to fade. The guide had mentioned hyenas lived nearby, and I wanted to be as far down the road as possible. It didn't matter that there might have been hyenas living near every place I had camped so far or that he might have been winding me up. The point was that, now, I had hyenas on my mind, and it would not make for a peaceful night.

I pulled off the gravel road where tyre tracks went down to a flat area, free of large rocks and sheltered from the road by some shrubs. There were signs of an old camp – the earth stained black from a fire long since extinguished. There were a few charcoaled remains, but the ashes had blown away. Around it were three rocks arranged in a triangle for balancing a pan above the fire. I looked closer at these rocks and realised they were chunks of petrified tree, and when I scoured the surrounding area I found many more scattered about. I did not have to pay to see these specimens.

Once I had cooked dinner, I lay down on the hard ground and looked up at the stars, but I couldn't relax. I had an uneasy feeling of being watched. *You're just being paranoid because of what the guide said.* I sat up and looked towards the road, but I could not hear any voices, and there were no headlights in the distance. There were definitely no other people about although that didn't make me more comfortable this time.

The lunar landscape was dimly lit by the stars, which cast shadows on every rock and crevice. *I hope the guide didn't mean this place.* The rocky hillsides no longer seemed like protective walls, but more like perfect hyena hangouts. *Don't be ridiculous.*

When I heard an unknown animal call in the distance I cleared up my gear, got in the tent and zipped it up, feigning a casual air that I was ready for bed, as if someone were watching. But I was only fooling myself that it wasn't a small dose of fear driving me inside. It is surprising how safe a flimsy tent can make you feel. I relaxed and read and soon fell asleep.

What was that? I opened my eyes, but it was pitch black. There was something outside the tent. I lay dead still barely daring to breathe, only straining to hear, and I bit the inside of my mouth to make sure I wasn't dreaming.

What if it's a hyena?

It's probably just the wind or a mouse.

What if it's a hyena?

Don't be ridiculous.

It's definitely not the wind, and mice don't sound like that. What if …

If I was going to be dragged out of the tent, it would be kicking and fighting. Slowly and quietly, I reached for my penknife and opened it up, wishing I still had my machete. *No point wishing, what else do you have? Bike pump or pliers … oh my God, am I seriously considering fending off a hyena with a bike pump?* I was. *Who in their right mind thinks they can batter a hyena to death with a bike pump?* I couldn't decide whether I would rather my remains were found with a bike pump as a weapon or with no signs of a struggle at all. I chose the pliers instead.

There I crouched, poised with a penknife and pliers, waiting for an attack that could come from any angle. And I waited and waited, and nothing happened. *Oh my God, it's a good job no one can see me right now.* The penknife and pliers only worked at fending off my own overactive imagination.

In the ensuing silence with only tiredness to fight off, when I could no longer keep my eyes open, I went to sleep with my weapons of choice close to hand. I should have just made a lot of noise, stormed out of the tent and looked to see what animal ran away. But there, alone, with no-one to bolster my bravado, I was simply a coward.

With daylight my fears dissipated, and I emerged from the tent to make coffee. That was when I saw them – an overactive imagination does not make paw-prints in the dirt.

* * *

The sun rose in the blue sky and beat down without remorse on anyone or anything that dared stay out. As far as I could see, I was the only one. There was not an animal in sight; even the insects had vanished. Not a blade of yellow grass moved, only I tried.

Where there is no shade, and nowhere to hide or take cover, you must make a stand, hold out, and endure the heat. What you know has an ending can be endured, like a race or a bad book. With the end of the day, the sun's siege would surely lift. First though, it must get hotter. The atmosphere was high voltage buzzing, electric static alive. But the air was dead still. That was when I saw the world with striking clarity, where every field of view was in perfect focus. Each tiny detail was sharply outlined and clearly defined as though the air around it had been cut away with a knife.

In the distance, I saw a cloud of dust rising and knew a vehicle was on its way. Tourists in cool air-conditioned cars peered through the windows at the world as it flashed by, catching glimpses of the rocks rising out of the orange earth. Maybe the observant passenger spotted one of the perfectly constructed weavers' nests in a tree here or there. Yet they were dissociated from their environment, separated by metal and glass and a 30 degree difference on the thermometer. They were merely seeing real-time photos like flicking through the pages of National Geographic.

They did not see the whole picture because to savour a sight you must hear and smell and feel and taste it too – hear the buzzing of the insects, and smell the sweat that runs down your neck onto your salt-encrusted shirt, and feel the hard earth defiant under your feet, and taste the fine dust that sticks in the back of your throat with your tongue sticking to the top of your mouth that even a gulp of sun-warmed water cannot moisten and does not satisfy your thirst either.

Advised against taking the back roads to the Brandberg Mountain because of the confusing myriad of tracks, I took a calculated risk and went anyway. As far as I could tell, it was not possible to get lost. I could see the Brandberg Mountain, an uneven plateau rising alone from the flat surroundings. There was supposed to be a lodge near the base along the riverbed. All I needed to do was follow any of the tracks in a downhill direction and eventually arrive at the dried-out watercourse because rivers do not defy gravity. Besides, I could see trees, which must flank the riverbed for they need water, if only occasionally, to live. If I then followed any of the tracks along the riverbed towards the mountains, I would surely find the lodge.

As the day wore on and the sun passed its zenith, so I wore out and passed my peak too. The gravel turned to dirt and took a meandering course like a stream. It rose and fell and wound its way around towering rocks, ever on down. There were no more corrugations to shake and slow me down, only my nerves and the strength in my legs to limit my speed. I raced recklessly until something caught my eye and then stopped.

There was a gentle breeze now. I felt it cooling my damp skin and saw it in the spiky yellow grass that rustled and followed the wind like an animal in the undergrowth. A tiny red lizard darted across the track, and when I heard a curious croaking I searched for the source of the sporadic sound but never found it.

I came to a farm spiralling slowly into decay with fencing fallen, and cars stripped and rusting. Dejected donkeys stood with heads down. The fierce sun had won the battle here. Even the colour of the earth had faded to a greyish-brown. The survivors sat defeated in the shade. Silence is a tangible thing, and here it hung heavily enveloping everything, as real as a thick blanket to fight off the cold.

Further down by the riverbed, I kept a keen lookout for desert elephants, but the only signs were of trees stripped bare long ago. I dragged my bike through the dry, sandy riverbed and pushed on up the other side. Eventually, I reached the lodge where I cooled down with a cold beer and then warmed up with a hot shower (that novelty had still not worn off).

It was here, sat by the pool, that I saw Rolf. He was running a 4x4 tour for a group of Germans. We had met before. Shortly after leaving Khorixas, trundling down the gravel roads, I had stopped to take a photograph. Rolf had stopped to ask if I was OK or wanted some water. It was a typical encounter in Namibia although sometimes I was given beer instead. We were both going to see the same sights, so as he drove off I called out, 'Nice to meet you and might see you again.' He had laughed at that then.

'I didn't expect to see you.'

'Well, I did say.'

'Yes, I know. But you are on a bike. It sounded ridiculous.'

'Not really. While you were sitting in the shade in the midday sun, I was cycling and while you have been talking and drinking around camp in the evening, I have carried on unconstrained. And on these rough roads, where vehicles must go slowly, we cover similar distances each day. Our paths were bound to cross if we were going the same way. Now I need to stop for a longer rest to relax and enjoy a cold drink. It's unlikely you'll see me after this.'

'I'm still surprised. Anyhow, let me buy you a beer.' We did meet again, on the coast.

From the Brandberg Mountain I went to Swakopmund, the harbour town founded for the German colony in 1892. Between the mountain and the coast is the mining town of Uis and not much else except a bleak washed-out desert like the Saharan *hammada*.

The wind blew fierce and unrelenting in my face, and my shirt flapped wildly behind me. It was late afternoon and with the sun hanging low in the sky. It was surprisingly cool. Still, I sweated as I battled against the elements, barely moving on the gradual upward incline. I cycled past a few weather-beaten shacks made of scrap metal and old wood. Large Castor Oil barrels, beaten flat and bolted together, were now someone's shelter in this barren wasteland, which was split through the middle by one road and a line of telegraph poles running to the sea.

In the last moments of light, I pulled off the road and pitched my tent under the burning orange sky. Scores of birds circled in a thermal until one-by-one they left the swirling column above the road and flew overhead so close that I could see their eyes locked on me, and then they landed on the ground to nest just one hundred metres away.

Predictably, the wind died down in the night and the morning brought with it a beautiful sunrise, soothing in this stark landscape. I would have liked to rest longer, but I knew I would regret it later when the intensely hot sun and unforgiving headwind returned. The coastal fog lingered low in the distance, yet where I was that early morning, the air was crisp and clear and the sky a bright blue.

A pale grey goshawk with golden beak, stood on a telegraph pole and watched me approach before taking flight. It glided ahead, then came to rest further on and watched me near, and then took off again to another telegraph pole. After a few more flights, it circled in a wide arc over the desert to my left and came up behind me as I pedalled down the road. It caught me up and passed so close I could have reached out to touch its black wing tip. But I didn't want to frighten it, so I only stared back at his watchful eye and admired the beauty of its feathers that weren't grey, but finely striped in black and white. When he had finished his inspection of this curious creature pedalling through the desert, he gracefully accelerated away and took up his watch on a telegraph pole ahead.

That was how I travelled with my winged guardian for many kilometres until he rose up in the sky and vanished over the desert. I wondered if he had gone far enough from his nest or seen something else of more interest. Then, in the distance, I saw a black mark moving across the horizon, and as I got closer and the silhouette took shape, I saw that it was another cyclist.

Oliver was another German and had a month to see some of Namibia. We stood there in the midday heat in the middle of the empty road that ran through the middle of the desert talking animatedly and rapidly as though we had not spoken to another soul in months and were worried that if we stopped talking we would never get another chance.

A vehicle came along the road, stopped beside us, and the driver wound down the window.

'Are you OK? Is there a problem?'

'Oh no, thanks. We're fine,' I replied.

'Oh, OK. Then why have you stopped here?'

'We came across each other going in opposite directions. It's not often we see other cyclists, so we've stopped to chat and, well, it's not like there's a rush.' The driver and lady passenger looked at us sceptically as the rare specimens and fools we were.

'But why didn't you stop in the shade then?' I looked around at the pancake-flat land and then looked at them as the idiots.

'If I knew there was shade, I would be stood in it. What shade?' I asked.

'There's always shade.'

'Really? Where?'

'Well, we usually see something every hour or so.' I suppressed a laugh.

'Yes, but an hour for you on this road is a day for us.'

This realisation stymied them with open mouths of surprise, and when the driver broke his trance it was to say, 'In that case, as you are OK, we shall be on our way,' and he drove off choking us on his dust trail. We went our separate ways shortly after; I could not stop in the sun for long.

A pool of water shimmered in the road ahead, but I was wise to mirages now. Although, when I saw an outline of hovering buildings faintly flickering through the haze, I wasn't sure if I was seeing a coastal town or just seeing what I wanted to believe.

It was Henties Bay and when the long road came to an abrupt end because there was no more land, I stopped and looked out at the wide blue sea and shrugged my shoulders. *Well, that's that. Where to now?* Rather than return the way I had come in Forrest Gump foolishness, I looked left, then right, and then went left, as I hadn't been going south much lately and that was, after all, the direction to Cape Town.

Besides, to my right lay only more of the vast Skeleton Coast, named because of the bleached bones that littered the shore from whaling operations and seal hunts, even some human remains. Notorious for its thick fog, shifting sands and uncharted rocks, these waters are dangerous and many ships that came too close now rust in their shallow graves.

That night I camped on a lonely stretch of beach, my tent sheltered among the small dunes where the sand had accumulated around the grassy tufts of earth. As the last light faded over the white crashing waves, the clouds came in and a fog slowly enveloped the wrecked fishing trawler in the distance that I had passed earlier. I had met a solitary fisherman sat by his *bakkie* sipping a sundowner there. We admired the harsh beauty where the desert meets the Atlantic sea. Now, I stood on the empty beach that continued without end and followed with my eyes the wild waves rising up and rushing at the wide sandy shore and was content to share it only with the seagulls that sometimes flew overhead.

I wondered what survivors of a shipwreck would have thought landing on this shore. Any relief brought from standing on solid ground would have been short-lived. The only way out was inland across hundreds of kilometres of wasteland without access to water. Even the San Bushmen called it 'The Land God Made In Anger,' and they, as well as anyone, were used to the desert environment. Death would have come slowly while suffering the torturous ravages of thirst, hunger and exposure, if rescue were not forthcoming.

Rescue did come for passengers on one ship, the *Dunedin Star.* It was carrying munitions and supplies for the Allies' war effort in the Middle East in 1942. Three weeks earlier, with more than 100 people on board, it had left Liverpool and in three days' time was expected to dock at Table Bay, which is overlooked by Table Mountain in Cape Town. That was when it hit the Clan Alpine shoal and began taking on water. On maps, it was labelled 'PD' like most obstacles in this region, meaning 'Position Doubtful'. The captain knew the boat would sink and chose to rush it headfirst to shore instead. He sent an SOS across the radio waves, which was picked up in Walvis Bay. The rescue effort was fraught with endless difficulties.

From where the boat ran aground, half of the passengers were evacuated onto the desolate Skeleton Coast shore through the rough surf using the on-board motorboat. But the engine failed, leaving the rest stranded on the ailing vessel. Both parties faced a bleak outlook. Those on shore had no food or water or shelter, and the other passengers and crew were on a boat that was at serious risk of breaking up under the strong swell.

A rescue tug arrived after two days and took some of the people from the boat, but on the way back to Walvis Bay, it ran aground too, and two of the crew died trying to swim for shore. The rest had to wait, unsure if they could be rescued.

Another three days passed when more boats came and rescued the remaining people on the *Dunedin Star*. Sea conditions were so bad that the boats could not reach the shore though. Instead, an aircraft was dispatched to make a drop of food and water. The plane then landed on a nearby salt pan with the aim of rescuing some of the women and babies. But the landing gear broke when it taxied for take-off and became swamped in the sand. In cruel irony, after four days of digging the aircraft free and repairing it, it crashed in the sea shortly after take-off. Amazingly, the crew survived and managed to swim to shore and return to the others.

Meanwhile, an overland expedition had begun to reach the stranded men and women, now in two different locations. All the while relief flights carrying supply drops were made from Walvis Bay until, finally, 26 days after the first disaster, the survivors were rescued.

The *Dunedin Star* was not the only ship to pass this coast on the way to Cape Town and beyond during the Second World War. Shortly before I left England to begin this journey, I received a kind letter from a man I had never heard of, who had read about my planned trip in the local paper. He wrote:

> Dear Helen,
> I read this morning in the dear old EDP of your exciting and wonderful mission in cycling to Cape Town. I wish you every success and good fortune.
> I took the easy way by troop-ship – Liverpool, Sierra Leone and Cape Town.
> You will no doubt get to the top of Table Mountain where I picked this leaf. Take it with you for every success. I picked it on 24 March 1941; I believe outside the post office shop at the top.
> Kind Regards, Colin

I had carried that letter and leaf with me through Africa and like a talisman, together with the Tuareg Cross and a chain of beads I was given by another cyclist, and the many whispered prayers from people I met, they were all given to bring me good fortune. I thought about Colin, who had passed these shores 60 years earlier, when I was alone on that beach. It was comforting to know that others were thinking of me even when I was not with them. I rarely felt lonely when I was alone, and perhaps that was because other people were in my thoughts and that connection was far stronger than anything physical. I can feel more lonely in a crowded market or bar, surrounded by other people, if we have no understanding of each other.

27

A Desert Thief, Broken Axle and 1,000 Beers

Namibia and South Africa

The coastal road passed through two towns, only 35 kilometres apart, which in a vast emptiness is not far. In 1884, present-day Namibia was made a German protectorate with the exception of Walvis Bay. The main port and only natural harbour along the Namibian coast, Britain kept control of. Walvis means 'whale' and was named because of the many whales that used to frequent the waters to feed on the rich marine life.

The Germans built their own harbour nearby and named the town Swakopmund. Swakop derives from a Nama word meaning 'excrement opening' because it is situated at the mouth of a river that when it floods, dead animals are carried downstream into the sea. As with the Caprivi Strip, the Germans got a bum deal at the 1884 Berlin Conference with this.

To the south is the Diamond Coast. There are no roads, only desert and diamonds. Instead, the road makes a right-angled bend inland, back across more barren desert with only isolated hardy shrubs and a couple of campsites. The campsites are unattended with no facilities or water. Run by the Namibian Tourism Board, you must pay for a permit to stay at them. You need a permit to travel anywhere off the main road in this region of the Namib Desert. This is less about protecting the natural environment than protecting the mineral wealth.

Some locals said that I might be able to get water at farms on the road up to the Gamsberg Pass, but couldn't guarantee it. Before then, I would have to camp two nights on the road. It would be even further before I reached somewhere with a shop. So I took 20 litres of water and carried enough oats, pasta and biscuits for a week, if I rationed it.

It was sweltering again, and as soon as the sea was out of sight, the breeze dissipated too. I dripped with sweat whenever I stopped cycling, and the salty shorts rubbed on my legs until they were raw. It was time to dig out the Tubigrip I had cut in half in Nigeria and wear them on my thighs for protection.

As the afternoon wore on, white sand dunes rose up in ghostly waves on the hazy horizon and the darkening sky threatened to swallow up anything that entered. I watched the headlights of vehicles emerging. When they reached me, one stopped and a highly strung lady leant out of the window.

'Just to warn you, the river is flooded,' she said. It had been unusually wet, even for the rainy season, except for the strip of desert that lines the coast, where it almost never rains. Rain was a hot topic among the locals.

'Oh really, which river? The Kuiseb?'

'No. The *whole* desert is flooded!'

'Right, thanks.' She struck me as a lady prone to exaggeration, so I dismissed her concerns.

By the time I reached the mound of rocks on the empty plain that I was drawn to subconsciously like a moth to light, for the hope of shelter it proffered, I was a sorry-looking drowned rat. I pushed my bike around the rocks and up the hillside. There were some overhanging rocks and to one side a dark opening. It looked the perfect size to pitch a tent. It was also the perfect size for a den. The entrance was littered with spoor of some wild cat. I decided against looking further into the cave.

On the other side of the rocks, there were vehicle tracks and several spots that had clearly been used for camping. I had inadvertently chosen one of the official camps as my place to sleep that night. When I saw a 4x4 parked under an overhang, I went to say hello to my neighbour. Simon was a British photographer, who had been with friends and was now by himself. I asked if he would mind if I camped near his vehicle. I was worried about camping with the signs of wild animals I had seen. He offered his spare rooftop tent.

I slept soundly until a piercing shriek ripped through the silent starry night. Now that I was safe on the top of a vehicle and not exposed in a flimsy tent, I stuck my head out and strained to see what animal it was in the shadows. There was a loud wail nearby, but I couldn't make out where it had come from, and then an animal returned the call in the distance over the plain.

'Helen? Are you awake?' Simon whispered from the tent.

'Yes.'

'Did you hear that?' he asked nervously.

'Hell, yeah.' I replied like an excitable child. I tried not to laugh; I was hearing myself ask the same question to Lars all those months ago, back in West Africa. How I had changed in that time. 'Any idea what it is? I can't see it.'

'No.' There were no more sounds after that. No longer did my heart beat faster with anxiety. After hundreds of nights camping in Africa, I was left only with wonder and fascination.

Now in the cool morning air, the open plain was no longer dripping in the honey of a golden sunset, but brushed with the harsh reality that day brings in these unforgiving places. It was time to start cycling.

Despite the heat, there were shallow pools of water from the recent heavy rains. They were shrinking by the hour and ringed by a dark brown mud whose surface was cracking around the outer edges as all the moisture was sucked out by the desiccating air.

It was a long, slow day. The sun was unbearable as my mind fried, crazed by the need for shade where there was none. When I finally saw a real tree, as opposed to one my mind had imagined from a rusting oil drum or solitary rock, I stumbled towards it and collapsed. I lay motionless as the afternoon wore on until clouds began to form and a stiff breeze blew.

The desert turned green beyond the wasteland. I had crossed the infernal purgatory and emerged into the land of the living. Grasses nourished by the rain spread across the valley, springbok grazed, and an ostrich pair herded their young through the open. It had not rained like this for 25 years, and the locals were driving into the desert to see it flourishing with colour. Flowers they had never seen were springing up where it had always been dry shades of yellow and brown.

Where the road rose up a ridge, out of the plain, there were quiver trees with stocky trunks and forked branches topped with long sprouting leaves reaching skywards standing prominently on the rocky hillside. They were like the prettier, younger sister of the baobab tree, and named because the Bushmen used to made quivers for their arrows from the hollow branches.

As I continued towards the Kuiseb Pass, which was more like a canyon that must first be descended, the road wound round rocks and ridges and gullies formed by infrequent floods over many millennia. A river flowed along the valley, carpeted in a thousand yellow flowers of a verdant spring that made me forget I was in the desert. But as soon as I left the valley, the soothing sound of the river was a distant memory, replaced by the searing heat and sand and rocks and a slow slog over the rough ground that had sweat running down my sunburned face and neck.

At the junction, I wavered about whether to rush on south or detour up through the hills. Tiredness set me off south, but I soon changed my mind and backtracked, determined to see more of the country while I could. I regretted it once the hill started, and was relieved when I saw the first building since the coast, but my tired legs rebelled, and I wondered why I was bothering to go through all this. My mind flitted back and forth, back and forth, like an indecisive schizophrenic until I saw a windmill and knew there was a lodge where I could stop and rest. But the lodge had been sold, and now it was empty except for a few loose wires hanging from the ceiling and walls.

I had got my hopes up of rest and shade, and they were shattered in an instant. All I could do now was ask for water from the one man there before continuing onwards and upwards and finding a place to pitch my leaking tent and weather the storm that was brewing. Tobias came back with my water bottles and added, 'The campsite is closed, but if you want it, there is a room in the lodge you can stay in. You don't have to pay, but it hasn't been cleaned as no one is working here now.'

'OK,' I jumped in before he could change his mind. And just like that I went from nothing to having everything – now I had a bed under a roof, beer and warthog goulash, someone to talk and listen to, and learn many things I never knew. We sat on the veranda and watched the sun set blood red and when the black clouds filled the sky and hid the stars, then the first bolt of lightning struck and the thunder bellowed. All around the sky wrestled as three storms converged overhead, and the rain streamed down on the distant hillsides that were lit up in a purple haze. It was a beautiful thing when viewed from a safe place.

When the next morning came, we sat drinking coffee. The sun was out – another scorching day. I knew I should leave before it was too hot, but I didn't want to because my legs were tired and because Namibia was a different country when I wasn't cycling through it. So when Tobias asked if I wanted to stay, I did.

We drove across the farm and checked the dams, which had flooded in the storm when usually they were dangerously low. We saw kudu and oryx, mountain zebra and steenbok, bat-eared foxes and ground squirrels and long-legged big-bodied corey bustards walking through the long grass. We walked over the meadow and up towards a rocky bluff, and Tobias showed me some ancient engravings. We looked out over the fields filled with yellow flowers, and when I looked closely, I saw dainty pale blue and lilac ones too. Then in the evening we had a *braai* and drank more beer. It was always good to drink beer and talk.

I cycled on through the Namib Desert's Valley of a Thousand Hills and up towards the Gamsberg Pass. At a dried-up riverbed, I took shade under a large nest balanced and overhanging the branches of a dead tree bleached by the sun. It was a communal nest that social weaver birds build. I saw many more in Namibia, some of them hanging precariously from telegraph wires. One weaver begins by building a nest, and then others come and add their own improvements and extensions and move in. Over time, more weavers join the nest and keep adding to it until one day, when the branches can no longer take the weight, the nest collapses and the weaver birds must build a new one from scratch.

It was fascinating that such a large, complex nest could be constructed by such small birds. It made me think of the endless mass action of termites whose creations emerge from the ground up, except I would rather share my campsite with weavers. It was tempting to climb the tree and peer inside the nest, but Tobias had warned me that snakes also find them attractive – they eat all the eggs and once the nest is clear of birds, they move in.

Once I reached the top of the pass, there was nowhere to go but down and I sped recklessly along the rocky track, switch-backing down the Spreetshoogte Pass and stopping only when my panniers fell off until I reached the first and only place nearby on the map: Solitaire.

This one-man town, which was nothing more than a gas station, general store, and bakery, was thriving when I arrived. It was the annual gathering of 'local' farmers, who came from hundreds of kilometres away, for one evening of festive fun and food and drink. Where homes and farms are so far apart, it takes an organised event to get more than two families together. Once I had pitched my tent round the back, I joined in and gorged on barbecued game washed down with beers. Everyone knew each other and was like one big family, and whilst everyone was welcoming, I was an outsider and could only get vague impressions from the gossip that meant little to me. It was like when you first move to a new area and don't know anyone there, and you listen intently because you want to be a part of it. The tales flowed through the night and got more raunchy and crude as the beer barrels emptied. When I could stay awake no longer because spending all day in the sun always tired me out, I crawled into my tent and slept a deep dreamless drunk sleep.

The next day I headed off towards Sossusvlei, in the heart of the Namib Desert. Surrounded by red dunes are salt and clay pans that tourists come to visit. I bought a delectable array of over-priced food at the gas station, so that my birthday feast would be more interesting than pasta. Once my tent was up in the shade of a tree on the edge of the campsite, I went to the bar for a beer, which turned into several more, and by the time I stumbled back to my tent, it was midnight.

What the … ! My camp spot was littered with rubbish, and the tent was on its side. 'Oh no!' I exclaimed to the night when I saw that it was the remains of my shopping. The only things left in the dirt were a few strands of spaghetti. I rummaged through the shredded bag in the hope that the chocolate was still there when clearly it wasn't.

Unbelievable! Who would do something like this? That was when I saw that the bottom of my tent now had a huge rip several feet long in it. Gradually, the scenario became clear – my desert camp thief was none other than a jackal. *Oh well, serves me right for leaving food unattended in my tent.* I duct taped up the rip. There was nothing else to be done.

So there was no birthday breakfast. Instead, I hitched a ride to see the famous Sossusvlei dunes. It was another case of too many people where there should be none. Half the beauty of the desert is its raw simplicity, and that was stolen by the trucks full of tourists who crawled like ants along the ridges of the towering dunes. There is more to beauty than appearances, but it seemed as though few people there realised it.

The highlight of the day was when I returned to camp and saw, scrawled in the dirt around my tent, a message wishing me happy birthday from John, who I had chatted to in the bar the night before. Little gestures go a long way, especially when you are by yourself on your birthday and a jackal has eaten your only birthday present.

When I finally reached the tarmac after another four days of gravel and dirt, I turned towards the coast along the one-way road to Lüderitz. At first, I had company from the wild horses that graze the desert fringes. Generations of them have lived in the desert for the last century. They have adapted so well to the environment that they can go up to three days without water.

During the First World War, a bomb was dropped amidst 1,700 grazing horses, and it is likely that the Namib horses from today are the descendants of some of those scattered in the attack. There had been several thousand in the area, from both the German Schutzruppe, the colonial force based in Aus, and the cavalry of the South African army that had set up camp at Garub. However, there are distinctive characteristics in today's Namib horses common to those bred for mining operations and racing at a nearby stud farm during the war.

They were lean and strong with sleek fine coats that glistened in the sun. Foals stood alongside the mares, and two stallions, fit and flighty, raced off. They bucked and kicked out and tossed their heads in the air and spun round to a halt and reared up at one another, and then galloped back to the group. I wondered how they could have so much energy to waste, but with so much recent rain the grass was good and water plentiful.

Part of the reason for their survival is the Sperrgebiet. The area, which the public are prohibited from entering, was created in 1908 and sole rights for mining given to the German Diamond Company. Although mining occurs only in a small area, the rest acts as a buffer zone. Then, in 2004, the Sperrgebiet was designated a National Park, so the land will continue to be protected from development.

Diamonds were first discovered in April 1908 outside Lüderitz. Immediately, everybody rushed into the desert in search of more. The first big deposit was found in gravel of the dry riverbed at Kolmanskop, and soon a town developed there. It boomed and prospered for 40 years until the diamonds ran dry and people moved away. Since then, it has lain abandoned, deserted except for the encroaching sands that pile up above the windows of the houses and hospital. It is what the deserted town in the Western Sahara will look like in a few decades, but at least this ghost town was once lived in.

Having cycled to Lüderitz and spent a lazy week in the quiet harbour town, I was ready for the last stretch of 1,000 kilometres to Cape Town. I had no intention of cycling the same road twice and was offered a lift back to Aus. As I removed the wheels to put the bike in the car, the front axle fell apart into several pieces.

The nearest place to get a replacement part was in the capital, Windhoek, in the wrong direction. With only two weeks left to cycle,

I debated whether I could limp on into Cape Town, but decided against it. It would have been a shame to prematurely end the trip because I couldn't be bothered to get a repair done. So I hitched a ride to Windhoek, talked my way into a hostel in the middle of the night, woke up early the next day, took the bike to the shop and waited while they fitted a new part, and then went straight to the bus stop and took the next bus to the main road to Lüderitz. It had taken 24 hours and a 1,500 kilometres round trip, but now I was set for the final stretch.

I cycled first to the Orange River that marks the border with South Africa and then continued south. The road signs counted down the kilometres to Cape Town – progress, now, was measurable and the end reachable. The road was smooth, the air cooler, and cycling was once again a pleasant, leisurely affair, and when I started passing vineyards, it was as though I were back in France.

After several nights camping by the road or more often in a tunnel underneath it, I checked into a campsite and showered. Now that I was clean, my stomach ruled my decisions. 'Do you know where there is a supermarket?' I asked one guy who was also camping.

'What do you need?' he asked in reply.

'Just something for lunch and maybe a few beers,' I said.

'Well, there are a couple of shops in town, but if a toasted sandwich and gin and tonic are good enough substitutes, then you don't need to go anywhere.' And that was how I met Rusty and Kim, who had been up to the Orange River for a holiday and were now on their way home. Some people you just know you will get on with. So when I passed by their homes in Velddrif three days later, I stopped to say hello and stayed.

* * *

The journey had been a trip of two halves, mirror images reflected at the equator. It had started in temperate Europe and become drier and hotter through Morocco to the Sahara desert as the tropic of Cancer edged ever closer. There was the Sahel and then the rains.

The flora flourished and my world became a thick forest creeping and crawling and sprawling, and when I had pushed through to emerge on the other side now south of the equator, there were the rains again. Gradually, they dissipated and the scorching desert, which I loved so much, returned. Now, here I was, close to the end of the continent, and I was in no rush to get there. I was content, instead, to spend time with new friends, just as when I had arrived in Morocco and met Youssef in Chefchaouen and later his brother Radi. I was in no rush to move on in case I should miss something.

A continent apart and 20 months later and in some ways nothing had changed. Sitting and talking and laughing was what made me happy, and we spent hours smoking and passing round a joint and concerning ourselves with only the little things like spending time with friends and what to eat for dinner. Rather than driving up into the mountains in search of a goat for a feast, we took the boat onto the river and cast lines into the water in the hope of catching some fish. The only difference now was that instead of the hot sickly sweet tea drunk from a small glass, we swigged cold bitter beer straight from the can.

I was inching towards Cape Town, whose climate was pleasant and agreeable and a lot more like Europe. The smooth roads, white faces in smart cars, hot showers, fully stocked supermarkets, and good restaurants had all returned. Even the winds had reversed. The winds that pushed me south through the Sahara, had blown full in the face across the Namib Desert. They had threatened to bring me to a standstill and rush me back to Africa's heart in the Congo, and I wouldn't have minded much if they did because there, too, was a place I had been happy and truly content.

It would have been too easy to stay in Velddrif longer. That I was so close to Cape Town was the only thing that persuaded me to continue and finish what I had set out to do. There were only 150 kilometres remaining – I could be there the day after tomorrow.

That night I camped on a hillside overlooking the sea although a fog had rolled in obscuring the view. Though, by morning it had cleared, so that when I woke and stepped out of the tent, I was greeted to my first view of Table Mountain rising majestically in the distance.

That made me happy – a broad smile and stretch-my-arms-in-the-air happy – I had finally made it. The last 50 kilometres were insignificant, and I knew there was nothing waiting for me in Cape Town. That morning is the moment I remember. It was then that I thought back to all that had happened since I left England 20 months earlier – when I had stood on the ferry, watching England slowly disappear from view, and wondered about what the next two years would have in store for me.

Just ten kilometres outside Cape Town, I saw another cyclist sat by the roadside in the shade, stopped for a snack. We were going the same way and agreed to cycle together. In all the cycling across Africa, I had only cycled with two other people: Lars and Wayne. Here was the third, and he was called Lars too. Lars Number Two was a towering Dutch guy who had double the luggage I did; for every item I had discarded or lost on my ride, he had acquired something.

'Where are you going to in Cape Town?' he asked.

'I don't know.' I honestly hadn't thought about it until now.

'But where are you finishing your ride?'

'Just Cape Town; it doesn't matter where. I suppose I'll head to the Waterfront.' I recalled a pub with an on-site micro-brewery from when I had visited Cape Town several years before. It was as good a place as any to go – bars were the places I usually gravitated towards. 'Do you want to join me for a drink to celebrate a journey of 1,000 beers?'

EPILOGUE

There was one final thing I wanted to do while I was in Cape Town. The following day I went with Lars to the top of Table Mountain and found a leaf like the one Colin had picked 65 years ago and I had carried nearly 25,000 kilometres across the continent. I stood there smiling, looking out across the bay at the future of endless possibilities that lay ahead of me, but all I could think about was how happy I was right then.

I would dare to say that you have not lived until you have slept on the hard earth, the darkness your duvet and stars your safety, and drifted to sleep with the earthy smell permeating your dreams as your chest rises and falls to a slow regular beat in sync with nature's rhythm. Happiness is when you lay down to sleep, your muscles relax and your body sinks into the earth; discovering that your inflatable mattress is riddled with holes from the thorny acacia is not. Happiness is realising that you don't care and that you sleep well anyway.

I would dare to say that you have not lived until you have spent a day not knowing where you shall sleep that night because then you can appreciate the impermanence and uncertainty of life. Our modern culture is obsessed with finding ways to help us live longer, but rather than hoping to cheat death, perhaps we should embrace it. Only by knowing that life is finite will we savour every moment and every breath.

I would dare to say that you have not lived until you have felt hunger gnawing at your belly or a thirst grappling with your brain. For it is only then that a morsel of food or sip of water can be truly appreciated for all its worth. Happiness is tasting the sweetness of water straight from the river and feeling each drop flow through you; finding unidentifiable insects floating in your water bottle is not. Happiness is fishing out the insect, letting the dirt settle to the bottom, drinking it anyway and not getting ill.

I would dare to say that you have not lived until you have lived outdoors, no matter the weather. Happiness is finding cool dark shade when the sun beats down, scorching the earth and everything on it, and of standing in the rain when all around is desert and washing the sweat and dirt from your sun-toughened skin; lying awake in a leaky tent during a storm as your ground sheet becomes a lake is not. Happiness is when the darkness breaks and the clouds clear and you emerge to another day knowing the sun will dry you out soon enough.

I would dare to say that you have not lived until you have spent time alone – alone in a tropical rainstorm with thunder crashing and lightning striking overhead, alone in the savannah where lions roam and hyenas howl, alone in the open desert with only the wind for company, alone at a crossroads that are unsigned and unmarked on the map. Only then can you put in perspective your place on this earth and how small and insignificant and powerless you are, and realise that, sometimes, the decisions you make can be crucial. Happiness is coming through all these with the feeling that you have been given another chance. Only when you have spent time alone can you realise the importance of your family and friends. Happiness is also being surrounded by those who care about you and filling your thoughts with those you care about.

Moments of happiness are easy to find when you take a simplistic view of life. Strip off the immaterial and remove the cosmetic, then you are left with the fundamental, where what you are looking for is easily found. But these are temporary feelings that pass like strangers in the night, touching us for the briefest time.

We follow our urges and desires, hopes and ambitions, with one aim: to be happy. How we achieve that is our own choice. I found happiness in something everyday in Africa. Now, perhaps, I will find a deeper, longer-lasting happiness inside.

Africa changed me. Anyone who has lived on African soil, even for the most fleeting of moments, cannot help but be changed. The irony is that many people go to Africa to change it.

It took me 25,000 kilometres and 1,000 beers to realise the true reason that I began this journey in the first place, which was to do something that would make me happy. If I can get through life and have a good time without hurting too many people along the way, and help those who ask for it and a few who don't, then that is enough.

I once had grander hopes of doing great things to make the world a better place. I've come to the conclusion that I'm never going to do that. I haven't come up with a way to do it and that, perhaps, is because I think the world is a great place to live in already.

But this story does not end in Africa. It is just the beginning.

ACKNOWLEDGEMENTS

There were many people I had the privilege to meet on this journey and they will remain with me long past our fleeting encounters. As John Donne poetically wrote, 'No man is an iland, intire of it selfe; every man is a peece of the Continent, a part of the maine; if a clod bee washed away by the Sea, Europe is the lesse, as well as if a Promontorie were, as well as if a Mannor of thy friends or of thine owne were; any mans death diminishes me, because I am involved in Mankinde; And therefore never send to know for whom the bell tolls; It tolls for thee …'.

When I finally wrote a letter to thank Colin for his letter and leaf he picked on Table Mountain, and to let him know that I safely made it to Cape Town, he had passed away. If the simple act of writing could have brought a small amount of happiness into his life, as his thoughts had to me, then it will be my everlasting regret that I did not write sooner.

There are countless people who helped me as I crossed the continent and only a few of them are mentioned in this book. I will remember them forever, but I won't name them here, namely because for every person I could list there are many more whose names I never knew.

My thanks go to all the people who helped me on the journey of writing this book. SJ and Dave, Savage and Marc, Catherine, and Al, all gave me a place to stay over the last year and Tony helped me get work when I needed it. Nancy Sathre-Vogel, Roger Bratchell, Iain Harper, Tom Allen and Alastair Humphreys answered all the questions I threw at them. And for their enduring efforts to make me a better writer and make Desert Snow a better book, I shall be eternally grateful for the help of Paul Lepisto and Sue Mitchell. Although, I know I still have much to learn. Finally, a special thanks to Mum and Dad, who have put up with my return to home and have been supportive throughout, as they are with everything I choose to do.

Lightning Source UK Ltd.
Milton Keynes UK
UKOW04f0609030116

265685UK00004B/189/P